16.75

Administration of Intramural and Recreational Activities:
Everyone can participate

Administration of Intramural and Recreational Activities:
Everyone can participate

John A. Colgate
Western Illinois University

John Wiley & Sons
New York • *Santa Barbara* • *Chichester* • *Brisbane* • *Toronto*

Cover photo: Bruce Roberts/Photo Researchers, Inc.

Library of Congress Cataloging in Publication Data:

Colgate, John A   1935-
Administration of intramural and recreational activities.

Includes index.
1. Intramural   sports.   2. Recreation--Administration.   3. Tournaments. 4. Student participation in administration. I. Title.

GV710.C64   796   77-9265
ISBN 0-471-01728-0

Printed in the United States of America

10 9 8 7 6 5 4 3 2 1

Copyright © 1978, by John Wiley & Sons, Inc.

*This book is dedicated to
the individuals who give of their
time to share in the joy others
receive from their efforts.*

Preface

This is written for the classroom teacher responsible for a course in intramurals or recreation, that deals with organizational procedures and programming. Although the book is concerned primarily with the intramural program, it can be used in the teaching of recreation classes because of the types of activities, tournaments, and administrative procedures that are included. Individuals working with intramural, recreational, YMCA and YWCA, and correctional-institution programs can use this volume as a resource. Many of the ideas presented here may be entirely new and provide information that may prove helpful in changing or improving programs.

One of the important features of this book is that the programs discussed are basically student-oriented operated. In this day and age, students need to identify with many factors in education and to participate in some type of athletic endeavor. Student involvement in the intramural program should include not only participation in activities but also in administration. Administrators in both higher and secondary education are continually being faced with drives to expand programs and increase opportunities for a wide variety of students. At the same time they are faced with considerations of costs; therefore, a method must be found to expand programs without greatly adding to the budgets of educational institutions. Student participation in the administration of the program may be the solution. This textbook makes clear how an educational institution, whether it be a college or a public school, can, by using tested techniques, expand a program and also limit the increase in costs.

An entire chapter is devoted to the methods and procedures required to operate the kind of office that is essential to a department conducting the many activities of an intramural program. A discussion of how to economize and speed up the administrative procedures involved in scheduling, duplicating materials, and record keeping is included.

A large amount of material that is relevant to programs at the elementary and senior high school levels is presented. Although a basic part of this book deals with the program that is now in effect at Western Illinois University, similar programs, using the same basic principles, have been started in other communities in elementary, junior high, and secondary schools. As most teachers upon graduation from college will obtain their first position in public schools, they may find information pertaining to programs at this level essential.

Activities are broken down into different areas of competition so that the reader interested not only in intramurals but also in other physical recreation areas can use this book to become acquainted with common rules and regulations which have proven successful in an existing program.

A chapter is devoted to simplified methods of drawing up and conducting various types of standard tournaments. It also introduces two types of tournaments that may be useful to anyone organizing activities based on progressive competition.

Sports clubs and co-recreational activities are on-going programs that will become more and more a part of the intramural program of the future; therefore, the structure and content of these programs have been described in detail in this book.

The author wishes to express his sincerest appreciation to fellow intramuralist Don Brady for his ideas and encouragement during the writing of this book, to Dean William Lakie for his candid comments, and to the "special" individuals who assisted with the typing of the manuscript.

John A. Colgate

Contents

The Flip of
the Coin

Before almost any contest can begin, there must be a meeting of the players' representatives to go over the ground rules for the game that is to be played. This meeting is generally brief and to the point so that the game may begin on time; here brief definitions of the terms necessary to compete in this game are given.

Intramurals are those activities carried out under the auspices of a particular institution and in which all the participants are members of the particular institution.

Extramurals are competitions between members of non-varsity squads of one institution and members of another institution.

Co-Rec refers to activities, structured or unstructured, engaged in simultaneously by both males and females.

Sports Clubs are organizations that are bound together by special interests. These clubs may be formed for the purpose of receiving instruction or for competition.

Free Play is unstructured activity for individuals made possible through scheduling and the availability of facilities.

Leisure is the free time when an individual does not have to perform tasks normally associated with an education or making a living.

Campus Recreation is any recreational activity which takes place on campus and is carried on by individuals or groups during students' leisure.

Director is the individual who has the responsibility of directing a specific program; the limits of this responsibility may or may not be defined. The term "intramural director" may be interchanged with "director" because this book is basically about intramural programs.

1

1. Looking at the Field

*All of us must consider our own responsibility
for the physical vigor of our children and or
the young men and women of our community.
We do not want a generation of spectators.
Rather we want each of them to be a
participant in the vigorous life.*

John F. Kennedy

Intramurals and recreation are a "way of life" on most college and university campuses as well as in the public school systems. Intramural personnel no longer need to look for motivational devices to interest the students in the program—rather they must work to diversify the program to meet the physical and social needs of the students. Students are very complex organisms who are attempting to promote their development through all available channels in the school systems. The intramural concept has been expanded to include many areas far beyond the traditional programs that included only a few types of activities mostly based on team or individual competition.

A BRIEF HISTORY

History reveals that intramural sports are the oldest form of sports in the American school system. A form of intramurals existed in Boston in 1701 when the city banned the playing of football, squibs, and the throwing of snowballs. Then in 1743 Benjamin Franklin recommended that schools have a "healthful situation" with gardens and fields, and a provision for students to engage in games, running, leaping, wrestling, and swimming.

One of the first accounts of unorganized intramural activity states that in 1807 students from Yale University played football on the public greens in New Haven.

The first-recorded organized intramural competition took place at Princeton University in 1857. During that year, the freshman class formed "The Nassau Baseball Club" and challenged the sophomore class to a game of baseball in which each team played with 15 men. This was followed in 1859 by the formation of intramural boat clubs at Yale University.

As early as 1860, English games were being played within the schools, although this was against Puritan philosophy. The strong urge and innate desire of young people to play and engage in some sort of competitive sports forced school authorities to give student sports academic respectability.

Intramural activities probably appeared on many college campuses, but two Big Ten schools, Michigan and Minnesota, began to emerge as leaders. In 1861, the Pioneer Cricket Club was formed at the University of Michigan. The first organized intramural football game was played at the University of Minnesota in 1878 between the freshmen and sophomore classes, and the first ski club was formed at Minnesota in 1886.

Very little is recorded regarding intramurals in the latter part of the nineteenth century however; competitions took place between institutions. Just before the turn of the century, public school and university administrators began to examine the situation on their campuses and worked toward faculty control of both interschool and intramural programs. This prompted the State of Wisconsin, in 1896, to become the first state to form a State Atheletic Association

The period between 1900 and 1920 was a very productive era for intramural and related activities. Cornell University is believed to be the first to have its coaches give special emphasis to intramural sports and in 1904 gave instruction to nonteam students. Then, in 1913, the University of Michigan and Ohio State University inaugurated the first intramural department under the direction of a faculty member. The importance of student participation in competition was advanced in 1905 with the formation of the first sports club on the west coast, the Stanford Crew Association, and the formation of the Association of College Unions in 1915.

During 1917, the Committee on Intramural Sports of the Athletic Research Society recommended a comprehensive classification of playing units. This recommendation was used by athletic associations to initiate better control over scheduling of facilities and equipment. By sponsoring "Athletics for All," the Committee also helped the athletic association to "take the heat off" from the criticism that their programs were conducted for only a chosen few. It was during this same year that the National Athletic Conference of American College Women was held at the University of Wisconsin, and it maintained a stand against varsity sports for women and promoted "Sports for All."

Intramurals received a strong boost from the National Education Association in 1918 when it listed "the worthy use of leisure time" as one of its "Seven Principles of Education."

World War I had its influence on intramurals when the Army had to place emphasis on more competitive sports because of the poor physical condition of the young men who were drafted or volunteered for the service. As a result of the new program, future leaders in intramurals and athletics received training in this area.

In 1920, the intramural director of Western Intercollegiate Athletic Conference (Big Ten) began holding annual meetings to discuss the problems related to intramurals at the college level. Then in 1923, the National Amateur Athletic Federation formed a Women's Division to select and administer activities which would provide athletics for all women, not just a select few.

In 1925, intramurals began to emerge as a strong factor in the educational society, when Dr. Elmer D. Mitchell published the first textbook on intramurals entitled *Intramural Athletics*; and Michigan State University became the first college to require its physical-education and recreation majors to take a course entitled "Organization and Administration of Intramural Sports." It was also in this same year that intramurals began to appear in high school programs. The 1930 meeting of the Big Ten intramural directors gave special attention to high school intramural programs and these then really began to flourish.

The first building ever built for intramurals was constructed at the University of Michigan in 1928. Many leaders in the field feel that the building was built due to the influence of Dr. Mitchell, who is considered to be the "father of intramurals" in America.

The 1930s, the depression years, were a fortunate "catch up period" for intramurals. First, there was the availability of federal funds to assist in the construction of expanded recreational facilities. Then in 1933 under the Federal Emergency Relief Administration, financial aid was offered to many students who worked in the intramural programs, thus allowing programs to expand. During this period industrialization and automation shortened the work week and created more free time; therefore, educational institutions had to prepare their graduates with some form of recreational outlet so that they would be able to cope with this situation in society.

During the 1930s, the status of intramurals within professional organizations was enhanced with more national recognition. The women's programs took on a national look in 1932 when the American Physical Education Association recognized the National Section for Girls and Womens Sports (Division of Girls and Womens Sports), as an official section of the organization. It was not until 1938, six years later, that the Division of Mens Athletics of the American Association for Health, Physical Education and Recreation recognized a section for men's intramurals. In 1933, the College Physical Education Association set aside a section for the discussion of intramurals at the college level.

In the 1940s, it became increasingly evident that intramurals would play an important role in education. First, the United States Armed Forces during World War II placed emphasis on physical training through a sports program, and when the veterans returned to college campuses, they wanted to continue participating in games of competition that they had enjoyed while in the service. Secondly, the youth of America were once again found physically inferior to youth of the same age groups in other countries; therefore, once again a need to provide more physical activities for youth was recognized. During this era American labor unions continued to expand in this highly industrialized nation. They worked out contract agreements which provided for higher wages and a shorter work week and thus created more leisure. Because of the new found leisure and additional money for the purchase of equipment, colleges and universities had to expand intramural programs, and industries and communities began to provide more facilities for recreation.

On February 22, 1950, intramural directors from nine southern negro colleges met at Dillard University, to lay the ground work for the first professional association of intramural directors and named it the National Intramural Association.

Midway through the 1950s the College Physical Education Association for men, the American Association for Health, Physical Education and Recreation, and the National Association of Physical Education for College Women jointly sponsored a conference in Washington, D. C., on intramural sports for college men and women. During the conference an attempt was made to establish a set of criteria by which intramural programs could be evaluated. Using these criteria, James Teaque of Texas Technological College devised a questionnaire which has been used and proved to be a valid instrument in evaluating and comparing college intramural programs. That same year Dr. Clarence P. Houston, President of the NCAA, pointed out that intramurals would continue to grow because they reached the greatest percentage of students on a campus.

The 1960s school and college population was increased by the "war babies" and caused an expansion of educational facilities at all levels. Some educational institutions benefited with the building of facilities designed for physical education, intramurals, and recreation. This was also the period when college students voted to use student-fee funds to build facilities for intramurals and recreation.

In 1966, the Division of Girls and Womens Sports and the Division of Mens Athletics joined together and two years later held the National Conference on College and University Recreation in Washington, D. C. It was strongly urged at the conference that the intramural program no longer be under the auspices of physical education, recreation, or athletics, but that intramurals report directly to an administrative officer at the vice-president level. This would alter the position of the intramural director in the university administrative framework.

The 1970s opened with intramural programs going through the greatest exposure ever recorded. Intramural programs had long been well established in colleges and universities and were now achieving their proper place in the public schools. The first half of the 1970s brought about two significant events which will continue to have a far reaching effect for many years on the improvement and expansion of programs. Although Mrs. Annette H. Atkins made a presentation at the very first National Intramural Association in 1950, women were not permitted membership in the NIA until 1971. In 1972, the United States Congress passed the Educational Amendments Act which brought about the writing of the Title IX. The Title IX guidelines have also had a far reaching effect on athletics and intramurals because they state that no person shall, on the basis of sex, be excluded from participation in, or be denied the benefits of, or be subject to discrimination under any educational program or activity operated by a recipient of federal support because of sex.

RELATED AREAS

Many different types of organizations and interest groups are concerned with planning general leisure activities or special activities. These groups may be publicly supported, church organized, or be private interest groups or commercial ventures. There is no way that an intramural department can be "all things to all people"; however, the personnel in a department should be willing to assist other programs whenever possible. In addition to providing professional guidance, a department can provide organizations with qualified officials for many activities because it trains student personnel who are capable of officiating at many different activities.

Before briefly discussing the types of organizations which provide programs for leisure, it should be pointed out that these organizations often give students and staff members the opportunity to

receive remuneration for their services. Frequently recreation department-
ments hire teachers and students not only to work as officials but
also to conduct various aspects of the program. In many smaller
communities, it is the physical education teacher, coach, or intramural director who organizes various types of recreational activities
which are not related to the school assignment in order to supplement
income during the summer months.

PUBLIC RECREATION

Public recreation and park programs are generally funded through
a tax levy and conducted by professional recreation personnel. In
some instances, the recreation department may have its own facilities in which it conducts its activities, but more times than not there
is a cooperative effort with the school systems and school facilities
are used for some activities. It is difficult to define the limits of
public recreation programs because each program differs in its scope
and service to a particular community. Most programs include activities for all ages, from the "tots" to the "golden agers." Some activities which may be organized by a public recreation director are discussed later.

The diverse nature of park and recreation programs makes it
impossible in this text to recommend a program. However, an individual working in intramural or recreation should be aware of commonly accepted guidelines for making recommendations for expanding a park and recreation program. These guidelines state:

Opportunities for recreation should be available to all the people
of a community, regardless of age, sex, creed, race, or economic
status.

Planning for recreation and park services should adhere to widely
accepted principles, standards, and planning processes.

In developing park and recreation programs and sites, consideration should be given to widely accepted principles, standards,
and planning processes.

Recreation and park facilities and services should be planned
on a neighborhood, community, and districtwide basis and
considered as related parts of a unified, well-balanced system
which provides maximal opportunities for all the people in the
area of jurisdiction.

A park and playground facility should be provided in each
neighborhood, preferably adjacent to the elementary school.

Each recreation area and facility should be located conveniently within the area it is to serve and should be accessible to all the residents of the area.

Park and recreation lands should be acquired even if the limited financial resources of the public park and recreation agency oblige it to delay complete development.

The park and recreation plan must consider the requirements for management, recreation programs, leadership, and maintenance, and the cost of these requirements.

Beauty and functional efficiency should complement each other in parks and recreation facilities, and should be considered equally important goals in planning.

Maximal effort should be directed toward the development of public understanding of plans for recreation and park services.

EXPANDED SCHOOL DAY

For elementary school students buildings are kept open approximately an hour and a half after school for supervised recreation. The buildings are opened again in the evening for supervised recreation for students at the secondary school level. A similar program may be conducted on Saturday, and in some school districts, this procedure has led to school facilities becoming the center for summer programs. The school district can either sponsor this type of program itself or work in cooperation with another sponsoring organization. This concept is not new and has been successful in large school districts as well as small and in many places it is the basis of the intramural program.

At New Trier High School East, Northfield, Illinois, the boys and girls intramurals sports organization conducted a different type of expanded school-day program: "Thursday Night Community Recreation." This program was open to the high school students and their families for a modest admission fee of 75 cents. The school's facilities were open from 7:30 P.M. to 9:30 P.M., and different areas were set aside for air hockey, backgammon, badminton, basketball, billiards, card playing, floor hockey, gymnastics, handball, miniature bowling, swimming, table soccer, table tennis, and volleyball.

YMCA and YWCA

These two organizations are semiprivate and have a worldwide fellowship designed for the purpose of developing Christian character and building a Christian society. The Ys are also very active in providing recreation programs through their physical education departments. They not only offer activities to their members but also to the community both at the Y facilities and, in cooperation with the school districts, at school facilities.

An example of the extent of the programs provided by a YMCA or YWCA is indicated by the following outline taken from the *Physical Educators' Policy for the Young Mens Christian Association of Macomb, Illinois.*

Objectives

1. Provide recreation and constructive use of leisure time.
2. To develop physical skills and healthful practices.
3. To strengthen family life by a creation of a friendly atmosphere.
4. To develop an atmosphere for social participation through physical activities and good sportsmanship.

Constituency

1. It shall be the policy of this YMCA to serve as many different groups as possible in the community in ways that are effective.
2. Service shall be provided to best accomplish the objectives of this YMCA for youth, boys and girls, young adults, men, women, and families.
3. It shall be the policy of the Physical Education Committee to direct its major attention on members who have signed up for physical activities as their primary interest.
4. It shall be the policy that organizational groups within the membership have priority over non-member groups, and that both sexes be served equally in accordance with percentage of total membership.
5. It shall be the policy that emphasis upon physical recreation, health and safety, be served to the entire membership, through activities, forums, consultations and recreational programs.
6. It shall be the policy of the Physical Education Committee to serve other organizations and related groups wherever possible, by helping them to make use of the YMCA facilities or the lay or professional leadership of the YMCA.
7. It shall be the policy of the Physical Education Committee to serve the entire community through the promotion of health, physical education, learning to swim, life saving, amateur sports programs, and the development of programs and leadership in sports, games and health education.

SPECIAL SPORTS GROUPS

A very broad catagory of organizations conducts specific-sport activities for the community as well as conducting local, state, and national tournaments. These organizations are concerned primarily with one particular sport. It would be impossible to name all the organizations, because new interest groups appear yearly to conduct tournaments in various sports. Most of the organizations deal with particular age levels as well as specific sports. They receive funding through recreation departments, fraternal organizations, church organizations, and fund-raising drives. A partial list of the sports for which state or national contests are conducted at different age levels includes:

Football	Gymnastics
Punt, pass, and kick	Rifle shooting
Basketball	Softball
Hop shooting	Track and field
Wrestling	Baseball
Swimming	Pitch, bat, and throw
Hockey	Go-carts

PRIVATE CLUBS

Private clubs are nothing new in the area of recreation. More clubs are being formed all the time to provide for many new activities. There is also great expansion within clubs themselves to include more activities for their members. Today golf clubs will often include tennis and physical fitness opportunities for their members. A good example of expansion within private clubs is shown by the changes in the Sheridan Swim Club of Quincy, Illinois, which was founded for the purpose of recreation and competitive swimming. In addition to the swimming activities, the programming was changed to capitalize on the activities which were dominant in the Quincy area and to bring the unique and "change of pace" activity to the club. The club successfully arranged for trout fishing in a pool, ice skating on an outdoor pool, and sky divers jumping into a pool. On the twenty acres adjacent to the club, they added a soccer field, jogging track, cross-country jogging trails, and most recently three all-weather tennis courts. In the spring, they also set up a target green for golfers of all ages.

Another key to their success in expanding their program was cooperation with other professional agencies. When members of their staff were not qualified to conduct a class, they found an agency that specialized in the activity and had them bring their program to the club. Examples of their planning and cooperation were successfully conducted beauty schools in cooperation with *Seventeen Magazine*, exercise classes with Western Illinois University, and ballroom dancing with a local dance studio.

Another concept in the expansion of private clubs led to the Chicago Athletic Club and a private suburban golf club entering into an agreement whereby the members of each club have privileges to use the others' club facilities for a nominal fee. This enabled the members of the Athletic Club to play golf and tennis and the members of the golf club to make use of the Athletic Club's recreational facilities which included handball and squash courts, exercise room, and sauna area.

COMMERCIAL RECREATION

Just as the private clubs have expanded to include more activities, commercial recreation now offers more opportunities. These centers are generally designed for both recreation and instruction in a recreational activity. The commercially run activities and facilities might include:

Bowling	Family recreation centers for billiards
Golf	Miniature golf
Tennis	Karate instruction
Boating	Judo instruction
Skiing	Fishing
Archery	Trap and skeet shooting
Go-cart tracks	Small-bore fire arm ranges
Horseback riding	Camping
Dance studios for all ages	Baton and cheerleading schools
Sports skill camps	Family game centers, with electronic games
Skin and scuba diving	Roller skating
Ice skating	

FEDERAL AND STATE AGENCIES

The federal and state agencies are basically concerned with the operation and maintenance of the federal and state park systems. These areas are primarily used for unstructured recreational activities such as picnicking, camping, boating, fishing, hunting, golfing, horse-back riding, bicycling, skiing, ice skating, and swimming. The federal government and some state governments also aid in other forms of recreation by providing funds for programs such as camps and sports clinics for inner city or underprivileged individuals, particularly during the summer months.

For a review of the role and responsibility of the federal and state agencies, the author has taken the liberty of citing the following passages from *Illinois Outdoor Recreation*.[1]

A multilevel system of government has evolved in this country, and each level of government is assigned a specialized role. The tenets that form the basis for delineating the specific governmental roles, relationships, and responsibilities proposed throughout this plan are identified as follows:

1. Government, on behalf of the people, is responsible and accountable for making sound decisions and carrying out programs that are in the public interest. To be effective, the government must be as close to the people as the individual situation permits. For this reason, it is necessary that both responsibility and accountability be entrusted to the lowest level of government having the resources and capability for providing the desired services. This responsibility should be transferred to the next appropriate higher level of government when the capability of the lower level becomes burdened or when the primary benefits of the services accrue to residents of an area wider than the jurisdiction of the government providing the service.

2. Local initiative and leadership are the fiber of American life and its institutions.

3. Higher levels of government are responsible for providing leadership to lower levels by assisting in the identification and achievement of the comprehensive objectives to be reached.

4. Governments must have confidence in each other and meet fully their respective responsibilities in working toward agreed upon common goals, avoiding expedient decisions that would endanger long-term benefits to society.

5. Participation by an informed public is required if government is to serve the needs of the people. The efficient delivery of a broad range of public recreation services can be assured if these tenets are understood and acted upon.

[1] *Illinois Outdoor Recreation*, State of Illinois, Department of Conservation, Springfield, Ill., 1974, pp. 77-78.

The Federal Government

The responsibilities of the federal government are:

1. To manage the elements of the total outdoor recreation system, such as the National Park System and National Wildlife Refuge System, that are of national or international significance.
2. To provide leadership to states by cooperatively identifying the comprehensive outdoor recreation objectives to be reached, particularly through national long-range plans and by assisting the states financially, technically, and by example in reaching such objectives.
3. To provide audience and give consideration to recommendations presented by states.
4. To provide leadership, programs, and assistance to states in the fields of leisure, outdoor, and environmental education.
5. To conduct and support research that will aid sound decision-making.

State Government

The responsibilities of state governments are:

1. To concern itself with the elements of the total outdoor recreation system that are of statewide or regional significance such as the state park system and the state wildlife management system.
2. To provide leadership to local government by cooperatively identifying comprehensive state outdoor recreation objectives, particularly through state long-range plans and to assist local governments financially, technically, and by example in reaching such objectives.
3. To provide audience for and give consideration to the recommendations presented by local governments.
4. To make recommendations to the federal government on policies, procedures, and programs.
5. To work cooperatively with other states.
6. To provide leadership, programs, and assistance to local governments in the fields of leisure, outdoor, and environmental education.
7. To conduct and support research efforts that will aid in sound decision-making.

Local Government

1. To provide a foundation of services by concerning itself with the elements of the total outdoor recreation system that are

of local significance, such as county and city park and recreation systems.

2. To make recommendations to state government on policies, procedures, and programs related to the total statewide outdoor recreation system.

3. To assist in reaching comprehensive outdoor recreation objectives by preparing and carrying out comprehensive plans for their jurisdictions.

4. To assume primary leadership in carrying out leisure outdoor and environmental education programs.

5. To coordinate and cooperate with other units of local government to assure efficiency and effectiveness in the delivery of public recreation services.

6. To conduct and support research efforts that will aid in sound decision-making.

Federal and state governments are also greatly concerned with individuals in mental and correctional institutions and for many years have hired personnel to conduct extensive recreation programs in an effort to aid in the rehabilitation of the individuals.

The National Advisory Commission on Criminal Justice Standards and Goals clearly stated the purpose of recreation in correctional institutions when it established Standard 11.8—Recreation Programs. The Commission stated that:

Each institution should develop and implement immediately policies and practices for the provision of recreation activities as an important resource for changing behavior patterns of offenders.

1. Every institution should have a full-time trained and qualified recreation director with responsibility for the total recreation program of the facility. He should also be responsible for integration of the program with total planning for the offender.

2. Program planning for every offender should include specific information concerning interests and capabilities related to leisure-time activities.

3. Recreation should provide an on-going interaction with the community while the offender is incarcerated. This can be accomplished by bringing volunteers and community members into the institution and taking offenders into the community for recreational activities. Institutional restrictions in policy and practice which bars use of community recreational resources should be relaxed to the maximum extent possible.

4. The range of recreational activities to be made available to inmates should be broad in order to meet a wide range of in-

terests and talents and stimulate the development of the constructive use of leisure time that can be followed when the offender is reintegrated into the community. Recreational activities to be offered inmates should include music, athletics, painting, writing, drama, handcrafts, and similar pursuits that reflect the legitimate leisure time activities of free citizens.

Mr. Jerry Colgate, Recreation Supervisor at the Colorado State Reformatory, Buena Vista, Colorado has incorporated a program of recreational activities for the residents of the correctional institution.

A look at the philosophy for the program indicates the importance of recreation in a correctional institution.[2]

The recreation department at the Colorado State Reformatory is structured somewhat similar to a small college physical education program with respect to classes and out approach to athletic competition. Each individual now and in the future needs outlets of enjoyment which he can use for the refreshment of his body and mind. Our program is made up of five distinct areas. These are recreation classes both inside and outside the institution, intramurals, arts and crafts, free time activities and programs such as movies, bands and plays.

Man is instinctively competitive and he continues to compete throughout life. This competition can be of a very high intense level or simply competing for the enjoyment. We feel that each individual at the Colorado State Reformatory should be given the opportunity to increase his ability in many leisure time activities so that his enjoyment increases. Many individuals who are placed in institutions failed to have a meaningful outlet to pursue in their leisure time so therefore, they commit crimes against society.

Emphasis in the recreation department is placed on lifetime activities which may be used by the resident once he is released. We are continually working with residents who fail in society in one way or another. Throughout the program we try to teach each individual that he can succeed and be competitive in activities of enjoyment. This type of competition can build the esteem of the man so that he can be proud of himself in a worthwhile activity. Not all men are athletically inclined so therefore, the out program is wide with many different facets. Our program varies from the competitive type sports to painting and handicrafts in our arts and crafts program.

---

[2] Reprinted with permission of Mr. Jerry Colgate. (See C. S. R. Recreation Program, Colorado Department of Institutions, Buena Vista, Colorado, p. 1.)

In order to implement the philosophy a program is scheduled as follows:

Activity classes. The activity classes are held on Tuesday and Thursday mornings and skills of the activity are emphasized. The rules and regulations of each activity are introduced with stress being placed on participation and enjoyment of a physical activity. The following are the activity classes taught throughout the year.

(a) Wrestling and tumbling
(b) Basketball and tumbling
(c) Weight training and handball
(d) Softball and track and field
(e) Handball, horseshoes and volleyball
(f) Flag football and speedball
(g) Basketball and handball

Special interest classes. These classes are conducted for individuals who have interest in a special activity. There is a group of classes taught within the wall and a group of classes that are taught in the surrounding communities and mountains. Each class has a two month duration and the classes are half a day, once a week, except skiing which is a full day class.

Inside Classes

(a) Net games
(b) Ice skating
(c) Gymnastics
(d) First aid

Outside Classes

(a) Skiing
(b) Golf
(c) Tennis
(d) Bowling
(e) Fishing
(f) Swimming
(g) Officiating

Club activities. The clubs are used to establish teams who are permitted to compete in leagues outside the institutions as well as compete with teams which travel to the reformatory to compete. Club sports consist of softball, basketball, weight lifting and swimming.

Intramurals. The purpose of the program is to give the residents meaningful competitive activities at all different levels. Intramural teams are made up of residents in different wings and different incentive levels. This causes an intermingling of residents which helps the socialization of individuals from wing to wing. All teams that participate in the intramural activities are to be integrated. The number of participants of each race is specified for each activity. The integration of teams helps each member of the team to understand different individuals and breaks down the racial overtones that might exist with teams of a single race. New activities are added when there is an interest shown by the residents. The basic intramural program includes volleyball, basketball, handball, small game tournaments, fast and slow pitch softball, baseball, flag football and wrestling. There is also a track and field meet held from which the times and distances are sent in for national competition.

Free Play. Free Play is scheduled for all residents seven days a week. The residents are scheduled by wings for the various recreational areas of the institution. It is during this hour and a half period that the residents have an opportunity to receive instruction and engage in leather work, wood carving, lapidary, metal art, painting and music.

2. The Director

*The most important motive for work in
the school or in life is the pleasure in work,
pleasure in its result and in the knowledge of
the value of the result to the community.
Such a psychological foundation alone leads
to a joyous desire for the highest possession of
men, knowledge and artist-like workmanship.*

Albert Einstein

The individual who is selected as the director of an intramural program will find that each institution presents its own unique situation in regard to administering a program. No subsititute has yet been found for individual ingenuity and initiative; therefore, through the use of personal attributes and the suggested guidelines for directing a program, an individual should be able to establish and conduct a program with a minimal amount of problems. This chapter will present a view of the responsibilities of a director in a student-oriented program and describe philosophy, financing, budget, promotion, legal responsibilities, and evaluation of the program.

PHILOSOPHICAL VIEW

The philosophy of intramural directors cannot concern only the intramural program. A good intramural director must have a broad philosophical view in regard to the total education of the students. The director must be eclectic and choose from various doctrines.

Intramural directors are *essentialistic* in that they believe there are certain educational values and experiences that all students must possess. They believe that students should and must acquire knowledge and skill. The students should develop the habits and skills to direct their lives and realize the enjoyment of life. They believe that students must develop their skills and intellect to their maximal potential, and to accomplish this educators must pass the proven facts of past experiences on to future generations.

Intramural directors are *progressive* to the extent that they believe in individual differences, student freedom of choice, within reason, and that in our dynamic society change is imminent and good. They believe that education can only be measured by the changes made in the students by their experiences and that there must be student involvement in the determination of objectives in order to generate the desired purpose and interest. They believe that pupil growth is the primary goal. They believe that there is always a social context to learning and that we must adapt our curricula to dominant changes in society.

Intramural directors are *realistic* in understanding that education does not exist by itself. Education at all levels is greatly affected by the changes of society. The knowledge explosion, advances in technology, the new awareness of the individual's rights and needs, the emerging concept of "personhood" are examples of causes and/or effects of changes in our society. Education seeks to prepare students for their role in society, and higher education, in particular, seeks to give meaning to the life of the student. Just as a cell in a living organism must change in response to changes in its environment in order to live, educators must be prepared to alter their programs to meet certain contemporary needs.

Intramural directors are *pragmatic* in recognizing that as members of an educational system they serve a function of assisting in educating individuals both liberally and professionally and that without students, their roles would be nonexistent. They view their programs as being just part—an important part—of the education of all students, because they work with the students as an entire entity, and through the involvement of the total student (mind and body) they strive to achieve the goals of education.

The intramural program should be consistent with the social philosophy of the American way of life and should contribute to the purpose of education in perpetuating, maintaining, and advancing the social order. The intramural program throughout its activities can be one of the most natural laboratories for the right social experiences. A sound program is an open and operative program through which a humanitarian view of the conditions of mankind can be developed. Students of both sexes, all creeds, colors, and races are placed together for a true social experience. The intramural program should develop tolerance of other people's opinions and levels of skills in the various activities conducted. All students should be encouraged to contribute their thinking. Thoughts and ideas should be respected by all, and settlement of a problem arrived at through the group process. A program which is operated under rules and regulations and experiences which require adherences to the law is a program that will succeed. These rules and regulations are similar to the laws outside of the college. Adherence to rules and regulations should be taken as a desirable and democratic necessity. The program should help develop students who possess *civic* responsibility and are able to think through issues in a calm, and intelligent manner.

The structure of the program that students will follow should consist of experiences that are planned for their needs as individuals as well as members of the educational institution. The program should be student centered, and the experiences gained by the students in the program should promote an understanding of basic concepts, principles, and relationships rather than only offering the motion of playing the contest. These experiences should guarantee the chance to demonstrate proficiency in physical skill and to develop desirable attitudes and essential personal and social qualities.

In the planning of the program, the students should be involved in cooperative efforts with the intramural staff. The election of experiences within the program should be determined by the interest of the students, their backgrounds, abilities, and needs. Once students have identified interests in being in the program, these experiences should begin as early as possible. The various opportunities for contact with fellow students and other recreational leaders may insure a well-rounded educational experience. The laboratory experiences which are provided by the intramural department must be appropriate to the needs and readiness level of the individual.

A continuous short-range and long-range planning program must be an integral part of any intramural program. To enhance the planning process, all aspects of the program should be continuously evaluated in terms of the basic concepts and objectives of the program. Directors as members of a profession, have the responsibility to contribute to this ever changing field. They are looked to by current and past students for leadership in these areas. They should instill in students an attitude so that they may become producers of new ways and not just users of the old. The practicing professional director should be one who is able to discriminate between the methods and materials which are good and those which are bad in the performance of his or her duties.

To summarize what the philosophical view means for the leadership role of the director who is planning an intramural program would be to say the director must be product oriented more than process oriented. The quality of the product—the student—should be of primary concern, not the how of developing a program.

PRACTICING THE PHILOSOPHY

In the student-oriented philosophy of intramurals, the director has the overall supervisory responsibilities, but must create an atmosphere in which everyone feels they have an equal say in regard to the program; therefore, they will assume equal responsibility for the success of the program. There should never be a communication gap between the director and the students. The students should feel free to express their ideas and philosophy in regard to the existing program.

The director works with the students and not over the students.

When the director assigns work tasks to the students and then joins in and helps perform these tasks, this creates an atmosphere in which the students feel they are a vital link in the program. This interrelationship between the students and the administrator may provide the student with a feeling of satisfaction when achieving a goal.

The phrase "everyone loves to play and no one wants to work" is not true in a student-oriented program because it provides the students with the opportunity to work at the administrative level in planning and supervising a program. The opportunity for educational benefits gained in assisting in the administration of the program are not ordinarily available to all students.

The director should instill everyone with the idea that service is the whole reason for the existence of the intramural department; therefore, everyone should go out of their way to assist students in any way possible with their requests. They should encourage all types of socially accepted recreational activities even though they may not be under the auspices of the intramural department. Intramurals offer the chance to bring the values of competition to the masses of students who are not good enough for "the varsity." Intramurals are based on participation with the aim of providing students with structured and unstructured playing opportunity in as near real-life situations as possible.

A good example of a student-oriented program is that at New Trier High School West, Northfield, Illinois, which is entirely student organized and administered through strong student leadership and a faculty sponsor. The intramural organization consists of a faculty sponsor designated as the "intramural director," a 12-man Student Board selected from the previous year's intramural staff (students that have volunteered their services as referees and to assist in administrative details), and 21 current members of the intramural staff.

Early in the school year, a preliminary organization and in-service training session is conducted over a weekend (Friday through Sunday) when the intramural board and the intramural director plan the year's program. The cost of staying at a nearby resort is defrayed by the participating students and the Dad's Club. The intramural board and the intramural director meet daily during a common free period, to carry on the various functions of the program. Special meetings are called during a 20-minute advisory period, with Fridays reserved for a meeting of the intramural staff. Organizational meetings of advisory representatives or individuals for activities about to begin are called after school.

In addition to working together to provide a good program for all students, the intramural board and staff have social functions, with many of their members helping to create a healthy atmosphere. All of the costs for their social events are assumed by the participating students. Once a month, a party is held on a Friday night; a carry-out lunch is ordered and the students remain at school for an evening of gym jam. Bimonthly, the intramural board and staff attend a professional sports event in Chicago, such as a basketball or hockey game. The group leaves school in the late afternoon, has dinner at a prominent restaurant, and then goes to the game At the end of the school year an intramural banquet is held at a local restaurant where symbolic awards are presented to particular staff members, and the following year's intramural board is selected.

There are four nouns which may be helpful in understanding the philosophy of student-oriented intramurals: participation, imagination, modification, and innovation. The suffix "tion" has been added to a verb in each case to make it a noun. Often individuals in administrative positions are quick to forget that the base of these four words is a verb—which indicates action. It is the action which is important in regard to the philosophy.

Participation. Every director should make an honest attempt to provide a wide range of activities which will enable all students to participate if they so desire. The program should be structured so that activities which interest the student may be added for their enjoyment. A director must be careful not to succumb to the pressures of our quantitatively-oriented society in which degree of success is measured only from a statistical standpoint. Too great a proliferation of intramural activities is not in the best interest of the students and staff. The enthusiasm of the students and staff may be undermined when just for numbers' sake a great many activities are added making it impossible to cope with demands placed upon their time. Directors should earnestly strive to make decisions in the interest of the students and not for the glorification of the program.

Imagination. Directors should never cease to make use of their imaginative ideas or the ideas of the students when it comes to planning the program. The imagination of the individual is unlimited, and programs can only advance if resourceful and creative concepts are put into practice.

Modification. The modification of many activities is the key to providing enjoyable activities for the students. Time, facilities, and ability levels may require modification of a number of activities. There are no rules "written in stone" which indicate that any activity cannot be modified to meet the needs of the intramural population.

Often the published regulations for certain activities are not particularly suited for intramural participants and may detract from enjoyment of an activity when the skills of the students are limited.

Innovation. The director should not be afraid to innovate and bring about new programs by changing established patterns. There is no end to the ways in which the director may improve the program by breaking from established patterns in order to provide more opportunity for the students to participate in activities during their leisure. Most programs have shown a trend of decrease in the number of individuals who participate in highly organized team events and an increase in the number of individuals who participate in individual, dual, and co-rec events. Two reasons for the trend to more individualized events can be offered. First, students can participate in the nonteam activities throughout their lives; and second, they may feel that they have participated in enough team games during their educational careers.

FINANCING

The intramural program at any level should be financed by the same means as the rest of the educational programs. Educators have long been aware of the values gained by the students through participation in intramurals; however, the recent trends in raising costs and decreasing support (taxes or student-fee funds) have once again brought about a financial squeeze on the budgets for intramurals. Because most intramural programs are conducted after school hours, individuals responsible for allotting funds believe these are extracurricular activities and, therefore, an unnecessary expenditure of educational funds.

If the intramural director properly plans and administers the program, the cost per student per year will be considerably lower than the cost for other phases of the educational of extracurricular programs. The cost per student participant in intramurals is considerably less because administrative overhead, coaches' salaries, teachers' salaries, special officials, elaborate travel, and expensive uniforms are not part of the program. Another factor in lowering the cost per student participant, is that the intramural program is designed and conducted for the entire student population and not for just a select few.

For several years there has been a question as to just where the intramural program should fall in the administrative structure. In the public school system it has been considered part of the physical education or athletic department, whereas at the college level, the program may be under the physical education department, athletic department, a separate intramural department, of the office of student affairs. The director should seek the administrative structure that provides the most adequate funding for the program. The following paragraphs will discuss the practices currently used to finance the program.

General Funds

These funds are generated from either taxes or tuition fees and are the best source of financial support for the program. The amount of money allotted from the internal budget should go directly to the intramural program. It may be administered by the physical education department, athletic department, or intramural department, but it should be a separate allocation just for the activities in intramurals.

Student Fees

Students pay a fee when they register, and the money raised is used to conduct student activities on the campus. The control of this fund at an institution generally rests in the hands of the student government organization and the intramural program receives an allocation just as other student groups do. Some schools have built their program through this form of "student taxation," and the money is either directly allocated to and administered through the intramural department or the office of student affairs.

Athletic Event Gate Receipts

Even though the receipts are generally returned to the general fund and intramural and athletics have separate established budgets, this is not a good source for financing the intramural program. The amount of revenue generated by this method is very unpredictable, and when gate receipts begin to fall off, the intramural budget will be the first to suffer because the athletic department will insist that they are generating the income.

Entry Fees and Dues

The charging of entry fees and dues will never totally finance a program but may supplement appropriated funds. This is not a good means of obtaining funds because it may detract from the original intent of intramurals by limiting the participation of those individuals who cannot afford to pay the dues or fees. The entry fee is charged to both teams and individuals when entering an event. The amount of the fee varies depending on the type of activity. Dues are charged to all individuals who wish to participate in the program. These dues are paid either on a quarterly or yearly basis. Either method is an "administrative headache" and creates too much red tape for the amount of revenue generated.

Forfeit Fees

Forfeit fees are not really established to generate much revenue but rather as an attempt to insure that there will not be forfeits. The fee is generally returned to the individual or organization if they do not forfeit. Once again this type of assessment discourages voluntary participation and requires a great deal of bookwork and the use of two types of receipts in order to keep records straight.

Other Methods of Generating Income

A number of methods have been tried to generate additional income for the intramural department. Just because a project has been successful at one place or another does not guarantee its future success or failure. When it is necessary to use this method of raising additional funds, the director must make a careful and adequate assessment of the situation before embarking on the project.

The citizens in any community are continually beset by one important fund raising campaign after another; therefore, careful planning and timing should be used. The director should never attempt more than one large money raising campaign during a school year. Professional fund raisers have indicated that organizations attempting to raise funds should aviod the month of September because of school costs, December and January because of Christmas spending, and April because of taxes.

A partial list of methods for supplementing the budget includes:

1. *Charging admission.* The intramural department may set up events for which an admission is charged. These events should be conducted in the evening so that parents and the general public may attend. The key to the financial success of any event is a good program, and proper advance publicity is an absolute necessity. Various intramural programs have had success with the following types of activities:

   a. Sports nights—evenings that are set aside for parents and students to participate in activities together.

    b. Carnivals and exhibitions staged by the student body as well as intramural athletes.

    c. Cosponsored performances by teams, such as the Harlem Globetrotters, a roller derby, professional wrestling, and other traveling athletes. These groups are generally looking for arenas to hold their events. They are willing to provide the posters for advance advertising and to give a share of gate receipts to the sponsoring organization. Intramural departments should be careful not to enter into any agreement that requires a guarantee.

    d. Cosponsored evenings of donkey basketball or donkey softball.

    e. Cosponsored presentations of professional carnivals.

    f. Exhibition games between IM champions, IM all-stars, faculty, and alumni.

    g. Showings of special sports films or old movies.

    h. School dances.

2. *Sales.* There are companies which provide schools with catalogs and items to sell for fund raising projects. These include magazine subscriptions, light bulbs, cookies, peanuts, special buttons, Christmas candy, orange and apple baskets for Christmas, and school stationery. A good method to motivate the students is to give them a percentage of the sales after they sell a certain amount. For example: no return up to $50 in sales, that 5 percent between $50 and $100, after which the percentage could go up to 10 percent. The intramural department can also hold bake sales and "white elephant" rummage sales.

3. *Percentage day.* A good method for getting additional income is to have a quick-food chain, or other commerical organizations, agree to donate a percentage of a day's proceeds if the intramural department will go out and promote the day for the commercial agency.

4. *Concessions, programs, parking.* These are good sources of additional income; however, most athletic departments are keeping these sources of revenue for their own purposes.

5. *Automatic vending machines.* The intramural department could examine the possibility of automatic vending machines, especially those which distribute orange juice, milk, and snacks that are sugarfree.

6. *One-day special projects.* Students may be willing to assist in one-day fund raising events which could include car washes,

paper drives, collecting bottles and cans for recycling, and volunteering for community service projects for which some businesses may compensate by contributing funds to the intramural program.

7. *Pancake breakfasts or wild-game dinners.* These can be big money makers if the local merchants and sportsmen are willing to donate the food and game.

8. *Equipment rental.* If the school or university has canoes, bicycles, tandem bikes, sleds, toboggans, camping equipment, or other unusual recreational equipment they may possibly gain additional revenue by renting out this equipment. Any rental agreement should require a deposit or security to the rental value of the equipment.

9. *Special programs.* Some colleges and universities have also had success in adding to their income by sponsoring excursions such as trips to foreign countries, trips to entertainment capitals, trips to football bowl games, and skiing, camping, canoeing, and scuba diving trips. Universities have had some success in generating additional income through extra teaching of various skills. Universities have occasionally large commercial concerns to underwrite special tournaments and events as an advertising device, and the intramural program has benefited from the profits of the activity.

As stated earlier in this chapter, ideally the intramural program should be financed completely through appropriated funds; however, in our present society it may be necessary to use a combination of methods to finance the program.

BUDGET

The director must be able to properly prepare and justify the budget proposal for the program. This individual should be well aware of the procedure used by the institution in preparing the "fiscal interpretation of the program." There are basically three phases of budget preparation: (1) determination of scope of the program during the fiscal period, (2) estimation of the expenditure necessary to properly conduct the program, and (3) estimation of the amount of revenue and receipts anticipated.

Before determining the scope of the program, the director must review operational costs and the expenditures that will be involved in reaching the goals set for the program. Properly examining the scope of the program while preparing the budget will make it possible to secure more items and services because a means for acquiring them will be included in the plan for spending the money.

To estimate the expenditures, the director must outline the areas for which funds will be spent. Careful consideration must be given to additional programming and inflationary costs in regard to equipment, commodities, contractural services, and personal services. The inventory report, which is discussed in Chapter 8, should be helpful in the preparation of the budget. An outline of expenditures would include:

1. Equipment.
   a. Game equipment.
   b. Permanent equipment such as goals, timing apparatus, and machinery.
   c. Office equipment.
2. Commodities.
   a. Office supplies such as pencils, magic markers, paper, dittos, rubber bands, staples, and paper clips.
   b. Awards.
   c. Photo supplies.
3. Contractual services.
   a. Printing of handbooks, newsletters, and bulletins.
   b. Subscriptions to professional journals.
   c. Telephone.
   d. Photographer's fees.
4. Personal services.
   a. Student help as office personnel, officials, lifeguards, and supervisors.
   b. Professional staff.
5. Other expenses if appropriate.
   a. Travel to professional meetings for staff.
   b. Travel for students to student meetings.
   c. Insurance premiums.
   d. Paint used for marking fields.
   e. School membership in professional organizations.
   f. Contingency fund.

The final phase in preparing the budget is to estimate the anticipated revenue that will be necessary to meet the predicted expenditures. If the funds to operate the program come from more than one source, a careful study of the income during the previous five years may prove helpful in identifying trends and assist in estimating the anticipated income.

Helpful Hints

1. Never pad the budget and anticipate a percentage cut because legislative bodies which appropriate the funds will soon become aware of this practice.
2. Always spend the yearly appropriation wisely.
3. Do not use a "slush fund."
4. Keep up to date on equipment costs.
5. Use sound accounting practices so that the books may be audited at any time.

PROMOTION

Most intramural programs will promote themselves through the enthusiasm of the students who participate. It is true that the best publicity an intramural program can receive is through the spreading of the "word" by the students; however, a director must continually promote the program. Although it is no longer necessary to sell the values of the program, it is important that the program is advanced through good public relations.

Promotion of the program, other than through student interaction, can be catagorized as involving four R's: getting the *R*ight information to the *R*ight people in the *R*ight way and at the *R*ight time. Each director should develop the best methods for accomplishing the four R's as they relate to a particular program.

Right Information

An intramural handbook can be a very important aid to any good program. A well prepared handbook will provide advertising and promotion for the program as well as inform the students of all the rules and regulations of the program.

All handbooks do not have to be printed in an elaborate fashion if it is not practical; however, the more professional the handbook, the more it will be respected by the students. It is most important that a handbook be available so that the students may refer to it and ideally every student has a copy. However, if this is not possible, a copy of the handbook should be located in each organizational unit of the program. There is no limit to what a handbook may contain, but the following areas should be included. (The regulations for each area will be described in a later chapter.)

Intramural Activities. The first section in the handbook should contain the activities to be sponsored, the dates entries are due, the dates of competition, and the type of competition.

Intramural Organization. The handbook should contain a clearly defined outline of the intramural organizational structure with special emphasis given to the governing body, membership, rosters, and league structures.

Eligibility Rules. The section on eligibility rules should clearly define who is eligible to participate in the program with subsections written to deal with varsity athletic squad members, letter award winners, squad members for playoffs, players using assumed names, players on more than one team, and with a special section devoted to student discipline.

Postponements. This section should establish the procedure that will be followed when an intramural contest has to be postponed. Special attention should be given to the replaying of a contest in a round robin or an elimination schedule.

Awards. This section should inform the students of the different awards presented in intramurals and how they may qualify for awards.

Point System. If participation is the basis of the program, then a point system should be developed and clearly defined in this section.

Description of Activities. A brief, clear description of each activity should help the students select activities in which they wish to participate.

Previous Winners. This section would contain the names of the individuals and the teams that are the defending champions in each activity. If the handbook is reproduced by professional printers, it is a good idea to include pictures of the winners.

Intramural Records. This section would contain the established intramural records in swimming, bike racing, cross country, golf, track, decathlon, and in any other timed or individual event. It is not good practice to keep records for most points scored in team contests.

If it is not feasible to reproduce a handbook, handout sheets may be used. It is also possible to put all of the above information on a desk blotter which may be passed out to the students to put on their desk or hang on the wall.

Although the handbook or other handout materials may be the best information to distribute to the students and interested individuals at the beginning of the program, the director must continually keep the students and news media informed as to weekly events and the winners from previous events.

Right People

The students are the first and most important group of the right people, because they are the potential participants in the program. They are also the best critics of the program. Figure 2.1 is an illustration of a student picking up information about entering an event. The second group is the school officials (administrator and faculty) who may have a direct or indirect influence on the program. It is extremely important that they are kept abreast of the developments as well as the needs of the program. The general public and parents make up the third population that should receive information regarding the policies and progress of the program in which their children are participating.

Right Way

Good publicity is the right way to promote the program. The director should make use of all available methods to bring about a harmonious interchange of information with the population. If at all possible, the intramural program should be publicized through newspapers, radio, and television. Time and space are valuable commodities when dealing with the news media. The director must develop good cooperation between the intramural office and these areas in order to make the best use of their expertise. Special attention should be paid to deadlines and to materials that can be used by the news media.

Not all programs will be able to disseminate their information through professional news media; therefore, the director should be prepared to use other avenues such as:

1. *Bulletin Boards.* There should be a place on the bulletin board to publicize coming events as well as the results of past events. If at all possible there should be a separate bulletin board or area where the activities of the day may be posted.

2. *Posters.* Commercial posters can be used to publicize the program; however, it is much more effective if the students use their imagination and create posters with popular characters. (Fig. 2.1)

3. *Slogans.* Catchy slogans or signs that use a play on words often attract attention.

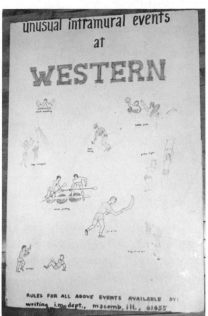

Figure 2.1
Student picking up an entry blank.

4. *Attention Getters.* These devices appear all of a sudden and not in the daily routine of the students. Examples would be a series of footprints on the floor leading to a special announcement or a large object, such as a pushball, placed on the roof of a building or the ceiling of the gymnasium.

5. *Printed Materials.* School bulletins, monthly IM newsletters, billfold-size schedule cards, or complete activity lists with entry and playing dates, as illustrated in Figure 4.1, can be used.

Right Time

It is always best to get the promotional material out well in advance of the event so that students can plan to participate. As recommended earlier, the yearly calendar should be available to all students and follow-up information should be posted to remind them of the event. This follow-up information in the form of posters, flyers, etc., should appear about one week prior to the event. Daily phone calls are a very good method of reaching organizations.

EVALUATING THE PROGRAM

The intramural program is continually being evaluated by the students as they are participating in the activities. The director should also continually evaluate not only the personnel involved in program, but the program itself. In order to make sure that the evaluation process is not left to chance, the director should develop a check list of criteria.

If the director permits distortions to creep in which divert the original purpose, thoughtless administrative practices can seriously impair the good inherent in an intramural program. In order to keep the program wholly within the original guidelines and democratic, the following characteristics should be well preserved.

1. The program should serve *all* students, providing participation outlets for everyone, no matter how small the group; however, the total program should not be dictated by the selfish interests of a few individuals or special groups.

2. The program should exclude no one, honor all who are deserving, be arranged to retain as many teams and individuals for the whole season as possible, and show no favoritism whatsoever in regard to sex, class, race, or any other distinction. Students who may lack in skill, ability, or have

physical handicaps should not be assigned meaningless tasks in the program, but rather they should be encouraged to participate through modifications of some activities.

3. Intramural programs sometimes are allowed to succumb to the lure of gaining a championship or a champion. The desire to attain supremacy may cause the use of elimination rather than round robin tournaments. Championships should not be the guiding goal in democratically administered programs.

4. Awards should not be the ultimate outcome of the program. Because intramurals are voluntary, the players should play for the values within the games—fun, friendship, or the exhilaration which comes from testing one's skill against that of one's contemporaries. Such simple pleasures are naturally supplemented by prestige and social approval.

5. Intramural programs provide a fine opportunity for the development of democratic experiences through leadership. Teams may be coached, managed, and captained by students; students should have a part in policy making and administration; officiating can be done by students.

6. The intramural equipment should be of the same high quality that is used by physical education and athletics. All students should be equal in their rights to use facilities, space, and equipment. When like standards apply to all programs much is done to convey a feeling of equality of opportunity to the rank and file of students.

A good evaluative check list which poses questions about the program before, during, and after the season was prepared by Craft Educational Services. Although prepared for secondary schools, the areas covered apply to most programs. However, one question which should have been included would have asked for students' input.

AN INTRAMURAL EVALUATION CHECK LIST[1]

Before the Season

1. Do I have adequate facilities?
2. Do I have adequate supplies and equipment?
3. Have I a good storage system?
4. Are all items marked and identified?
5. Have I planned for adequate safety supervision?

[1] Physical Education Newsletter, Croft Educational Services, March 1, 1966.

6. Have I scheduled a variety of seasonal sports?
7. Have I informed my administrator as to what we plan to do?
8. Have I involved as many faculty members as possible?
9. Have I informed and involved the PTA whenever practical?
10. Have I advertised the program by daily bulletins, PE class announcements, signs, posters, and newspaper releases?
11. Have I checked all community agencies to reduce conflicts in scheduling?
12. Have I planned seasonal activities that are neither too long nor too short?
13. Am I really enthusiastic about the program?
14. Do I have a standings bulletin board in a prominent place?
15. Have I posted a schedule of all proposed intramural activities?
16. Have I posted clear-cut rules governing all activities for all to see and do I insist that everyone understands and follows the rules?
17. Do I have well-trained student officials?
18. Do I have good captains who know their jobs?
19. Do the captains and team members know the rules of the league and the sport they're playing?

Seasonal Organization and Operation

1. Have I organized teams using a system that will work in our school?
2. Have I planned so that all who want to participate may participate?
3. Have I included activities for all grades and abilities?
4. Have I made being on a team attractive for all?
5. Do I have an effective means of checking attendance?
6. Do all teams know who, when, and where they play?
7. Have I developed a system to control absenteeism?
8. Do I have a plan to reorganize leagues if teams drop out?
9. Do I have a method of publicizing games (photography and journalism clubs)?

After the Season

1. Do I have a good awards program?

2. Have I based my awards on attendance and participation as well as ability?

3. Do I have team awards and trophies?

4. Do I have an all-star versus league champion game at the end of each season in each sport?

5. Do I have an awards day (father-son night, letter day)?

SAFETY, ACCIDENT PREVENTION AND MANAGEMENT

Intramural personnel should always be aware that the safety of the individuals who are participating should have a higher priority than winning the contest. When it comes to the safety of the participants, in addition to establishing the playing rules for the contest, a number of areas must concern all intramural directors.

Medical Examination. If it is a school policy that all students must have a medical examination before participating, then the director must implement a procedure which assures that no students participate who have not passed a physical examination. About the only way that a director can assure compliance is to use the "frozen roster system" which means that only those individuals who have have a medical examination and therefore appear on the roster, put out by the intramural office, can participate. This is a time consuming and restrictive method, but may be necessary in order to conform to a school policy. Most schools require physical examinations before students enroll in class and this serves to meet the requirement for any school sponsored function. A good number of schools do not worry about physical examinations for intramural participants because the intramural program is voluntary; therefore, the students are made responsible for determining their own physical limits when entering intramural competition.

Checking Facilities and Equipment. All playing areas should be inspected each day to assure that they are free from obstructions such as glass, sticks, holes, and metal objects that may cause bodily injury to the participants. Any time that equipment is to be used by the intramural participants, it should be checked carefully to assure it is safe. If the equipment is hand-me-down because it is no longer safe for varsity athletes it should not be used. Gymnastics apparatus and indoor playing surfaces should be clean and carefully checked before they are used by intramurals.

First Aid. When and if an accident does occur, all personnel should be instructed to administer the necessary first aid and provide comfort to the injured until the individual can be properly moved to a health care center, hospital, or doctor's office. Each institution will have its own procedure for moving an injured individual, and the intramural director should be sure that all personnel are aware of the institution's regulations. It is recommended that a communicative device (telephone, walkie-talkie, or CB radio) be easily available to the intramural playing area.

The intramural supervisor should have enough common sense to know that not all injuries necessitate having the individual moved by an ambulance or security officer. The supervisor should be able to determine the urgency and seriousness of the injury when it comes to sprains, broken bones, and excessive bleeding. A rule of thumb might be to never move an individual who has fallen on the back or neck or who has become unconscious while participating.

Injury Report. It is humanly impossible to file an injury report on every bump, bruise, sprain, or cut in an intramural program. The supervisors and officials should be made aware that a report should be filled out on any individual for whom a contest was delayed and for whom any form of first aid was administered. The individual who is filling out the report should not bother the injured person with a great number of questions but merely seek to determine the important facts from the injured individual, officials, teammates, or spectators. An example of an injury report appears in Figure 2.2.

LEGAL RESPONSIBILITY

Although not as directly related to the intramural program as setting up and maintaining a program, legal responsibilities may be of importance to the director. This section will in no way attempt to point out all the legal ramifications when it comes to legal liability but merely investigate what the problems might be, what can be done to prevent their occurrence, and what may be done in defense.[2]

Legal Terms

The following are the most common terms associated with legal liability. The definitions for these terms are taken from a law dictionary.[3]

[2] The author recommends that if readers really wish to examine precedent cases, they should refer to Herb Appenzeller books *Gym to Jury* and *Athletics and Law* which are published by the Michie Company of Charlottesville, Virginia.

[3] Henry C. Black, *Black's Law Dictionary*, Revised Fourth Edition, by permission. West Publishing Co., St. Paul, Minn. Copyright © Reprinted.

1. *Assumption of Risk.* Exists where none of fault for injury rests with plaintiff, but where plaintiff assumes consequences of injury occurring through fault of defendant, person or fault of no one.
2. *Defendant.* The part against whom relief or recovery is sought in action or suit.
3. *Loco Parentis.* In the place of a parent; charged factitiously, with a parent's rights, duties, responsibilities.
4. *Liable.* Bound or obligated in law or equity; responsibility; chargeable; answerable; compellable to make satisfaction, compensation, or restitution.
5. *Negligence.* The omission to do something which a reasonable man, guided by those ordinary considerations which ordinarily regulate human affairs, would do, or the doing of something which a reasonable and prudent man would not do
6. *Contributory Negligence.* Any want of ordinary care on the part of the person injured (or on the part of another whose negligence is imputable to him), which combined and concurred with the defendant's negligence, and contributed to the injury as a proximate cause therefore, and as an element without which the injury would not have occurred.
7. *Nuisance.* That class of wrongs that arise from the unreasonable, unwarrantable, or unlawful use be a person of his own property, either real or personal, or from his own improper, indecent, or unlawful personal conduct, working an obstruction of or injury to the right of another or of the public, and producing material annoyance, inconvenience, discomfort, or hurt, that the law will presume resulting damage.
8. *Plaintiff.* A person who brings an action; the party who complains or sues in a personal action and is so named on the record.
9. *Tort.* A legal wrong committed upon the person or property independent of contract. It may be either (1) a direct invasion of some legal right of the individual; (2) the infraction of some public duty by which special damages accrues to the individual.

Liability

All individuals who are working with students in the intramural program have a moral as well as a legal responsibility to conduct the events as safely as possible. There is no fool proof way to prevent bruises, cuts, and possible broken bones when students are competing against one another; however, the director, through rules and

Name of injured _____ Date _____

Local address _____ Phone _____

Nature of Injury

Place of accident _____ Time _____

Activity _____

First aid rendered _____ By whom _____

Circumstances of accident

Comments

Circle correct response

Removed from playing area by (a) personal car, (b) security officer, (c) ambulance

Taken to: (a) health center, (b) residence hall, (c) emergency room

Witness to accident _____

Officials on duty _____

Report filed by_____

File report with Intramural Director, Room 105, Western Hall

Figure 2.2
Intramural injury report.

selection of activities, should eliminate unneccessary risks to the participants.

Innocent as intramural personnel may individually feel themselves to be of wrongful conduct toward the participants, causes may arise in which students sue on account of injuries sustained by them while under intramural supervision. Each person has a right to freedom from bodily injury, intentionally or carelessly caused by others; yet in every human activity there is some possibility of injury. If the risk is great, the legal liability for possible injuries should be investigated.

Intramural personnel and teachers at the public school level do occupy a unique position in relation to their pupils as they are in *loco parentis* in all matters relating to care and guidance. A teacher takes the place of the parent in educational matters and the parent surrenders such powers as may be necessary to educate the child. Therefore, although teachers do not enjoy any more freedom from suits and liability than any other persons, this unique position of being in *loco parentis* does place him beyond the limit of common responsibility in many cases. The result has been a degree of confusion as to his actual status, with the courts frequently being called in to decide the issues.

Negligence in the Law

When individuals are held liable for an accident, they must pay out of their own pocket to the person whom their negligence has injured. Liability is a legal conclusion dependent upon a state of facts; when this state of facts spells negligence, liability follows. Conversely, no matter how serious the injury, if the facts absolve the individual of negligence, he will not be held liable. Negligence is the key to liability.

Essentially, the law of negligence deals with conduct, either action or inaction, which is claimed by the injured person not to measure up to the standard of behavior required by the law of all persons in society. The suit must be brought by the child. The parents cannot sue unless they have sustained some direct pecuniary damage. Briefly, that standard of measurement may be described as the manner in which a reasonably prudent person would act under the same or similar circimstances. Therefore, a person is negligent when he/she has failed to act as a reasonably prudent person would act under the circumstances.

Negligent behavior obviously is determined by the specific details of each case; however, the following types of behavior will give general boundaries to the kinds of conduct which create actionable negligence. An act may be negligent because:

1. It is not properly done, appropriate care is not employed by the actor.

2. The circumstances under which it is done create risks, although it is done with due care and precaution.

3. The actor is indulging in acts which involve an unreasonable risk of direct and immediate harm to others.

4. The actor sets in motion a force, the continuous operation of which may be unresonably hazardous to others.

5. The actor creates a situation which is unreasonably dangerous to others because of the likelihood of the action of third persons or of inanimate forces.

6. The actor entrusts dangerous devices or instrumentalities to persons who are incompetent to use or care for them properly.

7. The actor neglects a duty of control over third persons who by reason of some incapacity or abnormality he knows to be likely to inflict intended harm upon others.

8. The actor fails to employ due care to give adequate warning.

9. The actor fails to exercise proper care in looking out for persons whom he has reason to believe may be in a danger zone.

10. The actor fails to employ appropriate skill to perform acts undertaken.

11. The actor fails to take adequate precautions to avoid harm to others before entering upon certain conduct where such precaution is reasonably necessary.

12. The actor fails to inspect and repair instrumentalities or mechanical devices used by others.

13. The actor's conduct prevents a third person from assisting persons imperiled through no fault of his own.

14. The actor's written or spoken word creates negligent mis-representations.

Preventing Negligence. Perhaps the greatest opportunity for avoiding the imposition of liability is for the individual to be aware of steps that can be taken to prevent a case being built on negligence. Although they are not directly relevant to intramural programs, a good set of precautions to prevent negligence in the schools was suggested years ago by Thomas Steege:[4]

---

[4] Thomas Steege, "Negligence in Schools," *The American School Board Journal,* May, 1956, pp. 47-8.

1. Periodic inspections of buildings and grounds.

2. Teachers and pupils should be taught to alert the principal to dangerous or defective conditions observed by them.

3. Immediate action should be taken to eliminate threats to the safety of either the pupils or the public.

4. In school shops, teachers should give thorough instructions on the proper use of machines and on the safety regulations relating thereto.

5. Pupils guilty of dangerous conduct should be warned.

6. Machines should be provided with adequate safety devices and should be inspected regularly.

7. Signs should be posted to remind students of safety precautions to be taken and possible dangers to be avoided.

8. Teachers should set good examples in proper use of machines and in the application of safety rules.

9. Teachers in science classes should exercise great care in conducting and supervising experiments.

10. Chemicals and other materials should be carefully labeled and segregated.

11. Chemicals which may prove dangerous should be kept on locked shelves, and care should be taken in permitting pupils to have access to them.

12. Adequate supervision should be provided for athletic, social and other activities, for recesses, lunchtime, and other intermissions.

13. Adequate instructions on skills, techniques, safety rules and proper supervision of physical education activities.

14. Pupils should not be allowed to leave the school premises at other than the regular times. Principals should give their permission if any do leave.

15. Safety patrols under adult supervision should be organized to protect children on streets surrounding school premises.

16. Drivers of school buses should be carefully selected and thoroughly trained in their legal responsibilities and their vehicles should be frequently and carefully inspected.

17. Teachers and other persons in the individual schools should be trained in first aid, and first-aid kits should be placed in classrooms, the nurses room, and all vehicles in which children are transported.

18. An accident report should be made as soon after an accident as feasible.

19. In some jurisdictions, statutes and judicial decisions may require alteration of the foregoing suggestions.

20. In all jurisdictions, legal counsel should be sought regarding the problems of a particular situation.

Defense for a Negligence Action. First and foremost—call an attorney. There are four grounds on which a person may base his defense against being negligent, but before listing the defenses it should be pointed out that the laws dealing with such cases in the United States are derived from (1) federal and state constitutions, (2) statutes passed by state legislatures, and (3) "Precendents," which mean decisions the courts have made in previous cases. Most of the rulings handed down in liability suits are based on precedent.

A person can base his defense on the following:

1. *Contributory negligence* which is the failure by the person injured by the negligence of another to use care for his own protection. Such contributory fault generally bars the recovery of damages by the injured person if his misconduct exposes him to the injury resulting from the defendant's negligence, and combines and concurs with that negligence in causing the injury.

2. *Assumption of risk* which applies to the situation where the person subsequently injured may be said to have ventured into the relationship or situation out of which the injury arises voluntarily and with full knowledge of the danger. He thus relieves the defendent of the duty to protect him against injury.

3. *Immunity* (Neither our federal government nor any of the states may be sued *without consent*) which covers school boards and school districts and their officers *but not teachers.*

4. *Act of God* which applies when an uncontrollable act of the elements occurs.

The most important safeguard to use when directing a program is good common sense. The director should always study the activity that is going to be conducted and try to anticipate the dangers beforehand, and take all the precautions that are necessary during the activity to make it as safe as possible. Do not become overly cautious and give up an activity that the pupils need.

3. Role of the Students

*The galleries are full of critics. They
play no ball. They fight no fights.
They make no mistakes because they
attempt nothing. Down in the arena are
the doers. They make many mistakes
because they attempt many things.
The man who makes no mistakes lacks
boldness and the spirit of adventure.
He is the one who never tries anything.
He is the brake on the wheels of progress.*

*Washington Interscholastic
Activity Association*

The students' involvement in the intramural program is no longer limited to participation as players. Students assume many roles in the administration and operation of the total program. The majority of the students involved in intramurals are those who benefit from interaction with fellow students in competition; however, students also take an active part in programs as athletic chairpersons, officials, intramural assistants, office assistants, and spectators.

The value of student input for the program is unmeasurable. The students who suggest better methods of conducting an activity or rule changes for an activity to make it more enjoyable should be heard because they may be communicating the feeling of fellow students who are playing in the contest. Students are the best judges of their peers because they have the most intimate contact with their classmates.

Students are continually seeking ways in which they can identify with the institution by becoming involved in campus activities. When it comes to the intramural program, the students seek out and welcome the opportunity to become part of the decision-making process. Students' involvement in all phases of the program can assure that the program will perpetuate itself from season to season.

PARTICIPANTS

Students participate in an intramural program for various reasons, and it is impossible to classify individuals as to why they participate and the benefits they receive from the program. It has been established for some time that active participation in physical competition has many merits for the individual. Some students participating in the intramural contests are concerned with their physical fitness; some with the learning of rules and regulations, but it is not difficult to generalize that most individuals participate for the enjoyment they receive from the particular contests in which they compete.

The participants seek their own goals at their own levels in intramurals. True, there are individuals who strive for superior performance and excel in various aspects of the program. Some students participate in intramural activities primarily for the vigorous physical activity which is involved and so that they may improve their cardio-respiratory endurance, their muscular coordination, skill, and agility. Many students participate to test their skill, learn a new skill, or test their mental endurance as demanded by the various activities themselves.

Special interest groups and individuals who have an interest in and enjoy activities which may not be currently popular should never be excluded from a program. A number of students probably participate because of the enjoyment they receive from interaction with fellow students when it comes to planning strategy, working out practice seasons, and actually playing as a member of a team working toward a common goal. The comradeship that is created through their efforts is enhanced through celebration in victory or the "agony of defeat." There should be an opportunity for those individuals not only to participate in their chosen avocation but also to expand their program by introducing their activity to other students. Many students use the "open rec" periods to practice their "thing," or they may ask for an area to be reserved for their club or interest group. Many of these students act as teachers and help fellow students develop skills in new or different activities.

Students also enjoy participating in activities which require no previous experience because they may feel they then have an equal opportunity to excel. Students may have far more interest in new activities because they are pursuing the experience for recreation and therefore do not feel it necessary to spend many hours practicing the skills needed to participate in a contest. Another reason students may select new activities, is that, as a rule, they are not as time consuming as the most familiar activities.

Many more students are participating in co-rec, both scheduled events and free play. The growth of co-rec activities is mainly the result of the social factors involved in the structure of these activities. Students realize that there is a wider range of ability levels and the contest is more relaxed which comes in part from individuals helping each other while playing the contest.

Reporting for Events

One of the keys to the smooth operation of a student-oriented program is to have all participants aware of the standard procedure for starting events. If the basic procedures are the same for all events, then participants will be able to report quickly to the central area so that the events can begin as scheduled. Although students may enter the playing areas from different directions, they should be aware of the central reporting station where the intramural assistant will be located. For outdoor activities, if there is no check-in building to identify the area, it is a good practice to set up a card table at the same spot each day.

In order to assure that students know when to report for the different events, either list the reporting procedures in the intramural handbook or post the procedure for each event on the bulletin board at the time the schedules are posted. The following suggestions may assist in bringing about uniformity in reporting for events:

Outdoor Events (football, softball, and volleyball). All teams report to the playing fields where the officials will have equipment and score cards. Teams playing the second game should get the score card from the official and fill it out before the first game is completed.

Basketball. The team captain or a representative should report to the check-in table and fill out the score sheets before the previous game is over. The intramural assistant should set out the score sheets in the same order as the floors are numbered to assist teams in knowing where they will play. When games are over the scorekeepers should report to the check-in table and give the previous game's score card to the assistant and pick up the score sheet for the next game.

Indoor Volleyball. All teams report to their courts where officials have all the equipment. Teams playing second games should fill out score cards while first game is being played.

Swimming. All competitors should report to the check-in table to sign up for events. This table should be located away from the starting area.

Track Meet. Participants in the field events should report to the official at the field event. Participants for all running events and relays should sign up at the check-in table which should be located near the center of the field.

Individual-Skill Events. Participants should report to the intramural assistant to be paired with a student from another organization so that they can record the scores for each other in the event.

Table Tennis, Paddleball, Handball, and Tennis. Players should report to the assigned court at the assigned time to meet their opponent. It is a good procedure to have an intramural assistant at the playing area for all first-round contests.

Distance Running and Bike Races. Teams and individuals should report to the starting area to fill out cards and begin the race.

NonIntramural Facilities. Participants should pay their fee for use of the facility and then report to the intramural assistant with evidence of having paid the fee.

STUDENT OFFICIALS

The students play a very vital role in the intramural program when they serve as officials. Students perform some official functions in almost every contest in which they participate whether they are paid, volunteer their services, meet a class requirement, or make the calls when competing in individual or dual events.

Teams and individuals in the program should be made aware that it is not always possible to provide officials for all contests, and that, therefore, the participants should be prepared to officiate certain contests. A great number of intramural programs enlist the students who are competing in single or dual activities to serve as officials while they are waiting their turn to participate in the tournament. These are institutions which operate on the "honor system" in which no officials are assigned to certain activities. At Western Illinois University, all individual and dual activities as well as the entire slow-pitch softball program are part of a system whereby each team must assign an official or agree on a volunteer official.

No tests have been devised that can guarantee the success of an individual as an official; therefore, the intramural department will have to actively recruit officials. The individuals who get along well with their peers and are able to officiate are the ones who display the personality traits of conscientiousness, self-assurance and serious mindedness. There are three general categories from which the officials may be selected for the program.

Paid Officials. If funds are available for hiring officials, the director has the opportunity to select more highly qualified individuals. High pay often can attract those individuals who are more competent and conscientious about their performance and the intramural director can weed out those who are less competent. The best source for paid officials are those individuals who have just become registered with local officials' associations and who need the actual experience of officiating contests in the sport for which they are registered. These officials should not be limited to their sport only, because most state associations do not have all the activities which are conducted in intramurals. These officials can gain valuable experience in other activities by conducting contests. Professional officials who are not students should not be hired because students can, in addition to gaining compensation, gain the educational advantage of associating with their peers.

Classes Requiring Laboratory Experience. When students enroll in a class which requires a laboratory experience in officiating they generally indicate an interest in the sport to be officiated. The key to motivating the officials to do a good job is to weigh the laboratory experience very heavily in the final evaluation of the student. The individuals who complete the class and are good officials are in part motivated by the thought that if they do a good officiating job they could possibly be selected for one of the paid officiating positions in the future.

Interest Groups. It has long been known that good officials are those individuals who have participated in that particular activity. One of the best sources of officials for an intramural program comes from the interest groups, varsity athletic teams, or sports clubs. The director should never hesitate to use these individuals to conduct intramural activities in their field of interest, not only because they have knowledge about the activity but also because it will create good will between the groups and the intramural department. For example, the weight lifting club could be asked to conduct the intramural weight lifting contest. If the officials from the interest groups are not volunteers, the financial compensation can be paid either to the student official or the organization.

Training Officials

After the officials have been recruited for the program, they should undergo an established course of training to help them carry out their particular duties. This training may consist of workshops, knowledge tests, actual practice for officials on field or floor in mechanics, or just an informal meeting to discuss how to conduct the activities. As part of the training, the officials should be informed as to proper dress when conducting an activity.

Workshops. Preseason workshops or clinics are the most widely used method of training the officials for the coming season. The workshop can either be conducted by the intramural director or a guest official who is registered with the state officials' association. The clinic should include films, slides, rule interpretation, and mechanics as well as serve as a means of being sure that all officials understand the intramural procedures. The clinic should be kept as brief as possible yet cover all information necessary for the individual to successfully officiate. If the workshop-clinic method of training perspective officials is used, officials should be required to attend to assure uniformity in rule interpretations. Clinics should not be limited to officials only; team captains or teams should be encouraged to attend the clinic for information as to how the contests will be conducted.

Knowledge Tests. All officials should be given the same type of a knowledge test in the rules of the contest that they are going to officiate. The intramural department can devise their own test or obtain a copy of the test that is used by the state high school association. Officials should be required to make a passing score on the test as well as to discuss the questions which they missed either at an informal meeting or in individual conferences with the intramural staff. A very good basic knowledge test is to ask the official to take a true-false exam on the basic fundamentals of a sport which are listed in the rule books, because if they answer "false" to any question, they lack the knowledge of a guiding principle of the activity.

Practicing Mechanics. A good method of training officials is to have them actually work on the field and floor mechanics among themselves. Officials then become aware not only of the positioning they must take but also of what the participants might do in the contest. The officials should realize that proper positioning is important to controlling the contest. Hand signals should be improvised as they are tools of communication between the officials and the participants. The most important mechanic that all officials should learn is to speak out clearly so that there is no misunderstanding as to the call. Officials may have trouble mastering the hand signals, but they should not be permitted to officiate if they have trouble communicating verbally.

Informal meetings. Informal meetings with the officials and members of the intramural staff are a good method of in-service training that could be carried on all season. Some individuals are more apt to ask questions and seek advice in a less structured atmosphere. For many of the activities in the program, the informal meeting of the officials just before the contests are to begin may be the only time that is available to go over the special rules. A successful method of assuring that the officials know how the activities are to be conducted is to have them all meet before the contest and discuss the rules and problems which may arise. Then the officials should meet with the teams—not just the captains—to explain the activity and answer any questions. The training of officials is a continual process carried on through everyday contact with the individuals and the problems that they face. Officials should be made aware that they serve an important position in the program and that the contests they are officiating are very important to the individuals who are playing.

No matter which method or combination of methods is used to train the official, one requirement should be made very clear—professionalism. The good officials are the ones who take a professional attitude toward the job. The more officials act as though they know what they are doing, the more easily the teams will accept their judgement. Professionalism includes a good knowledge of the rules, neat appearance, proper mechanics both during the contest and while conducting the pregame conference, an authoriative manner tempered with courtesy, and the ability to "sell" one's decisions in such a manner as to leave no doubt about the call.

At some point during the training of the officials, the intramural department should make sure that they are familiar with the standard procedure for conducting all contests. The following suggestions may assist the officials in meeting their obligations.

Pregame. The first time a team competes in an event, assemble the teams to discuss the rules and answer any questions. Then proceed to have the necessary coin flips, and check to see if the score sheet is filled out properly. If equipment is to be checked out to a team, it should be assigned to the captain.

During game. Officials should maintain control of the contest and talk only to team captains. They should explain rulings when feasible, but not go into details on judgment calls. Officials should also be aware of the procedure in handling:

1. Injuries. A seriously injured player should not be moved until proper methods of transportation are available. The official should make a note on the score card and report all injuries to the supervisor.

2. Protests of a game. The time of the protest and the score at that time should be noted. Officials should never permit a protest based on the judgment of an official.

3. Flagrant misconduct of players. The official should note this on the score card and indicate the nature of the misconduct.

Postgame. Report flagrant problems to the supervisor. Note all irregularities, ejections, and problems on the back of the score sheets so that these problems can be corrected. Indicate if any equipment is missing and what team has the equipment and be sure to sign the score sheet

Evaluating Officials

The intramural department should be continually evaluating the individuals who are officiating. The positive approach to evaluation should be used. Evaluations should serve as confidence builders and motivate the official to do a better job. Evaluation of an official serves no practical purpose unless it assists in the training of the official.

Due to the nature and scope of most intramural programs, it is impossible for the intramural director to personally evaluate each official; however a periodic evaluation by the official's peers has proven to be effective. The daily evaluation comes from the field supervisor who may merely comment on the good as well as the bad points about a contest and answer any questions which the officials may have. Written evaluations may be obtained from supervisors, fellow officials, selected players, or individuals assigned to rate the officials. The rating should always be made available to the official, but the raters should remain anonymous.

When using a written evaluation, the rater should be permitted to use either numbers or letters to rate each area. The letters should carry a number value so they may be added together to derive a letter grade for the evaluation. Students understand a letter grade more than a numerical grade because these symbols are used in the educational system. However, the most useful information in assessing the official is the written comment by the rater. Figure 3.1 is an example of a student evaluation form which has proven effective for intramural officials as well as class officials.

Another good method of evaluating the officials is by self-evaluation. The direct approach to self-evaluation is not as effective as the suggestive approach. To initiate self-evaluation the intramural department can put out an officials' newsletter or post on the bulletin board any of the weekly comments which may cause the officials to examine themselves. Comments that might catch officials' eyes are:

"Blow your whistle; don't talk through it."

"Speak out—both with signals and mouth."

Name	Knowledge of game	Judgment	Control and handling	Enthusiasm	Overall rating	Comments

Rating key			Point value
Excellent	=	A	5
Good	=	B	4
Average	=	C	3
Fair	=	D	2
Poor	=	F	1

Rater

Figure 3.1
Officials rating sheet.

"More fouls—less jump balls."

"No 3 seconds without team control."

"Don't kill the grass—move around."

"Hand signals—practice your signals even when you are in the shower."

"Get something early—so that they are aware that you are there."

"Work both ends of the floor—no squatters rights."

"Take your Time—when it's yours, but hustle on our time."

The officials who are selected for the championship contest should be those same officials who have been working that event throughout the competition. The teams who are involved in the championship contest should have a certain amount of input as to which officials work their contest. A successful method of selecting officials for championship events has been to ask all teams who reach semifinals to list three officials who they might want to have in their championship contest. These individuals are then put in a pool and at least one of the officials selected by each team should be assigned to the championship contest. At no time should the officials be informed as to which team selected them. The director should be very careful that his information is not let out so that the students will not feel neglected or hurt.

Scheduling

Once the officials have been selected, the director must establish a definite pattern for scheduling them. Each director may have his own preference, but it's advisable not to schedule officials ahead more than a week at a time because of cancellations, and the officials should have enough interest to check in the IM office at least once a week.

The intramural department should have a definite place on the bulletin board where the officials will be able to see the officiating schedule as well as any information which may pertain to the program. Officials should be instructed to review this officiating schedule each Monday and indicate by a check that they have seen their assignment for the week. Figure 3.2 is an example of a weekly assignment sheet.

Along with the weekly schedule, there should be a list of all officials with their telephone numbers and days of the week when they are *not* available to officiate. This information is essential for the student who is assigned but unable to meet the assignment and who must get a substitute (See Table).

Name	Phone	Monday	Tuesday	Wednesday	Thursday	Friday	Saturday
Joe	295-2912		No			No	
Pete	295-1283	After 8					
Bill	295-1555						No
Jack	295-1768		No afternoons		No afternoons		

Please check when you read schedule

Day	Date	Time	Duty	Name	OK
Mon.	3 - 17	3 : 45	Co-Rec Umpire	Joe Doe	
		3 : 45	Scorer	Bill White	✓
		6 : 00	Polo Timer	Sid One	✓
		6 : 00	Polo Official	Ron Blue	
Tues.					

Figure 3.2
Weekly working sheet.

OFFICE ASSISTANTS

The students who assist the intramural department in the office may be male or female. It is no longer an accepted practice to have only male officials and female office help. Experience has proven that only those individuals who enjoy their fellow students and have an active interest in the program are successful as office assistants.

Office assistants perform a very valuable service for the intramural department. Probably the least recognized and one of the most outstanding contributions which these individuals make to any program is that they can serve as the ears for the intramural department. Often an office assistant can bring ideas to the department which otherwise would be lost because they were student suggestions.

Like any other student who is working in the intramural program, the office assistant must be given a certain amount of freedom in which to work; however, there are very definite tasks which must be assigned in order to have the office function properly each day. In addition to meeting the public, the office assistants could be held responsible for the following:

1. Making daily phone calls to organizations that are going to participate in activities for the first time that day.
2. Posting on the bulletin boards the results of the previous day's play. When posting the results, the scores are placed on the schedule as well as the won-loss records marked on the schedule sheet (Figure 9.11).
3. Posting in a prominent place the winners of each event.
4. Making and distributing posters and bulletins which are necessary to announce coming events.
5. Listing on the participation records individuals who have taken part in the previous day's events.
6. Recording information from the score cards about the officials who work and bringing to the director's attention any comments on the score cards.
7. Indicating on the entry check-off form those organizations who turned in entries for coming events.
8. Typing and duplicating any information regarding upcoming activities.
9. Duplicating the schedules and making them available to the students.
10. After schedules have been drawn up by the intramural director or administrative assistants, filling in the field and floor

books (discussed in Chapter 4) for the entire season.

11. Using the duplicated schedules, filling out the current day's activities on the score card from the field and floor books.

A detailed description of the entry check-off form, mentioned above, is discussed in Chapter 4.

ATHLETIC CHAIRPERSONS

The athletic chairperson plays an important role as the liaison between the intramural department and the students who are participating in any organization. This individual is generally elected or selected by the student organization to work with the intramural department on behalf of their organization. The athletic chairpersons are the individuals who generally make up the intramural council for the institution. There is a great deal of merit in rotating the athletic chairpersons as often as possible so that many students may be exposed to the responsibilities that go with the position.

The athletic chairperson should be held responsible for the following:

1. Entering the teams in the desired activities by the announced dates.
2. Thorough understanding of the intramural rules and informing the organization of the rules.
3. Notifying team members of the date, time, and place of each contest for the league, checking the tournament drawings, and notifying members when they are scheduled to participate.
4. Familiarizing the organization with the department's eligibility rules.
5. Writing the first and last names of players on the score cards.
6. Notifying the intramural office if it is necessary to reschedule a contest.
7. Submitting a list of the total membership of the organization at the beginning of each school year.
8. Submitting written protest 24 hours after the contest was played.
9. The general conduct of players and spectators from the organization during a contest.
10. Assigning a member of the organization to officiate when the rules of the contest state that the organization must supply an official.

INTRAMURAL ASSISTANTS

The student intramural assistant is actually the long fingers of the intramural director, and it is very important that the fingers manipulate correctly and effectively. These students should be made to feel that they are playing an essential role in the administration of the program. They should be given the authority to make decisions in regard to rules and regulations which might effect the outcome of a particular event and in turn they should accept the responsibility that goes along with the position.

The intramural director must be very careful in selecting the individuals who are to serve as the student intramural assistants. It is extremely important that these individuals be well respected among the student population. The director should be able to identify the individuals from their work as participants, officials, or athletic chairpersons, and select the individuals who have carried out their previous tasks to the best of their ability.

The student intramural assistants should have a complete knowledge of the rules and regulations for all the contests which they are administering so that they can answer questions and, in an emergency, officiate.

The exact duties of the student intramural assistant will vary with each program; however, a list of responsibilities for these individuals might include:

Field Duties

1. Taking the field and floor book and score cards to a central location at the playing area.
2. Assigning officials to their respective fields and checking the equipment out to the officials for their fields.
3. Directing the teams to their assigned playing areas.
4. During the contests, circulating through the playing areas and generally observing the contests and evaluating the student officials.
5. Being prepared to administer first aid, when necessary, before an injured player is moved to the health center or hospital.
6. After completion of the contests, collecting the equipment and indicating in the field and floor book the winners of the contest.
7. Noting on the score cards any irregularities regarding the contest.

Administrative Duties

1. Assisting in the publicity and promotion of the program.
2. Serving on the intramural council.
3. Assisting the athletic chairperson with schedules and dates.
4. Posting the rules and regulations for the activities they are responsible for conducting.
5. Working with the office assistants in handling the paper work.
6. Making recommendations to the director regarding any aspects in the program.

SPECTATORS

The basic philosophy of intramurals leads to attempting to prevent "spectatoritis" by providing activities for all students; however, a good program will attract a number of spectators who want to watch their fellow students display their athletic talents. The spectators at an intramural contest may not be limited to students only; when the leagues or tournaments reach the championship stage, family and faculty may be in attendance at the contest.

One of the values of intramurals to spectators may be that the students have the opportunity to identify with a particular group or organization, and that is why it is important that spectators be allowed on the sidelines for the contest and not be sent off to the stands. If it is convenient to provide stands for the spectators this is all well and good; however, at intramural contests spectators should not be required to sit in the stands unless they directly interfere with the playing of the contest.

The conduct of the student spectators at an event should be the same as that of a competitor. If students display actions which are unsportsmanlike or detrimental to the contest, they should be removed from the area.

There should never be a charge for attendance at any intramural contest, and it is an especially bad practice to charge the students for championship events when they have attended all other contests free of charge.

4. Center of Operation

The successful manager of men derives his satisfaction from achieving with people. He takes real pride in surrounding himself with strong people and in helping them achieve. He recognizes that in a world which is changing economically and socially and which is accumulating technical knowledge rapidly, he and his people are confronted with the need to cope skillfully with these changes. To keep his business competitive in an ever-changing society, he holds a very strategic position. Helping his people grow with the times is his opportunity and his challenge.

Mack T. Henderson

The "center of operation" is the intramural office where the students and staff combine efforts to efficiently put into motion the machinery necessary to get the program started. This chapter will detail a method of office operation using only students that has proven economical, efficient, and effective. All of the forms and score cards, discussed in regard to the office operation, can be duplicated and serve more than one function in the program. By using the same form for more than one purpose, the cost of operation can be cut and information centrally located.

Efficiency in the office is created by following "ten administrative steps" when dealing with each activity. A joint effort by the director and the student office assistants is needed to assure a smooth operation when working with students participating in the program. Several of the ten administration steps are discussed more thoroughly in other chapters.

ENTRY DATES AND
PLAYING DATES, STEP I

The director should establish a calendar that lists the important dates in the program. The intramural handbook, which is discussed in Chapter 2, provides the director with a good opportunity to distribute the dates for the program to all students. In addition to using the calendar, it is a good practice to duplicate a running schedule for all events which can be distributed to the students when the first set of entry blanks are passed out (Figure 4.1). In addition put a bulletin board in a prominent place which lists "Intramural Today," and each day post not only a copy of the field and floor for that day (Figure 4.7) but also a reminder of what entries are due or what one-day event is to occur.

FALL QUARTER

Activity	Entry Dates		Playing Dates
1 One-day football	Sept. 4		Sept. 6
2 160-pound football	Sept. 5		Sept. 10
3 League football	Sept. 5		Sept. 8
4 Paddleball singles	Sept. 8		Sept. 10
5 Paddleball doubles	Sept. 8		Sept. 15
6 Bowling	Sept. 9		Sept. 15
7 Fast-pitch softball	Sept. 10		Sept. 15
8 Soccer	Sept. 13	9:00	Sept. 13
9 Golf	Sept. 15		Sept. 17
10 Outdoor volleyball	Sept. 17		Sept. 22
11 Football skills	Sept. 18	3:00-6:00	Sept. 18
12 Field archery	Sept. 18	3:00-6:00	Sept. 18
13 Tennis singles	Sept. 20	9:00	Sept. 20
14 Putt putt, 2 ball	Sept. 22	3:00-9:00	Sept. 22
15 Coed putt putt, 2 ball	Sept. 22	3:00-9:00	Sept. 22
16 Inner tube water polo	Sept. 23		Sept. 29
17 Coed volleyball	Sept. 24		Sept. 29
18 Bike road race	Sept. 25	4:00	Sept. 25
19 Pushball	Sept. 27	9:00	Sept. 27
20 Fall relays	Sept. 30	3:30-6:30	Sept. 30
21 Slide-a-puck	Oct. 1		Oct. 6
22 Racketball	Oct. 2		Oct. 6

FALL QUARTER (Continued)

Activity	Entry Dates		Playing Dates
23 Tandem bike	Oct. 7	5:30	Oct. 7
24 Coed tandem bike	Oct. 7	5:30	Oct. 7
25 Cross-country running	Oct. 10	4:00	Oct. 10
26 Tennis doubles	Oct. 11	9:00	Oct. 11
27 Team handball	Oct. 11	9:00	Oct. 11
28 Rifle shoot	Oct. 13,14,15	5:00-9:00	Oct. 13,14,15
29 Coed rifle shoot	Oct. 13,14,15	5:00-9:00	Oct. 13,14,15
30 Guys and dolls basketball	Oct. 15		Oct. 20
31 Knee tackle football	Oct. 20		Oct. 22
32 King of the hill (bowling)	Oct. 21		Oct. 29
33 Canoe jousting	Oct. 22	6:30	Oct. 22
34 Coed football	Oct. 25	9:00	Oct. 25
35 Billiards	Oct. 28		Nov. 3
36 One-on-one basketball	Oct. 30		Nov. 3
37 Water volleyball	Nov. 1	9:00	Nov. 1
38 Bloodmobile	Nov. 3 4, 5, 6		Nov. 3,4,5,6
39 Tug-of-war	Nov. 4	6:30	Nov. 4
40 160-pound tug-of-war	Nov. 4	6:30	Nov. 4
41 Coed tug-of-war	Nov. 4	7:30	Nov. 4
42 2-man volleyball	Nov. 11	6:30	Nov. 11
43 Fitness day	Nov. 12	6:30	Nov. 12
44 Turkey trot	Nov. 15	12:30	Nov. 15

Figure 4.1
Entry and playing dates.

PUBLICITY, STEP II

The combining events should be advertised using all available media that will reach the students who may participate in an activity. The publicity should include where and when entry blanks are available and how to return them so that a student may be entered in an activity. Methods of publicity and promotion were discussed in Chapter 2.

ENTRY BLANKS, STEP III

All entry blanks for the year's program should be duplicated before the school year begins and checked against the calendar of events to assure that the dates on the entry blanks agree with the calendar. It is a good practice to send a packet which contains one of each of the entry blanks for a quarter to the intramural managers. There should also be a central place in the IM office where entry blanks may be picked up. A stand-up magazine rack serves very well for holding entry blanks, because all entries are clearly visible to the students and the rack takes up little space in the office. See Figure 2.1. This rack should be close to the entrance of the office and to the area where the entries are to be returned. A definite place where the entries are to be returned is required. It is a good idea to have a "mail slot" cut in the office counter with a sign indicating that entries should be placed in the slot. It is also possible to put the mail slot in the door if the catch box is large enough so students can place entries in the box when the office door is open.

To avoid confusing the students when different activities are played at the same time, there should be four different types of entry blanks. It is useful to use a different colored paper for each type of entry blank. Although each entry blank may be used differently, it should contain information which will assist the students who wish to enter as well as provide the necessary data for the intramural office. All entry blanks should include: (1) name of event, (2) entry due date, (3) playing date, and (4) basic information about the event such as number of players, type of tournament, participation points, and specific rules.

Team Entry

The entry blanks, which must be turned into the office prior to competition, should also have a space for the names of the participants, the organization's name, manager, and phone number (Figure 4.2). For events such as bowling and golf, a space is needed where individuals indicate the times they prefer to participate.

160 FOOTBALL
(Lightweight)

ENTRIES DUE: Tuesday, September 14
PLAYING DATE: After September 16

1. Persons can play on only one intramural football team no matter what league.
2. Eligibility rules apply.
3. Players must weigh 160 pounds when they play or when they weighed in on either September 10 or 13.
4. Weigh-in will be from 3:00 to 6:00 in P.E. locker room and individuals must have ID card.
5. Procedure for challenge of weight—only two individuals may be challenged. Officials must be immediately notified, and officials must notify players. Players challenged must be weighed or it is assumed they are overweight.
6. Six men play at one time.
7. Participation points: 6 points for each game played plus 15 points for winner and 5 for second.

_____   _____

_____   _____

_____   _____

_____   _____

_____   _____

_____   _____

_____   _____

ORGANIZATION_____

MANAGER_____ PHONE_____

WEIGH-INS: Friday, September 10, or Monday, September 13: 3:00-6:00

Figure 4.2
Team entry blank.

One-Day Entry Blanks

The entry blanks for one-day events and meet events, which are not turned in prior to the date of competition, should serve as a reminder to the students in addition to containing the rules for the event so that the office does not have to duplicate separate rules (Figure 4.3).

Girls   Boys

    TAG A BOY   TAG A GIRL

CO-REC FOOTBALL

ENTRIES DUE: Saturday, October 23 at 9:00 a.m.
PLAY BEGINS: Saturday, October 23 at 9:00 a.m.

One-day double elimination tournament.

1. Each team will consist of four men and four women.
2. Rosters are limited to eight men and eight women.
3. Intramural rules apply as far as eligibility is concerned.

RULES

Co-rec touch football is played using the regular intramural football rules with the following exceptions:

1. No down field blocking (this includes punts and kick-offs).
2. No rushing on punts.
3. On punts and kick-offs, no players on offense may advance until the ball is kicked.
4. On a scrimmage play, once blockers have taken a position they may not move to ward off defensive players. Defensive players may not run into a blocker.
5. Teams have five downs to make the line to gain.
6. The individual who receives the snap from the center must alternate between men and women players.

Figure 4.3
One-day entry blank.

Individual or Dual Event Entry

In addition to asking for other information, this entry blank should emphasize the fact that phone numbers are required for each participant (Figure 4.4).

FALL GOLF ENTRY BLANK

ENTRIES DUE: Monday, September 20
MEET WILL BE HELD: Wednesday, September 22

1. Teams and individuals turn in entry blanks to IM office.
2. Tee times will be posted.
3. Each organization can enter as many members as they want; team championship will be determined by the total of the five best scores. Individuals are also invited to enter.
4. Nine-hole medal play.
5. Player must play with assigned partners and at assigned time.
6. All golfers must pay their own green fee of $1.25
7. Tournament will be held on WIU course.
8. Tee times will be assigned between 12:00 p.m. and 4:00 p.m.
9. No scores will be counted unless a player from another organization verifies the score.
10. Participation points: Total of 5 if five play, plus 5 for first team and 3 for second team. Also, 2 for first individual and 1 for second.
11. ESPRIT DE CORPS EVENT.
12. PLEASE LIST PREFERRED TIME.

Name	Phone	Time	Name	Phone	Time

ORGANIZATION_____

MANAGER_____

PHONE_____

Figure 4.4
Individual or dual entry blank.

Meet Entry Blanks

The meet entry blanks should provide information about the number of trials as well as number of events an individual may participate in. When conducting an intramural meet, the starting time of the first event should be stated and all other events listed in order. It is a good practice to put meet records on the entry blanks so that students and officials can determine quickly if new records have been established (Figure 4.5).

FALL RELAYS

ENTRIES DUE: Tuesday, September 21 between 3:30 and 6:00 p.m.
EVENTS WILL BE RUN: September 21 between 3:30 and 6:00 p.m.

1. Fall relays will be individual events with time and distances of the three competitors added together to determine the score of the event. Team winner based on 8, 6, 5, 4, 3, 2, 1.
2. Organizations may enter as many teams as they desire. However, the designated three persons per team must have entered before the event.
3. Events will be run against time, and champions determined by adding the three scores together.
4. Contestants may come and run anytime between 3:30 and 6:00 p.m. Team members must be listed prior to running any event.
5. Participation points: 3 points for each event entered (total 18) plus 10 points for team winner and 5 points for second place team.

EVENTS AND RECORDS
220	72.9
440	2:50.6
660	4:35.4
Broad jump	58'5"
Shot put	138'4"
High jump	17'6"

ENTER AT ANY TIME OF EVENT!

Figure 4.5
Meet entry blank.

ENTRY CHECK-IN STEP IV

The entry check-in method can save a great deal of time because in order to total the number of entries and determine the number of sections, or the number of individuals entered in a tournament, the director need only add up the numbers which appear on the entry check-in list. When the entries are turned into the intramural office, the entry check-off sheet is used to indicate which teams have chosen to enter. In arranging a team event, the office assistants indicate a team entry by placing an OK by the organization name (Figure 4.6 under Lincoln). For an individual or dual event, the office assistant indicates the number of entries which have been received from each organization. Four names above the hash line would indicate four entries in singles, two underneath the hash line would indicate two entries in doubles (Figure 4.6 under Olson).

At the same time that the office assistants indicate on the entry check-off list that a team has entered, the athletic chair person's name and phone number are placed on a second check-off form, as in Figure 4.6 under Wetzel Hall. This provides a quick and ready reference when it is necessary for the office to contact the individuals who are responsible for a particular team. Often there are different managers for different events, and students who are responsible for a contest must be contacted directly by telephone.

SCHEDULES, STEP V

The formulas necessary to determine the number of sections and amount of playing time will be discussed in Chapter 9. The forms that are to be used for a round robin tournament or the forms with brackets for an elimination tournament should have been previously duplicated so that the director and office need only fill in the names and dates when drawing up the schedules. These forms are also illustrated in Chapter 9.

To save time, the department may use one of two methods to prepare the schedule to be duplicated. First, if the director has access to the school's Spirit Master machine, the schedules are drawn up on a work sheet and then photographed and duplicated. The second method is to have previously drawn round robin blank work sheets on dittos and actually write on the dittos so that the schedule may be run off immediately from the ditto. Schedules may be neater if typed; however, in the interest of time, it is acceptable to write the schedules in longhand before they are duplicated. After the schedules are duplicated, they should be checked for errors. Then two complete sets of all schedules should be put together for the office. One

Event _____

LINCOLN	OLSON	WETZEL	HENNIGER	SEAL
2	2a	4 *Bill Jones*	2	1
3 *OK*	2b	5 *5-4218*	3	2
4	3a *4/2*	6	4	3
5	3b	7	5	4
6 *OK*	4a	8 *Joe White*	6	5
7	4b	9 *5-1607*	7	6
8 *OK*	5a	10	8	
9	5b	11	9	HURSH
10 *OK*	6a *4/2*	12	10	1
11 *A OK*	6b	13	11	2
12 *B OK*	7a		12	3
13	7b		13	4
14	8a		14	
	8b			

TANNER	THOMPSON	FRATERNITIES	INDEPENDENTS
4	3	AGR	*Run-offs OK*
5	4	Delta Sig	*8-Balls OK*
6	5	KAP	_____
7	6	Phi Sig	_____
8	7	Lambda Chi	_____
9	8	Theta Chi	_____
10	9	Theta Xi	_____
11	10	TKE	_____
12	11	ATO	_____
13	12	Alpha Sig	_____
14	13	Delta Tau Delta	_____
15	14		
16	15		
	16		
	17		

Figure 4.6
Entry check-in form.

of these sets should be posted on the bulletin board and the second set used by the office to fill out the field and floor book.

It is a good practice when posting the duplicated schedules on the bulletin board to list the first games for all teams and have a sign over the first game notices which ask the students to place a check mark by their names or team after they have seen the schedule. This will tell the office staff which teams have seen the schedule thus eliminating some unnecessary calls to notify the teams when they play.

In the interest of economy, for leagues that have many teams, the sections should not be stapled together, and the athletic chair person should be instructed to pick up only those sheets with the schedule for their organization. For example, if there were 20 sections with 2 sections per page it would necessitate 10 pages being put together if each team were to receive a complete copy. With 6 teams in each section, the intramural department would need to use over 1200 sheets of paper to give each section a complete copy. By having athletic chairpersons pick up only the sheet for their section, only about 120 sheets of paper are needed, thus allowing a considerable saving to the intramural department.

When the work sheets for making schedules are duplicated, they should also have a section for posting the won-loss records for each team (Figure 9.11).

FIELD and FLOOR
FORM, STEP VI

The field and floor form is the intramural office's record of the games that are being played in the different leagues each day. When the office assistants fill out the forms they should use different colored pencils to indicate the different leagues. These should be the same colors that are used to fill out the score cards. This book serves five purposes. First, it is a quick and easy reference which the office personnel can use when teams call to inquire if they are playing that day. Second, a duplicate of the day's or week's field and floor forms can be placed on the "Intramural Today" bulletin board. The third use of the form is to have the field supervisor take it to the playing area to assist the teams in finding the time and field or floor they play on. After the games are over, the supervisor should circle the winners and record the score of each contest so that it will be easy to mark the results on the won-loss section of the schedule. Fourth, the field and floor form serves as a ready reference for the director when it is necessary to reschedule games on an open floor or teams wish to schedule practices on areas not scheduled for league play. The fifth use, discussed in Chapter 9, is as a checkoff list when scheduling. Figure 4.7 is an example of a football field form for a week's activity, and Figure 4.8 is an example of a softball field form.

INTRAMURAL RULES, STEP VII

A copy of the intramural rules should be posted with the schedule on the bulletin board. There should also be a supply of rules with the schedules that are to be picked up by the managers. It is also possible to put the rules on the backs of schedules or to hand them out to each organization. A copy of special intramural rules for most activities appears in Chapter 7.

SCORE CARDS, STEP VII

The next step in the office operation is to fill out the score cards for each day's activity. The score cards should be filled out using the field and floor form for that event. It is also advisable to fill out all the cards for the entire season, so that when games must be rescheduled, the director merely needs to change the dates on the top of the score cards. The completed score cards should be kept in a place known to all office personnel so that they can be easily located when they are to be used. When filling out the information on the top of the score cards, it is a good idea to use different colored pencils to represent different leagues. For example basketball might use blue for the regular league, red for the 160-pound league, and green for the 5-foot 9-inch league.

The intramural department can save time and money by duplicating all of the score cards necessary for the program. The 5 X 8 index cards make good common score cards because they are sturdy enough so that officials can fold and carry them in their pockets while the game is in progress. One duplicated score card can be used for all events except softball and basketball. Figure 4.9 is an example of the front of a common score card which has lines for the following information:

1. Name of event.
2. Date of event (both sides).
3. Time of event.
4. Field or floor.
5. Name of teams.
6. Place to indicate winner and score.
7. Place for names of participants.

Day		1	2	3	4	5	6	7	8	9	10	11	12
Monday	4:00	TKE PS	AGR ATO	L-8 W-6	O-2 T-6	H-14 OI-3	T-4 H-3	W-7 Th-7	Hur 4 T-8	T-10 W-5	OI-6 T-13		
	5:00	LCA TX	TC SPI	S-2 T-9	H-7 S-1	L-14 W-3	Th-8 Fish	H-5 W-9	Th-9 Owls	Th-5 OI-9	Th-6		
Tuesday	4:00	DTD KAP	CATS White	T.D.'S 605	L-6 L-10	Hur-2 H-4	Runts Giants	H-2 L-4			H-9 S-3		H-13 Th-4
	5:00	Kicks Holders	Reds Birds	Balls Jets	L-12 H-6	Sams Tap	Walts Mill	S-2 Hur 3			L-2 S-4	H-10 TH-2	Hur 1 Th-3
Wednesday	4:00												
	5:00												
Thursday	4:00												
	5:00												

Figure 4.7
Football field and floor form.

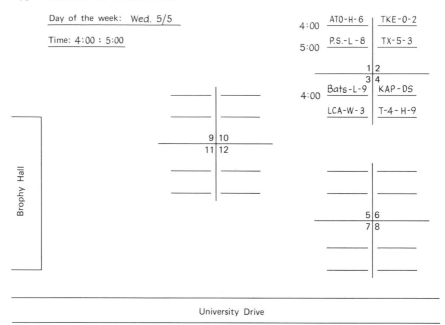

Figure 4.8
Softball field form.

Figure 4.10 is the back of the score card which is arranged to hold the following information:

8. Running score for volleyball or other event.
9. Play countdown for football.
10. Place for time-outs.
11. Signature space for officials and score keepers.

The score cards for softball can be run on 5 × 8 index cards and all the information placed on the front of the cards (Figure 4.11).

Individual-skill event score sheets and basketball score sheets should be duplicated on 8½ × 11 paper because it is economical. Two basketball score sheets can be obtained from each sheet, and different colored paper used to indicate different leagues (Figur 4.12). Five individual-skill event score sheets can be duplicated on a page, and it is easy to tally the sheet to determine team and individual winners when using this method because the sheets can be cut and clipped together which prevents having to rewrite the scores. This method also eliminates a chance for error in recording the scores (Figure 4.13).

Date _____ Time _____ Event _____ Date _____
Name _____ Winner _____ Name _____
Field _____

Figure 4.9
Common score card (front).

_____ 1 2 3 4 5 6 7 8 9 10 11 12 13 14 15 16 17 18 19 20 21
_____ 1 2 3 4 5 6 7 8 9 10 11 12 13 14 15 16 17 18 19 20 21

_____ 1 2 3 4 5 6 7 8 9 10 11 12 13 14 15 16 17 18 19 20 21
_____ 1 2 3 4 5 6 7 8 9 10 11 12 13 14 15 16 17 18 19 20 21

_____ 1 2 3 4 5 6 7 8 9 10 11 12 13 14 15 16 17 18 19 20 21
_____ 1 2 3 4 5 6 7 8 9 10 11 12 13 14 15 16 17 18 19 20 21

1 2 3 4 5 6 7 8 9 10 11 12 13
14 15 16 17 18 19 20 21 22 23 24 25
26 27 28 29 30 31 32 33 34 35 36 37
38 39 40 41 42 43 44 45 46 47 48 49 50

Time—outs
_____ 1 2 3 4
_____ 1 2 3 4

Scorer _____

Officials _____
_____
_____

Figure 4.10
Common score card (back).

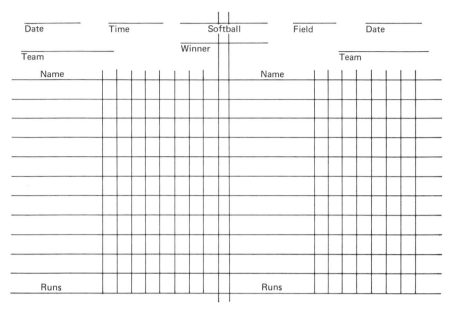

Figure 4.11
Softball score card.

When the score cards are returned to the office they are checked
for any comments regarding protests or misconduct of participants
during the contest, and the official who worked the contest is given
credit. If a team has forfeited, the office assistant will make a note of
the team and call the athletic chair person to inquire if the team is going to continue in the league. The office assistant then cuts the score
card in half and places the date and event on the half of the score
card that does not have this information. The cards are then placed
in the folder to be used when recording participation.

PERMANENT PARTICIPATION
RECORDS, STEP IX

Each intramural director may have a special method of keeping
records of participation; however, the use of the 5 × 8 score card and
a second 5 × 8 index card for each organization has proven effective,
efficient, and economical in both time and money.

A definite procedure is followed after each event to assure that
all records are complete and accurate. For team events half of the
score card is placed in the file under each organization name and is

Figure 4.12
Basketball score sheet.

81

Skeet Shooting

Name _____ Team _____

Attempts   1 2 3 4 5 6 7 8 9 10 11 12 13 14 15

Hits   1 2 3 4 5 6 7 8 9 10 11 12 13 14 15

Score _____

Skeet Shooting

Name _____ Team _____

Attempts   1 2 3 4 5 6 7 8 9 10 11 12 13 14 15

Hits   1 2 3 4 5 6 7 8 9 10 11 12 13 14 15

Score _____

Skeet Shooting

Name _____ Team _____

Attempts   1 2 3 4 5 6 7 8 9 10 11 12 13 14 15

Hits   1 2 3 4 5 6 7 8 9 10 11 12 13 14 15

Score _____

Skeet shooting

Name _____ Team _____

Attempts   1 2 3 4 5 6 7 8 9 10 11 12 13 14 15

Hits   1 2 3 4 5 6 7 8 9 10 11 12 13 14 15

Score _____

Skeet shooting

Name _____ Team _____

Attempts   1 2 3 4 5 6 7 8 9 10 11 12 13 14 15

Hits   1 2 3 4 5 6 7 8 9 10 11 12 13 14 15

Score _____

Figure 4.13
Individual event score sheet.

used for keeping the participation record in that event. Each time a team plays, a mark is made on the first score card to indicate which individuals have participated. Any names which appear on the additional score cards that are not on the first card are added to the original. This method of using the actual score cards to keep participation records gives the intramural department a quick reference when questions arise as to whether a player has participated on the team. When the league and play-offs are over, the figures are totaled for each individual and transferred to the organization's 5 × 8 permanent record card. Whenever information is transferred from one card to another, a large "R" is written on the card to indicate it has been recorded.

For tournament, individual, or dual events, the office assistants record the amount of individual participation for each member of the organization. The individual's name is placed on the card along with the ID number for the event and the number of times the individual participated in that particular event. An R is placed by the individual's name in the tournament bracket when the information has been transferred to the organization's card. The example below would indicate that Joe participated in golf, played four matches in tennis, and twice in slide-a-puck. The ID number is the same number that appears on the entry and playing date list (Figure 4.1).

Joe Smith (9)   (13—4)   (21—2)

WINNERS AND AWARDS, STEP X

At the conclusion of each event, the winners and runner-ups should be marked on a record sheet that is kept in the file. A notice of the winners should be posted. When appropriated funds are used for awards to students, accurate records of who receives the awards must be kept, as discussed in Chapter 5.

Office Tidbits

In addition to the ten administrative steps, several other factors in the office operation are essential for a smoothly running program.

1. Next to the phone, the file cabinet is probably the most important physical item in the intramural office. In order to simplify filing, Western Illinois University converted to a number scheme for all activities. Each quarter's activities are placed in a file drawer, and a file folder corresponds with the numbers on the entry and playing date list of activities. A copy of the entry and playing dates list is

A. Entries
B. 6-team work sheet
C. 8-team work sheet
D. Won-loss work sheet
E. 8 bracket
F. 16 bracket
G. 32 bracket
H. 16 double elimination
I. 32 double elimination
J. Field and floor
K. Team and individual totals
L. Individual and team event sheets
M. Heat sheets
N. Participation (forms)

O. Participation (dittos)
P. Officials' class ratings
Q. Choice of officials
R. Student time reports
S. Accident reports
T. Play-off notices
U. Forfeit notices
V. Trophy forms
W. Intramural equipment
X. 24-place tournament
Y. 32-place tournament
Z. Procedure for all games
AA. Sigma Delta Psi
BB. Ditto Masters

Figure 4.14
Work drawer directory.

placed on the front of the file drawer. Using Figure 4.1 for fall events, any information on guys and dolls basketball would be found in the file under number 30. All other duplicated forms (such as work sheets, tournament brackets etc.) not related to a specific sport are classified by a letter, and this information is placed on the front of the file drawer which contains all the work sheets (Figure 4.14).

2. In the file folder for each event there is also a copy of the procedure for conducting the event. Having the procedure clearly written up insures that the event will be conducted the same way each year and provides a guide for the individual who must conduct the event. The procedure can either be typed right on the folder or pasted to the folder (Figure 4.15).

3. Because the field and floor form is so important for use in the office, each activity should have a binder in which the forms are placed for the season. The office assistants should be instructed to place the score cards for each day's events in the field and floor book and then to place these books in a common area so that the event supervisor can easily locate them.

PROCEDURE FOR CONDUCTING SPRING RELAYS

1. Get the microphone from the equipment room
2. Obtain the key from the equipment-room attendants to open the press box.
3. Turn on all electricity in the press box and turn on the P.A. system.
4. Plug the P.A. system into the socket down field.
5. The items you will need to conduct the meet will be: (a) starting gun and shells, (b) eight stopwatches, (c) shot put, (d) discus, (e) two footballs, tape for triple jump, tape for measuring shot, discus, and football throw, finishing string, marker for throwing events, eight batons, racks for long-jump pit, and high-jump standards.
6. Make up sheets for each event and place them on the boards. Be sure to list record and number of attempts.
7. Make up the team total sheet and place it on the board.
8. First event is the 100-yard hurdle relay against time. Set the hurdles at low hurdles every 10 yards with 10-yard start.
9. Steeple chase is started in the northwest runway. Flight of hurdles should be put across the middle of the track on the southeast corner of the track and the northeast corner of the track.
10. Everyone gets two attempts in all throwing and jumping events.
11. After completion of the tournament, be sure that you have all equipment. Close the press box and return the equipment to the equipment room.
12. Place all results in the IM office on the desk to be recorded.

Figure 4.15
Procedure for conducting event.

4. The entry check-in form (Figure 4.6) is also used to record the team participation points for each event as well as being used to periodically post the participation leaders. This same form is used for individual events to record participants; scores beside the organization name enable the recorder to pick the top five for the team title as well as the best scores for the event.

INTRAMURAL HEAT SHEET

Time   I   From   Time   II   From

_____ _____ _____   _____ _____ _____

Time   III   From   Time   IV   From

_____ _____ _____   _____ _____ _____

Time   V   From   FINALS

_____ _____ _____   _____

Figure 4.16
Heat sheet.

SPRING RELAYS

Organization _____
                1._____   3._____

                2._____   4._____

                TIME _____   PLACE _____

880 RELAY

Organization _____
                1._____   3._____

                2._____   4._____

                TIME _____   PLACE _____

SPRINT MEDLEY

Organization _____
                1._____   3._____

                2._____   4._____

                TIME _____   PLACE _____

MILE RELAY

Organization _____
                1._____   3._____

                2._____   4._____

                TIME _____   PLACE _____

Figure 4.17
Relay entry sheet.

Team Totals
Indoor Track Event

Scoring
IND   7 5 4 3 2 1
Relay 10, 8, 6, 4, 2, 1

Name	70 Dash	Long Jump	High Jump	220	70 L.H.	Shot Put	880 Run	880 Relay	Mile Relay	Total
Theta Xi	4	1	7	2	5		3		10	32 2nd
Tke		5			1	7		8		21
Hen 9	5		5	3		1			6	20
0-1 6A		7			2	2	5	6		22
Road Runners	3		4	5	7		2	1	4	26 3rd
BSA	7		3	7		3	4	10	8	42 1st
01-6A		4			3		7		1	15
α-14	2		1	4	4		1	2		14
Seal 3	1	3	2			4			2	12
Hursh		2		1		5		4		12

Figure 4.18
Team totals.

5. There are times when it is necessary to put event sheets or tournaments on a clipboard. A piece of good cardboard makes an excellent clipboard for intramurals if the sheets are stapled to the smooth surface and a pencil on a string is attached to the top.

6. The intramural department will also on occasion need heat sheets, relay sheets, and team total sheets for different events (Figures 4.16, 4.17, and 4.18). These sheets should also be duplicated.

7. All forms that are to be used by the department should be duplicated before the year begins. The ditto and mimeograph rosters

TO: Intramural Chairperson
FROM: Intramural Director
RE: All-University Play-offs

This is to notify your team that they have qualified for the All-University Playoffs in _____.Your first game is _____ at _____ . Please keep your team posted as to when they play in the play-offs.
Thank you.

                                                    _____
                                                    Date

TO: Intramural Chairperson _____
FROM: Intramural Director

Your team forfeited their first scheduled league game in _____ on _____ .Your team is scheduled to play again_____ .
If they are not going to continue in the league, please notify the intramural office immediately.

Figure 4.19
Play-off and forfeit notices.

should be numbered to correspond with file drawer numbers before being placed in a designated area.

8. The intramural department may also wish to send reminders to the teams when they either forfeit a game or qualify for the play-offs. Figure 4.19 shows examples of notices which can be filled in and sent to the teams.

5. Policies

Education means to acquaint young with the best heritage of the human race. But while much of this heritage is expressed in words, it is effective only if these words become reality in the person of the teachers and in the practice and structure of society. Only the idea which has materialized in flesh can influence man.

Erich Fromm

The policies for an intramural program should be clearly stated and available to all participants. Several methods can be used to ensure that the students are aware of the policies.

Constitution. If the intramural program has a governing board which uses a constitution, then all of the policies should be stated as part of the constitution and students should be made aware of this fact.

Handbook. When an intramural program is fortunate enough to be able to publish a handbook that is passed out to the students, policies should be part of the handbook and thus be readily available to readers.

Bulletin Boards. If there is no other method of informing the students as to the policies, an area on the bulletin board in the IM office should be set aside for policies.

General policies govern the operation of the program and specific rules pertain to each sport. A director should be careful not to over legislate. The regulations set down for the program should be limited to those areas which need covering. Regulations should be carefully written and condensed as much as possible to prevent the chance of one regulation being used to interpret another regulation.

Directors should establish policies that are specific to their program. Although programs will need to cover the same general areas, unique factors within each program will prevent one set of standards for all programs. The general topics that should be covered by written policies are eligibility rules, postponements, protests, and awards.

ELIGIBILITY RULES

The basic concept for having eligibility rules is to provide equality in participation. The regulation should not eliminate anyone who needs the opportunity to participate but it should establish uniformity in the program. The intramural eligibility rules should be reviewed periodically, and if it is found that exceptions to the rules have been made then it is highly questionable if those rules are necessary. Rules should be written specifically to define an individual's eligibility and specifically for a team's eligibility.

An example of a set of eligibility rules for the individual follows:

Rule 1. Any individual displaying conduct unbecoming to an intramural participant may be barred for further competition.

Rule 2. Individuals who have earned a letter, either major or minor, at any institution giving collegiate work shall not be eligible to compete in intramural tournaments in the sport or related activity in which they won the letter until one full calendar year has elapsed since the letter was awarded.

Rule 3. Members of varsity or JV sport squads are not eligible to compete in intramurals in that sport or related activity.

Rule 4. Sports club members may not make up more than one half of the number of players necessary to participate in an event related to their club activity.

Rule 5. Individuals not members of a varsity sports squad due to scholastic standing are not eligible to compete in intramurals in the sport in which they should be varsity members, if the coach indicates they would otherwise be members of the squad.

Rule 6. Members of varsity or JV squads who leave the squad are not eligible to compete in intramurals in that sport if a coach indicates they would make the squad.

Rule 7. Members of varsity or JV squads who are dropped from the squad because they lack ability will be approved for intramural competition in that sport upon presenting to the director of intermural sports a written statement to that effect from the coach of the sport concerned.

Rule 8. Students who are classified as professionals under AAU rules shall not be eligible to compete in intramurals in those sports in which they have competed as professionals.

Rule 9. To be eligible to compete in all all-university or league championship play-offs in any sport, a player must have competed in at least one league game.

Rule 10. Any student using an assumed name shall be barred from that sport during the quater in which such offense is committed and the team with which the student played shall forfeit all contests in which the student competed.

Rule 11. No player may compete as a member of two teams in the same sport. Any player violating this rule shall be ineligible for any further competition and the team shall forfeit the contest in which the player participated when discovered.

Rule 12. Students participating in intramurals are responsible for their own eligibility. Any questions should be referred to the intramural office and rulings obtained prior to participation. Although a student is ruled eligible on the basis of facts presented, if other facts are presented later which make that student ineligible, the student shall be declared ineligible.

Rule 13. No one shall be allowed to participate while under the influence of alcohol. Any such cases brought to the attention of the intramural director could result in immediate suspension of the violator.

Rule 14. Any student who is on an athletic grant shall not be eligible in the sport of related activity while the grant is in force.

Rule 15. Students not eligible to compete in an intramural sport may participate as officials.

Individual Eligibility

No uniform regulation defines the individual's eligibility when it comes to scholarship, varsity team membership, club membership, awards and professional athletic status. Each institution has its own unique situation to which these rules must apply.

Scholarship may be a factor in eligibility in an intramural program in a public school system. It is almost impossible to require students in colleges and universities to abide by a set of academic regulations because students may not carry "full class loads." There is really no logic in keeping a student who has academic problems from participating in an enjoyable recreational outlet. Undoubtedly, if students are having grade problems, they do not need to be frustrated further by a set of rules which prohibits them from participating in intramurals.

Members of varsity sports squads and club team members are generally prohibited from competing in the same intramural sports in which they participate or in some programs the number of such persons on a team may be restricted. Basically, these restrictions arise because varsity coaches may not wish to have the athletes competing during their season and because in order to be fair to intramural participants, these individuals, who have special practice privileges, should not be permitted to participate. The limitations on squad members generally apply only to their sport so that they are permitted to play in other activities; however, no special time scheduling should be used to allow them to participate.

There is always going to be a problem with the individual who leaves a squad and wishes to participate in intramurals; therefore, a rule must be clearly stated to cover this individual. Some programs publish a list of varsity squad members which may be used to determine eligibility. A more effective method is to have the coach of the squad that the player leaves rule on his status. An individual may go out for a squad without being deemed a varsity squad member.

Team Eligibility

Regulations regarding team eligibility are extensions of the individual eligibility rules and regulate team activities. These rules should clearly define organizational units and policies regarding using ineligible players and transferring of players from one team to another. An example of team eligibility rules follows:

Rule 1. A roster of all members of an organization should be turned into the intramural office, and when entry blanks are turned in any members of the organization are eligible if they meet individual eligibilty rules.

Rule 2. Independent teams may use those individuals that appear on the entry blank or they may add players until they have completed two scheduled games.

Rule 3. Any team permitting students to compete who at the time of the contest are not members of the organization they represent shall forfeit all games in which they participated and they shall be dropped from competition in that sport for the year in which such an offence was committed. Students who at the beginning of a season were members of an organization in any sport shall be permitted to compete during the remainder of that activity with the team with which they entered play. Competition in any new sport may be with the new organization.

Rule 4. A team winning a game by forfeit may list as participating team members up to twice the number of players required for that activity.

POSTPONEMENTS

In general, postponements should be discouraged in an intramural program; however, there may be circumstances in which teams are unable to participate. If the postponement is deemed necessary by the intramural office due to weather conditions or any other unforeseeable occurrence, then the games should be rescheduled. If it is not possible to reschedule the contest due to limited time or facilities, each team should receive credit for a win and they should not be eliminated from a play-off or eliminate other teams if the game was unable to be rescheduled.

If teams or individuals must postpone contests, there should be a set of regulations which they must follow in order to avoid confusion and unnecessary delay.

These regulations might include the following statements:

1. If necessary, intramural contests may be postponed, but such postponements must be arranged and approved by the intramural director and the manager of the opposing team at least 24 hours in advance of the time originally scheduled.

2. In round robin tournaments it is recommended that arrangements be made at the time of the postponement, for such postponed games must be played before the regular league schedule is completed.

3. In elimination tounaments, postponed contests must be played before the date on which the winner is scheduled to play the next match.

FORFEITS

It is impossible to completely eliminate forfeits in league play or individual tounaments that are drawn in advance. The intramural department should continually work to cut down on the number of forfeits by working with the teams having difficulty fielding their members. The department should attempt to make personal contact with the team as well as send a notice to the team's representative (Figure 4.19).

A definite set of rules for forfeits must be established to insure that teams will not be "short changed" if they are on time for a scheduled contest. Rules expressing forfeit policies could include:

1. Teams who fail to report to the playing area 10 minutes after scheduled time shall forfeit the contest.

2. Teams who report late to any event that is being timed with a master clock should begin the contest two points behind their opponents for each minute up to 10 minutes.

3. Individuals who fail to report for a scheduled contest within 10 minutes of scheduled time shall forfeit the contest.

For some activities it is also necessary to establish a minimum number of players that must be present to play the contest. The only time this type of rule should be used is if permitting a limited number of players on a team will make a travesty of the contest or give the short-handed team an advantage as in bowling. The students should be informed of the minium-number rule on both the entry blank and the rule sheet.

A policy should also be established that if a team forfeits a second game they will be dropped from the league. It is important to notify the team that was to play the team that has been dropped that it has won the scheduled contest so that it may find a pick-up game during this time. Whenever there is a pick-up game between a scheduled team and other players, the officials should still be assigned to the contest and they should handle the contest as though it was a league event. It should be clear to all students that if they participate in a pick-up team this will not count against them as playing for a second team.

Two policies which have proven successful in encouraging the students to continue in the activities even though they may have forfeited the first contest are:

1. If teams or individuals are unable to make contests and forfeit, they may ask their opponents to reschedule the contest and the intramural office will honor the rescheduled contest. The intramural office does not say that they have to play the contest but the philosophy is that a team signed up to play should play—so they are encouraged to reschedule.

2. Teams that forfeit their first contest in a league are not eliminated from the play-off if they play the rest of the schedule and the first loss would have kept them from going further.
   In such a situation, the team which forfeits is scheduled to play the team they forfeited to for the right to enter the play-off tournament.

PROTESTS

It is impossible to completely eliminate protests. One method of decreasing the number of protests is to have competent officials working the contests. However, even with the best officials, participants may feel they have a legitimate protest regarding a game.

A good rule to follow is that the official judgement is final in calling a play. The intramural director must always back up the official judgement on a call. However if a rule has been misinterpreted then there is grounds for a protest.

As no provisions for handling protested contests are to be found in most of the rule books, the intramural director or protest committee must rule on each case individually. Before the protest is taken before the protest board, the director should obtain a written statement from the officials regarding the play in question. If the protest does not eliminate the team from further competition, it should be acknowledged as a legitimate protest, although the game will not be replayed. When it is necessary to replay the contest, the game must be played from a point that would be fairest to both teams that were involved.

A set of regulations for teams filing protests might include the following:

1. Officials' judgements may not be protested.
2. If the game is to be protested, the officials should be notified and a notation made on the score card.
3. For league contest, the protest must be turned in, in writing, at least 24 hours after the contest not including weekends). See Figure 5.1.
4. In elimination tournaments, the protest must be turned in, in writing, no later than 9:00 a.m. the following day (not including weekends).
5. Protest on individual eligibility may be made at any time.

AWARDS

The intramural program fortunate enough to have funds to present awards should clearly state the policies regarding the awards that will be given. Statements of policies should cover the number of teams which will receive awards based on the number of contests in which they must participate to be eligible for awards, and the number of places that will receive awards in the individual events.

Over the past few years there has been a definite trend to cut back on the number and types of awards given because the programs have increased in number of activities and the cost of awards has increased. Directors have determined that funds can be better used when adding additional activities rather than when putting the money into awards. Most programs which have either eliminated awards completely or cut back on types of awards have experienced no lack of interest in participation.

It is true that students would like to receive some type of award or recognition for their efforts. The following suggestions are for

PROTEST FORM

Protesting team: _____ Date: _____

Final score: _____ Winner: _____

Please Check (X)

_____ Protest based on eligibility of players

_____ Protest based on rule interpretation

      (Judgement call is not protestable)

                                    Situation

Score at time of protest _____

Team leading: _____

Time left in game: _____

Description of the incident:

Names of officials: _____ _____

Team manager: _____ Phone _____

Office use: _____ Received by: _____

                                Date _____

                                Time _____

Figure 5.1
Protest form.

different types of awards which may be given at any level and are for the most part economical:

Certificates of achievements may be designed and reproduced very economically. This type of award is meaningful to students because they can place it on their bulletin boards. (Figure 5.2)

Pictures can be taken by the school photographer or by the intramural department if they have a camera. The pictures may be used in three ways: (1) the winners pictures may be posted in a permanent place, (2) the school or local newspaper may run the picture, or (3) each member of the winning team may be given a picture of the team.

Ribbons may be purchased from a commercial outlet; however, it is much more economical to make the ribbons. The intramural department can either purchase the ribbons or ask florist shops and funeral homes to donate the ribbons when they are no longer useful on flowers. The ribbons can either be prepared by the intramural office or it may be possible to ask the home economics class to cut the ribbon and the typing class to type the events on the ribbons.

Homemade Awards can be used at the junior high and high school levels if the industrial arts class makes the awards. The students who make the awards will feel just as proud of the awards as the individuals who receive them.

T-Shirts have become very popular with all students. The intramural department can either purchase T-shirts or make arrangements with a local sporting goods merchant to give the winners a special rate on shirts with the name of the school and of the event they won.

There is also a possibility that local merchants may be willing to donate food items for events held around Thanksgiving and Christmas so that the winning team can present these donations to a charitable organization or needy family.

Different methods are used to present awards. First, the awards may be presented to the winners at the time of the event. Second, all winners may be able to report for their awards on a given day so that pictures may be taken. Third, the intramural department may arrange with a local soft drink distributor to have them supply the soft drinks for a party which will be held in honor of all winners after school during a regular intramural period. Fourth, an assembly may be arranged where all students are presented their awards in front of the student body. Fifth, an awards banquet may be combined with an

WESTERN ILLINOIS UNIVERSITY

DEPARTMENT OF MEN'S INTRAMURALS

PRESENTS THIS

CERTIFICATE OF ACHIEVEMENT

TO

FOR INTRAMURAL EXCELLENCE IN

DURING THE   SCHOOL YEAR.

INTRAMURAL DIRECTOR

Figure 5.2
Award certificate.

athletic banquet or held separately. In order to limit expenses at these banquets, schools have been having parents bring a covered dish and asking local merchants to donate meat.

If students are to receive awards for outstanding performances on the playing courts, the intramural director should not neglect the students who assist the program. It is a good policy to recognize the outstanding intramural athlete. Some schools even recognize all-star teams and make special presentations to show the individuals on them.

6. Planning for All

It is a general human weakness to allow things, uncertain and unkown, to set us up in hope, or plunge us into fear.

Garris Caesar

The sport of play and the desire to participate are very important to the existence of intramurals but often are not enough to ensure participation for all interested students. The intramural program needs something to offer those individuals who may be shy, unskilled, not having time to practice, or just want to play for fun. Programs are needed where the emphasis is placed on widespread participation for enjoyment as well as programs geared to the pursuit for the all-school championship.

Earlier in this book it was pointed out that intramural and recreational activities are beneficial for all ages and both sexes. Planning for intramurals is basically a challenge to find means to provide individuals with an opportunity to participate. Individuals probably do not set objectives when they plan on participation in an activity; however, the director who is planning a program should keep student objectives in mind. The scope of the program should be broad enough to provide students with the chance to achieve the following objectives:

1. To experience competition. Nearly everyone enjoys competition, win or lose, if a contest is fairly even.
2. To have fun. Relaxation and recreation are necessary at all ages, and if students can learn to play and continue to play, the program has been of real service.
3. To learn cooperation and self-control.
4. To learn to use leisure wisely while in school as well as in later life.
5. To acquire a knowledge of and liking for sports and activity.
6. To develop physical fitness, grace, strength, stamina, and maintain physical vigor and well-being.

Many school districts, and some colleges and universities throughout the country, are in a financial squeeze due to the fact that bond issues and educational referendums have failed. Financing is largely dependent on the local community, and if the community is aware that a majority of the students are participating on a volunteer basis in an efficient program then possibly they will come to the aid of the school district.

This chapter is devoted to planning activities for students at different education levels and also presents an example of an intramural program for an entire school district. Although the chapter is divided into sections based on educational levels in order to effectively deal with each, it should be kept in mind that no boundaries for types of activities exist when it comes to "planning for all."

ELEMENTARY SCHOOL PROGRAM

Intramurals at the elementary level afford the director an opportunity to assist in the physical and social development of the students. In an effort to give each child satisfying, meaningful, and safe activity, professional judgement must be used and awareness of the differences in level of readiness, maturation, and tolerance that are critical in conducting specific activities.

A prime concern should be the creation and the maintenance of interest in the activities themselves. Children at this age generally greatly admire their peers who excel in movement skills; however, most of them have a very strong urge to belong to and participate with a team. The desire for personal glory among elementary school children is often submerged because as a team member they are loyal, and they want to win for the team.

Intramural activities offer a golden opportunity to channel the interests of most children with favorable outcomes. Children's personalities let them approach competition in various ways. There are the self-centered egotistic individuals who command and secure constant approval, the unruly youngsters who need much support and encouragement to get going and keep going, the independent individuals who find great satisfaction in being able to do things by themselves. A director must be careful not to develop excessively competitive sports that may induce uncontrollable aggressions.

Students should be given the opportunity to try and work things out for themselves, to try to plan strategy for games or patterns for the activities they are going to join. Students like to act as helpers with equipment, game officials, team captains, and bulletin board managers. Children have their own ideas as to how things should be accomplished, yet they want excellent leadership, to assure them that they will be able to play using common rules and procedures.

When planning a program for elementary school students, it should be kept in mind that scientists for years have told us that children in the formative years need between three and five hours of vigorous activity each day. Along with the vigorous physical activity, the student should be given the opportunity to develop the basic physical skills of running, jumping, skipping, and throwing.

Generally the program will be coeducational, and most activities will be done as a group. When conducting any activity requiring skills, students should be made aware of the importance of the individual's contribution to the total team as well as of personal achievement. By stressing the importance of each individual contribution to the team, the teacher helps students to attempt their very best and to be encouraged to do so by fellow students. Certain activities will not be done individually, and the director must select a method of grouping the students for competition. Children may be grouped for competition based on class level, age, performance level, height-weight, or interest as suggested by the AAHPER publication,[1]

Intramurals for Elementary School Children

Classroom or Grade Level. This type of classification is often preferred where there are at least three or four classrooms in each grade level. It utilizes ready-made loyalties, age groupings, and administrative structure. For optimum particpation, depending on the activity involved, two or more equally balanced subgroups can be organized from a room. Moreover, activities conducive to coeducational participation are easily incorporated.

Age. Another simple and convenient grouping index is age. With this method each team has the same number of students from each age group, or all teams are composed of children of the same age group.

Performance. Allowing for differences in skill and motivation helps establish equal teams for competition. Specific-skill tests are available for various activities in a program and can be used as a means of classification. In addition, batteries of performance tests can be used to obtain estimates of overall ability.

Height-Weight. Extreme differences of height and weight may affect performance in some activities; therefore, an extension of the age-grouping method may be indicated.

Interest. When physical differences are not significant factors in the performance of an activity, groups may be organized on the basis of interest alone.

[1] Intramurals for Elementary School Children, Athletic Institute, Chicago, Illinois, 1964.

Students at this age do not need much outside motivation to enjoy competition; however, with proper planning individual skill testing or competition may be turned into an enjoyable event. For example, if the students are studying Latin American countries in social studies or geography, then possibly the director should relate the intramural activities to activities of the Latin American countries. As soccer is the main South American sport, it would be a fine time to have some type of soccer lead-up games in the intramural program, and the teams could be named for the countries in Latin America. Every four years when there is an election, interest can be created by dividing the group into Democrats and Republicans, and playing would determine who was going to win the election. Each day the team that wins a particular contest for their party could have another seat in the Senate. Activities may thus become more meaningful and enjoyable to the individuals.

When it is an Olympic year, most of the activities can be related to traveling to the Olympics. In any activity in which student accomplishments are measurable, they can be informed that their accomplishments will be converted to measurable miles to the Olympics. For example, individuals would receive a mile for every basket they score or every goal that they kick. Thus the program is enhanced by injecting the incentive to see which team can reach the Olympic site first through excelling in skills.

Motivation can also be increased in physical education classes that need to measure growth and development of individuals as well as their skill. If properly planned, the tests for levels of efficiency or growth can be enjoyable to the individuals. For example, to measure leg strength, individuals jump to see who is going to be the jumping jack champion of the school; and students can be motivated to do their best, although they all won't be the champion, by having teams who receive recognition based on their total efforts.

Most elementary schools have a gymnasium or cafeteria as well as a hard-surface playground area that can be used for activities. Often in elementary schools, one can improvise and use the classroom or the hallways for playing areas. In using a classroom or hallway one must be extremely careful to keep the area safe. Individuals are highly keyed up in competition; therefore, they are not as aware of dangers arising from walls being too close, chairs sticking out, pencil sharpeners, or open desks. Rules must be modified and games must be adapted to the situations in which they are being played.

Activities

An endless number of different activities can be incorporated into the intramural program at the elementary level. The following is an abbreviated list of activities that are recommended because they help to develop the basic movement patterns which are so important at this age level. Although most of the activities are for students in upper elementary schools they could be used for first through third graders by modifying the activity so that the students will experience success.

Lead-up Games

Football	Punt for distance	**Volleyball**	Ball keep-up
	Pass for accuracy		Serving for accuracy
	or distance		Volleying relays
	Punt-back game		One-bounce
	Passing relays		volleyball
	Team football		Beachball volleyball
	keep-away		Modified volleyball
	Modified touch		with lowered net
	football	**Softball**	Throw for accuracy
Soccer	Dribbling for time		and distance
	Obstacle dribbling		Base running for
	Goal kicking		time
	Dribbling relays		Batting for distance
	Circle soccer		Long base
	Passing relays		Kickball
	Line soccer		Wiffleball
Basketball	Shooting contest at		Modified softball
	lowered basket		with an adult
	Obstacle dribbling		pitching to both
	Dribbling for time		teams
	Twenty one		
	Dribbling, shooting,		
	passing relays		
	Sideline basketball		

Individual Skills

40-yard dash	Modified shot put	Headstands
220-yard distance run	Standing hop, step, jump	Forward-roll relays
High jump	Shuttle relays	Back-roll relays
	Handstands	

Miscellaneous Games and Contests

Marbles	Paddle tennis
yo-yos	One-wall handball
Jacks	Tetherball
Four squares	Table tennis
Newcomb	Modified field hockey

Balance beam Good measure of balance. Timed event for individual and team. Call it a race across the Golden Gate Bridge.

Bike race Use students' bikes. Call it "Grand Prix" or "Little Indy 500."

Obstacle run A timed team event as well as individual event.

Pushball ride Students ride a ball either for distance or for time. Or make it a contest between large animals that could be ridden.

Rope climb Attempt to climb Washington Monument. Have the rope marked so each 3-inch distance counts toward achieving the goal.

Stilt race Using fruit juice cans for stilts have a moon-walk race.

Vertical jump Measure distance then convert this to distance of equivalent jump on the moon; this could result in a great jump due to lack of gravity.

Gym scooters Have races using different methods such as back to back and wheelbarrow or auto races, train races, and swimming races.

Fitness champions Individual event as well as total fitness scores can be used.

Floor hockey Use the plastic floor hockey equipment. Teams should be named after professional teams.

Bowling Gym bowling with plastic equipment. Can be done in the halls. A variation would be bank the ball off the wall.

Micky Mouse Intramurals It should be kept in mind that some intramural activities might well be those which students engage in during their free time, such as chess, checkers, yo-yos, jacks, marbles, and kite flying. It is also possible to use the electrical team games and racing track that are of great interest to students, and the students would probably be willing to bring these games to test their skills against classmates.

Jumping Jack. The winner would be the individual who earned the highest total score on the following activities:

a. Standing broad jump.
b. Long jump.
c. Sargent jump.
d. High jump.
e. Rope jump for 30 seconds (Two taken off jump total for each miss.)
f. Triple jump (hop, step, jump).

Odd-Hand Olympics

1. Opposite-hand softball throw for distance, three tries.
2. Hit softball off tee from opposite side of plate for distance, three tries.
3. Opposite-hand dribble for distance in 10 seconds.
4. Roll softball at pins, take total number of pins in three tries.
5. Opposite-foot 20-yard foot dribble of soccer ball, for time.

Playground Intramurals

The summer months provide an excellent opportunity to conduct intramural type activities on the playgrounds. The participants are generally broken up into age groups for activities and instruction. The playground intramural program not only offers competition in team and individual events but provides for instruction in athletic skills, passive games, art and crafts, music and dance, as well as hiking and excursions.

Most summer playground programs have a weekly theme to which all the games and arts and crafts are related. These themes might be used for:

Hobo week. Dress and activities are related to hobo life and may include sleeping under the stars.

Ecology week. Talks and visits can be made to organizations interested in ecology. The week may be culminated by making a modern art design out of metal cans, etc., that were collected during the week.

Nature week. Activities can include field trips.

Independence week. This is generally the Fourth of July week and features a pet and doll parade.

River boat week. Interest easily can be turned to water and water-related activities.

Good Neighbor Week, Circus Week, Western Week, Hobby Week, Campus Week, and *Superstar Week* are other events commonly held.

Dr. Larry A. James of the University of Northern Colorado best defined the objectives of a playground intramural program when he stated[2]

1. To provide the playground participants with an opportunity to participate in a wide variety of worthwhile activities based on the needs and interests of the participants.
2. To provide opportunities for social interaction in which friendships and democratic human relations can be developed.
3. To create new interests and skills for constructive use of leisure time.
4. To create an atmosphere that contributes to the personal fulfillment and happiness of each participant.
5. To offer an opportunity for the development of imagination and creative ability.
6. To emphasize safety as an integral part of the playground program.
7. To develop community awareness through organized field excursions.
8. To develop a deeper awareness of nature through selected activities and sound conservation practices.
9. To have fun and satisfy the need for activity.

JUNIOR HIGH PROGRAM

The intramural program at the junior high level may have a great and lasting effect on students. It is difficult to state that intramurals are more important at one age than another; however, the junior high age student is going through a period of rapid physical and emo-

---

[2] Larry A. James, *Twenty-fifth Annual Conference Proceeding*, National Intramural Association, **52**, 1974.

tional growth. Personality patterns which may be retained throughout life could be effected by the enjoyable experiences gained with peers. Both boys and girls experience rapid changes in height and weight which may result in poor body mechanics. Activities should be planned in which individuals will not feel embarassed by their clumsiness. Intramurals may help alleviate the awkwardness by providing activities which allow the participants to repeat basic body movements.

When planning a program of activities for the junior high age student, the director must keep in mind not only the rapid changes but also the differences which begin to appear between boys and girls. The young ladies are going through a visible physical change and they are concerned with becoming "grown up," while boys are more aggressive, and their peer society has a great influence on their activities.

Students at this age want approval from the adult world and at the same time they seek a certain degree of independence. Adult approval may be influenced by the achievement of the individual; however, a program should never be designed just to obtain a champion. The junior high student is more apt to accept criticism from his peer than from the adult world; therefore, team activities that are well organized will be of great benefit to the student.

Active games appeal to both the young men and young ladies, but at this age level they have no real desire to compete in the co-recreational activities. The boys feel that they must be aggressive and masculine while performing an activity. The girls do not wish to have the boys view them in active games for fear they will lose their "ladylike" image. Coed activities which are not strenuous and permit for equal competition may be accepted by both boys and girls. The program should also provide certain activities which enable youth to satisfy their aggressive drives through combatives; however, not all individuals are interested in these activities and they should not be required to participate.

Competitive Units

There are several methods of organizing teams for competition at the junior high level, and no matter which method is selected the director should continually evaluate the process to be sure that the correct social outcomes are being derived as well as equal competition. Team play may replace the desire for "gang" membership, when properly organized in the program.

Counciling room. This method of organization has been used for years because students have always been identified by this method so it makes for a natural unit.

Interest groups. With this method students get together to form their own teams. Its advantage is that individuals will be playing with peers by choice. The disadvantage is that some students may be left out of competition because of "clicks."

Alphabetical classification. The students, both boys and girls, are grouped alphabetically. This random method of selecting could lead to unbalanced teams.

Pool method. All those interested in participating are placed on teams by the intramural director. Captains may be appointed when using the pool method, but they should not be allowed to do the selecting of team members. This is the best method to assure equal opponents because the director can place the more highly skilled individuals on different teams.

Physical education class. Within the class period teams are organized and individual events are conducted. This method of organizing teams makes interclass play unlikely as other periods are usually scheduled for the other classes.

Programming

The range of activities at the junior high level is broadened and scheduling takes in more hours due to the various interests and levels of skill of the students. Facilities, consolidation, and bussing cause the program to be scheduled before school, during the noon period, and during physical education classes in both junior and senior high schools. Consolidation and bussing may provide a period that could be used for intramural activities. For example, the students who ride the first bus may have time before school whereas those who arrive on the second shift of buses would have time after school while they are waiting for the buses to return.

It is very important at this age level that the parents as well as the students have a definite schedule and know when the activities are planned. It is a good practice to put out a monthly schedule so that all parties concerned are aware of activities that are offered and when they are scheduled (Figure 6.1). This handout can also serve as an intramural newsletter if information is printed on the back of the calendar.

Noon Program. Noon programs have been established for many years in a number of schools and are becoming more prominent in

October

Sunday	Monday	Tuesday	Wednesday	Thursday	Friday	Saturday
1	2 8th, Football 9th, Tug–of–war Check schedules	3 9th, Football 7th, Tug–of–war Check schedules	4 *No activities*	5 7th, Football 8th, Tug–of–war Check schedules	6 9th, Soccer	7
8	9 8th, Football 9th, Tug–of–war Check schedules	10 9th, Football 7th, Tug–of–war Check schedules	11 Frisbee golf All grades	12 *No school* Teachers conference	13 8th, Soccer	14
15	16 8th, Football 9th, Tug–of–war Check schedules	17 9th, Football 7th, Tug–of–war Check schedules	18 *No activities* Make–up date for rain out	19 7th, Football 8th, Tug–of–war Check schedules	20 7th, Soccer	21
22	23 8th, Football 9th, Tug–of–war championship Check schedules	24 9th, Football 7th, Tug–of–war championship Check schedules	25 Cross–country All grades	26 7th, Football 8th, Tug–of–war championship Check schedules	27 Pushball All grades	28
29	30 8th, Football Check schedules	31 9th, Football Check schedules	*All events begin at 3:30*			

Figure 6.1
Junior high monthly schedule.

more schools every year. The concept in back of the noon program
is to provide a variety of activities in open tournaments. Most of the
activities in the noon programs have been of a quiet nature; however,
if it is possible to schedule the use of the gym or outdoor playing
areas, then short active contests can be held during this time period.
The more active events can be selected from the list that appears
later in this section. Quiet activities which might be part of a noon
program includes:

Box hockey	Dominoes
Card games	Electrical games
Checkers	Jarts
Chess	Word games
Darts	

Hallway Program. For years hallways have served as a supplemen-
tary area for intramural programs due to lack of available time
in gymnasiums. In some schools those hallways now have become a main area for scheduling intramurals due to Title IX
which requires equal use of facilities by boys' and girls' interscholastic teams. The hallway may be used during the noon
program, but more often they are not used until the afterschool
program because of the equipment that must be set up or the
nature of the activity which requires a hallway to be closed
for that activity only.

If the hallways are relatively safe from hazards and the school
board will grant permission to use them, an endless number of
events may be run in the hallways. The most common activities to be held in hallway are: bowling, table tennis, shuffleboard, and horseshoes (rubber). With adequate safety precautions, it is also possible to conduct: tug-of-war, floor tennis,
BB-gun shooting, two-man hoc soccer, fitness events (push-ups,
sit-ups, shuttle runs, distance runs for time, maze runs, stair
runs, and standing long jumps).

Physical Education Period. The physical education class period
offers a fine opportunity for conducting certain intramural
activities in conjunction with evaluating the student's ability in
physical activities. A great number of skill tests, given in con-
nection with physical education units, can serve to identify an
individual intramural champion and, when combined scores
are used, to recognize a team champion. For example, after a
unit of competition in archery, all members of the class could
be given a test requiring shooting 30 shots and the scores

attained by the students could be used as a partial evaluation in the archery unit as well as help determine the intramural champions. By keeping a running total of the various skills or fitness scores, a director may determine fitness or sports skill champions for each class which may motivate the students to do their best on all tests of skill. The following is a partial list of skill-testing activities which were used to evaluate students in the physical education class as well as determine intramural winners at North Junior High School, Collinsville, Illinois:

Archery (30 shots at 60 feet)
Backward race (220 yards)
Balance beam
Baseball accuracy throw[2]
  (30 throws)
Baseball distance throw
Base running (60-foot bases)[2]
Basketball distance throw
50-yard dash
100-yard dash
220-yard dash
440-yard dash
880-yard run
Mile run[2]
Discus
Football distance pass
Football distance placekick
Football distance punt
Golf distance drive[2]
Hop, step, jump[2]
120-yard low hurdles
Leg lifts (1 minute)
Long jump

Obstacle race
Peg board
Pillow fight
Pull-ups

Push-ups (no time limit)
Rope climbing (distance)
Rope climbing (for time, 20 feet)
Rope jump (1 minute)
Running high jump
Shot put (12 pounds)
Shuffleboard
Sit-ups (1 minute)
Soccer accuracy kick
Soccer distance punt
Soccer endurance kick
Softball distance hit
Standing high jump
Standing long jump
Squat thrusts (1 minute)
Verticle jump
Weight lifting

[2] Ninth grade only

If students are aware that the aforementioned skill test will effect their grade as well as count for intramurals, they will probably practice the skills outside of class—this is one of the few times that physical educators may have to motivate students to do "homework." It would also be a very good idea to establish records in these events for each grade level so that students have a chance to attempt to put their names on the school record board.

Afterschool or Saturday Programs. This time period is generally set aside for team and individual or dual activities. The leagues should be set up for each grade as well as for both boys and girls in some activities. It is not good practice to schedule leagues that have seventh graders playing ninth graders; however, in some individual or dual events it is possible to have all school play-offs between the winners and runner-ups from each grade level. Activities for these periods might include:

Team Sports (Boys and Girls)

Baseball	Softball
Basketball	Speedball
Broomstick hockey	Swimming
Field hockey	T-ball
Floor hockey	Track and field
Football (touch)	Tug-of-war
Line soccer	Volleyball
Soccer	Water games
	Wiffleball

Individual and Coed Activities

Archery	Handball (one wall)
Badminton	Horseshoes
Basketball goal shooting	Paddleball
BB-gun shooting	Paddle tennis
Bicycling	Roller skating
Bowling	Skiing
Canoeing	Swimming
Dance	Table tennis
Deck tennis	Tennis
Distance walking race	Tetherball
Free throws	Track and field
Golf	Tumbling
Gymnastics	

Clubs. It is only natural that interest clubs begin to appear at this age level because of the importance of peer acceptance. Sponsors for the various clubs are either assigned by the administration or volunteer according to area of interest; however, there are a number of club activities which might be sponsored by the intramural director. The clubs are generally one of the strongest socializing factors at the junior high level because both boys and girls want to participate. When students elect to join a club they are reaching out for new experiences and often receive a good deal of self-satisafaction from their accomplishments. Of the many clubs formed at the junior high level, those which might fall under the direction of the intramural director are:

Archery

Bicycling

Bowling

Canoeing

Chess

Dancing

Fishing

Go-carts

Hiking

Horseback riding

Minibike (motor)

Outing

Roller skating

Sledding

Tumbling

The Macomb-Adair School District, Macomb, Illinois, recently eliminated the study hall from the junior high curriculum, and instead during this period they have "Special Assignment," led by outside resource people, in which students may elect to participate in special programs, such as physical fitness, arts and crafts, karate, photography, and needlework. The special assignment concept permits the school district to provide students with a chance to expand their interests and participate in club activities during this period.

HIGH SCHOOL PROGRAM

The intramural program at the high school level should place more emphasis on the carry-over type of activities because a good number of high school graduates will not further their education and the intramural program should provide the student with an opportunity to participate in activities which will be of value in adult life. Many high school curriculums do not require physical education every year that a student is in high school; therefore, many students, especially girls, lose interest in physical activity. The intramural program should not be used to replace physical education, but should provide an outlet where students may get the physical activity necessary to help maintain sound physical fitness as well as continue with the development of skills.

All students at this age level need to participate in some form of recreational activity. The intramural program has an opportunity to help students develop the learned skills and put them to practical use in competition that is enjoyable and meaningful because it is voluntary participation.

Social life is very important to the high school age students, and intramurals should try and help the students develop socially and acquire new and lasting friendships through co-rec programming. Many of the values gained through interaction with fellow students both male and female carry over into adult life.

The students play a very active role at this level in assisting with the administration and operations of the program. Well trained intramural officials and intramural assistants are essential if the program is to succeed, and students welcome the opportunity to serve in these positions if they are afforded the proper respect that should go with the duties they are performing. Although the students like to "do their thing," they need guidelines as how to conduct the program and respect for the administrator that sticks by the rules and regulations. If the students can break rules and regulations and get away with it, they may soon lose interest in the program and undertake less desirable activities during their leisure.

Competitive Units

Competition in high schools is generally conducted between units at the same class level, and an all-school championship is determined by competition between the class champions for selected events. There are some events in which team membership is made up of students from all classes. When teams are formed using this method, it is a good practice to have a regulation which states the exact numbers that must represent each class.

The most widely accepted method of forming teams is to permit friends to form their own teams. It is also possible to form teams by using counciling units or clubs, or to form special teams for students who must ride buses; the "pool method" has all interested individuals sign up for the events, and the director arbitrarily assigns players to a team. Intramural teams may be formed in physical education class but at the high school level there should not be intramural competition during class periods because this time should be devoted to the teaching of skills in carry-over activities as well as to maintaining the physical fitness of the students.

Co-rec activities should not be restricted to class competitions because boy-girl relationships are not regimented by classes. One of the social values that may be gained in co-rec activities is to provide an opportunity for individuals who are dating to compete in a recreational activity.

There should be very few regulations which limit the students participating in the program. Athletic squad members should not be permitted to participate in sports which are related to their sport while it is in season. Students should not be required to maintain the same academic standards as those in interscholastic competition, but they might be restricted from competition if school policy prohibits students from extracurricular activities as a disciplinary measure. There should not be two standards for disciplines that is, the same regulations which prohibit a student from participating in intramurals should apply to the athletics.

Programming

Programming methods for high school are very similar to those discussed in the previous section on junior high; however, there are some special considerations as to what groups and types of activities should be scheduled during available times.

Noon Programs. This period provides the director with the opportunity to run structured or unstructured tournaments in a variety of activities. This may be the only time in which team contests may be held for those individuals who are bused to the school, and these leagues should have priority in the use of facilities for team contests.

Afterschool Programs. Generally these hours are used for scheduling team events, and because of limited indoor facilities the indoor activities are generally limited to fall and spring.

Evening Programs. At the high school level these programs are practical, because students are old enough to return to school after the evening meal. In many cases, this offers the only opportunity to use the indoor facilties, and high school age students welcome an activity scheduled in the evenings so they may socialize with their peers.

Saturday Programs. One-day events in either team or individual activities can be conducted on Saturdays. This is also a good time to use the indoor facilities which are heavily scheduled during the week.

Commercial Facilities. These should be used to conduct as many activities as possible. The director should work with the proprietors of the facilities to establish the best possible rate for the students when they are using the facilities for regular leagues.

Recreational Agencies. Agencies which serve the community can assist the director in joint planning for areas and facilties, and this mutual planning may provide the students with a wider choice of activities.

Informal Recreation. The weight room, swimming pool, and gymnasium should be scheduled to provide the students with opportunity to pursue their recreational interests.

Sports Clubs. These groups may want to conduct their particular activities for their members and other students. Special interest clubs should be encouraged because they generally display evidence of good student leadership.

Activities

There should be no restriction as to the number of kinds of activities which may be offered at the high school level. The scope of the activities in the program should never be limited by personnel. If the students are truly interested in participating in a wide variety of activities, the director should be able to seek out interested students to assist in conducting the program. The specific types of activities may be selected from those listed either in the section for junior high or in Chapter 7.

An Actual School District Program

This section presents an example of an actual intramural program conducted by a school district at the elementary, intermediate, and high school level.

The Macomb-Adair District Number 185, Macomb, Illinois, intramural program includes a wide range of activities involving both boys and girls in grades fourth through twelfth. The program is based on the philosophy that values participation in preference to competition and winning. To achieve its goal, the program offers a wide diversity of activities ranging from individual passive activities to highly organized team sports. The program is divided into three levels—elementary, intermediate, and secondary. It was organized on a total district basis to give continuity throughout the program and to give the students an early background in carry-over lifetime activities.

Elementary Program. The intramural activities program for fourth, fifth, and sixth grade students are offered in six different elementary schools. All of the programs are coeducational and are scheduled two days a week. The programs are organized to fit the individual school's daily schedule. Three of the schools offer early bird activity before school which lasts 40 minutes, and the other three schools operate a noon-hour program.

An important factor in the elementary program is the full-time staff member. The district has three qualified instructors assigned to teach physical education and the administration of the intramural programs. Each staff member is responsible for conducting the elementary intramural program in two primary schools. The staff works in cooperation with the district intramural director in setting up the basic program activities which include:

Touch football	Tetherball
Soccer	Four square
Soccer jamboree	Kickball
Basketball skills	Softball
Basketball league	Relays (teams)
Football skills	Track and field
Floor hockey	Wiffleball
Volleyball	

The physical education classes provide the skills, rules, and basic background needed to successfully participate in the intramural activities. Following a major activity such as soccer or volleyball, the elementary staff and director organize a "jamboree play day" in which all interested students participate in a districtwide one-day tournament. Certificates and team pictures are given to the winning team. A picture of the entire group is also taken to aid in motivating the students and publicizing the program.

Intermediate Program. The junior high intramural program is carried out during the student lunch periods and also during a special intramural activity period that is provided twice weekly. The special intramural period is obtained by shortening the eight normal 40-minute periods to 35 minutes each on Monday and Thursday. This allows 40 minutes of time at the end of the day for intramurals. Each of the eighteen homerooms are encouraged to participate in every activity, with competition taking place between homerooms of the same grade. For those students not wishing to participate, alternatives are offered in other areas of the school curriculum. Activities are co-educational, but separate tournaments and leagues are offered in some team and contact sports. In team sports such as football and basketball, games are divided into equal periods with boys competing against boys and girls against girls, and the winning team is determined by combining the boys' and girls' scores for each homeroom.

During the fall, the students compete in frisbee and football skills during the noon program period. The touch football league is conducted during the special intramural period, and upon completion of the football league, the students participate in a soccer league. Winter noontime activities include king of the beam, basketball skills, wrist wrestling championships, and recreational games. The homerooms for the afternoon intramural period are assigned to one of three areas: the gymnasium, the rear of the auditorium, and the cafeteria. The gymnasium is used to conduct the basketball and volleyball program while table tennis is being played in the rear of the auditorium. The cafeteria is used for box hockey, chess, checkers, and basic card games. The scheduling is arranged so that each homeroom has equal time for competition in all areas. The spring noontime intramurals include four square, three-man volleyball, two-on-two basketball, team free throw contests, tandem bike races, and other activities requiring little organization. During the afternoon activity period, a round robin schedule, which includes all of the homerooms, is conducted in softball.

Supervision for all activities at this level is a joint effort between the individual assigned to the intramural staff and the homeroom teachers. The intramural staff is responsible for the noon program supervision as well as for the special period. The homeroom teachers accompany their classes to the assigned area during the special period and assist in the supervision of the activity.

Secondary Program. The elementary and intermediate programs provide the opportunity for the introduction of skills and techniques and the development of good habits and sportsmanship. The secondary program is organized to provide students with an opportunity to continue using the skills as well as exploring new physical and mental challenges. The secondary program offers activities during the three 45-minute lunch periods and after school. During the lunch periods, the cafeteria is set up with three table tennis tables, three foosball games, floor tennis, five decks of cards, four checker sets, and four chess sets. Two staff members are assigned to the noon program during which individual activities and games requiring little organization are scheduled. The activities include:

Table tennis ladder tournaments	Card hockey
Team free throw	Chess league
Jarts	Checker league
Tandem bike races	King of the beam
3-man football	Wrist wrestling
3-man volleyball	Frisbee golf
4 point pitch	Hole-in-one golf

Table tennis league

Foosball singles

Foosball doubles

Limbo

3-on-3 basketball

Leagues and tournaments are conducted in the above activities. The duration of each activity depends upon the number of contestants and the interest generated. A master schedule is made, and the contestants are responsible for arranging and officiating their matches. Following a contest, the winner will report the score to the intramural supervisor on duty. The contestants must organize their 40-minute lunch period so eating and playing is possible. All leagues and tournaments are scheduled to be completed in three to four weeks. The players must play all matches before the deadline or forfeit all unplayed games. Following all noon hour leagues and tournaments, the top four finishers from each noon hour advance to the all-school championship which is held on specially scheduled nights. The three champions and the second place finisher with the best record receive a first round bye in a twelve-team double elimination tournament. Winners of the events receive a T-shirt naming the event in which they were champion. The top three finishers also receive a certificate of achievement.

The afterschool activities include team and individual events which require additional time and facilities. The program includes:

Table tennis invitational
    tourney

Racquetball

12-inch softball

Badminton

Coed badminton

Weight lifting tournament

Tug-of-War

Football league

Football minitournament

Super bowl

Soccer league

Volleyball

Coed Volleyball

1-on-1 basketball

2-on-2 basketball

Basketball play-offs

All-star basketball game

21 elimination

Free throw contest

Floor hockey league

Floor hockey tournament

Fishing Derby

Putt-putt golf

Billiards

Bowling

Water basketball

Water polo

Swimming meet

Superstars event (ten activities)

The intramural activities are conducted throughout the various school facilities within the district, and other facilities in the community accommodate several special activities which constitute an important part of the secondary program. Among these special facilities are the Western Illinois University bowling lanes and billiard areas. The community facilities include the putt-putt golf course, park district softball diamonds, and Macomb Country club golf courses. Community cooperation enables the intramural staff to prepare the students in many of the enjoyable carry-over activities.

In addition to the schools' daily bulletins and school newspapers, publicity concerning the intramural activities is posted on the intramural bulletin boards located in the schools' lunchrooms. Monthly newsletters are very helpful in keeping the students up to date on coming events, vital statistics, and other information concerning the IM program.

Complete intramural records are kept at the high school which aid in the scheduling of events, budgeting, and staff distribution. Records are kept on the total number of participants as well as on individual participation. Students are responsible for reporting their own participation to the IM office. The intramural office prepares a 3×3 record card for all students who are enrolled in the school. When a student turns in a participation sheet (Figure 6.2, top), the office transfers this information to the permanent record card (Figure 6.2, bottom).

Program Potpourri

1. Special intramural leagues or tournaments may be conducted on buses by using portable chess and checkerboards or by playing pencil and paper word games. Champions may be determined for each bus route, and the champions may meet to determine the "bus champ."

2. Single skill activities, such as hole in one, Frisbee throw, and most consecutive free throws, make good noon period activities or quick activities to conduct just after school.

3. Students may enjoy competing in a telephone meet where their scores are compared with scores from other schools in the area. This type of a meet may be conducted in any of the events that achieve individual scores, times, or distances.

4. Physical fitness activities and weight lifting scores may be posted on a challenge board, and students should be encouraged to have their name put up on the board by scoring a higher mark.

5. "No-champ leagues" may be scheduled in some activities for those individuals who are not concerned with who is champion or participation points but merely want to compete in an event on a regularly scheduled basis.

Macomb High School

Physical Education and Intramurals
Macomb, Illinois 61455

Individual participation sheet

Number of
event _____

Event _____

Playing site _____

Total participation _____   Name _____

MACOMB DISTRICT 185 INTRAMURALS

PARTICIPATION RECORD

Class _____

Name _____   Parents or Guardian _____

Address _____   Phone _____

Lunch Hour

1
2
3
4
5
6
7
8
9
10
11
12
13
14
15

16
17
18
19
20
21
22
23
24
25
26
27
28
29
30

31
32
33
34
35
36
37
38
39
40
41
42
43
44
45

Figure 6.2
Participation records.

125

6. Allow ten weeks for a thirty-mile swim in the pool.
7. Conduct field events one day and running events the following day for a track meet.
8. The top qualifiers of a free throw contest can "throw-off" at the half time of a varsity basketball game.
9. Exhibition games are scheduled in various sports prior to the regular league schedules to familiarize old and new players with rule changes, etc.
10. Arrange for the cross-country meet to end at the half time of a soccer or football game. The finish line is the middle strip or 50-yard line.

COLLEGE OR UNIVERSITY PROGRAM

Although each institution (junior college, community college, commuter college, and campus college and university) has its own unique problems, it is possible to explore the intramurals and recreation programs at this level. The typical college student cannot be catagorized or characterized in regard to growth, maturity, or interest; therefore, the college program must be prepared to offer a widely diversified program to meet the interests and needs of a population. One of the biggest assets to an intramural-recreation program— besides that of the participation by the students—is that the students are not catagorized when it comes to the intramural program. In many of the large universities, students have lost their individual identity as a result of large classes and ID numbers. Intramurals can provide its students with an opportunity to be an individual and receive recognition as an individual and not as just a number.

The men and women who participate in the intramural-recreation program often use this experience as a social stepping-stone. Through active participation in the program, they are afforded an opportunity to meet many different students who may not be in their academic discipline in college. The importance of the social aspect of the programs is reflected in the rapid growth of the co-rec programs at most colleges and universities.

Structured Program

The structured programs provide the students with a guarantee that they will have the opportunity to participate in the activity of their choice at a given time and place. This program includes leagues and tournaments for men, women, and co-rec, which are generally conducted on a regular basis during the week and on Saturdays.

The scheduling of the structured program is not only affected by the facilities that are available but also by the type of college or university. The director of a commuter college must keep in mind that most of the students in the program do not live on campus; therefore, activities must fit the schedules of the students who travel to school in car pools or by commercial buses. The structured program for the commuter college may be run in the evening or after school on a limited basis; however, the director should examine the possibility of conducting activities during the school day when facilities are available and the students have free time. The colleges and universities that have the majority of their student population living in housing units on or near the campus may schedule the structured program in the afternoon, evening, and on Saturdays and Sundays. The director of this type of program must be careful not to over schedule structured activities, thus preventing the students, staff, and faculty from using the facilities for open recreation. On campuses that are fortunate enough to have intramural-recreation buildings, areas can be set aside for both structured and recreational activities during the same time period.

The director must examine all possibilities when scheduling the structured program to assure the students an opportunity to participate. A suggested list of rules and regulations for the college level is presented in Chapter 7.

Unstructured Program

Unstructured recreational activities are almost an absolute must at the college level. It should be realized that not all students are competitive by nature and therefore welcome the opportunity to participate without the pressure of a competitive program. Students at this level understand that they are about to leave the highly structured educational world, and they begin to show more interest in the activities which they must initiate themselves.

Definite periods should be set aside when the students may use the facilities for open recreation. During these open recreation periods, the students should have access to the equipment and be able to use all of the facilities, including the pool. Although these periods are scheduled as open recreation periods, it may be necessary to establish certain regulations that will assure more adequate use of the facility and prevent special interest groups from dominating the areas. These regulations might include:

1. No full-court basketball games will be permitted if others are waiting to use the area. When students are waiting to play on a basketball court, individuals must vacate the court every 30 minutes.

2. In order to assure badminton or volleyball players a chance to participate in their activities, it may be necessary to assign an area for their activities only.

3. Tennis players should not be permitted to dominate an indoor basketball court when it could be used by more students for some other activity. Likewise if there are baskets on the tennis courts, there should be a definite time when no basketball players are permitted so that tennis players may use the courts.

4. When working with handball courts, it may be necessary to either set up scheduling regulations or state that individuals must vacate the court after 45 minutes of activity.

5. Regulations should also be established for the throwing of footballs, baseballs, and softballs in indoor areas.

6. Bikes and pets should not be permitted in the facilities.

7. Swimming pool regulations should be posted in regard to taking a shower and use of floatation devices, masks, fins, and balls. An area should be set aside for diving and a lane for lap swimming.

Students will find many uses for outdoor facilities which are convenient to their living areas. There should be a system whereby organizations may check out any equipment necessary for weekend or evening recreation. Just as with the indoor facilities, there should be an established period when outdoor facilities are not scheduled and may be used by students for free play.

During recreational hours on the tennis courts a set of regulations should be established to assure individuals an opportunity to participate. Racket boards should be placed on the outside ends of the courts, and individuals who are waiting to play should place their rackets on the boards to indicate they are waiting. Regulations regarding the courts might include:

1. Play on all courts will begin and end *each hour on the hour.*

2. Individuals must place their rackets on the racket board for the court on which they desire to play. The left side of the racket board could be for odd hour play, and right side for even hour play.

3. Four rackets on a peg indicate that four players will share that court for an hour by playing doubles or by playing equal periods of singles. A single racket on a peg does not give possession of a court but entitles the individual to share that court with the owners of other rackets on the same peg.

4. Players may not racket a court more than 2 hours in advance of the time they wish to play.

5. When others are waiting, it is requested that only doubles be played on all courts.

6. Only one court may be racketed at a time by any two players.

7. No individual who is playing or has just completed play may reracket a court until all other persons who have racketed courts and are waiting to play have taken possession of their courts and all individuals who have been waiting to racket courts have had an opportunity to do so.

8. Rackets not claimed when play changes on the hour may be removed from the racket board. A court made available by nonappearance may be taken by the individuals who have racketed for the next hour's play if they wish to accept it, if not, the court is available for immediate use by the next individuals in line.

Campus Recreation

The intramural department plays an important role in the total campus recreation program, not only through providing equipment but also through its leadership. The intramural director and all staff members should encourage all forms of acceptable leisure activities, but must be careful not to insist on input into student activities unless the students ask for such input. The department should serve as a "resource and supply center" to assist any campus organizations in their efforts to provide structured or unstructured leisure activities. The department should not attempt to conduct all the leisure activities, but should encourage and assist the organizations in setting up their tournaments, getting equipment, and obtaining good officials.

The residence halls, fraternities, sororities, and independent organizations often wish to conduct their own tournaments and need assistance from the intramural department concerning playing areas, equipment, and officials. They will generally conduct their tournaments using the same format as intramurals because the students are familiar with the intramural rules. These tournaments should be scheduled whenever it does not interfere with the regular scheduled program. Sundays, when most facilities sit idle, have proven a very effective time to schedule their activities. To encourage these worthwhile activities, the intramural department should publicize the fact that student organizations may seek assistance with equipment and personnel which they may not have, such as officials, shirts, whistles, clocks, and score sheets.

Colleges and universities have constructed more married student housing which encourages married couples to go to school or to stay in school, and this group of students may require assistance from the intramural department in providing activities for their leisure recreation. The husbands and wives who are students should have the same opportunity to participate as any student. It is also a good practice to permit both husband and wife, no matter if one is not a student, to participate in all coed activities. The married students who have children should be permitted to use the recreational facilities during the same period that is scheduled for staff family recreation. The intramural director should make an extra effort to inform this group of students that they are eligible to use the department's equipment for their family and recreational outings.

One of the purposes of the student union is to encourage student programming as well as to provide recreational areas. The intramural department should work very closely with the student union in coordinating and conducting their activities. The intramural department may make use of the student unions' recreational areas, such as those for bowling and billiards, to conduct the IM program and should be willing to assist the student union in conducting some of their activities using the intramural facilities and equipment. Students who work on programming for the student unions not only conduct activities such as dances, bridge, bowling, and table games but also sponsor activities such as homecoming week, winter carnivals, and "thank goodness it's spring" which may stretch over an entire week. Probably the biggest assistance that the intramural department can give is to provide the required officials.

The faculty-staff program is another area which must be considered by a university intramural director. Although the faculty-staff program should never take precedence over the student program, a good faculty-staff program may create a certain amount of esprit de corps among the faculty of different disciplines. This group of individuals is basically interested in obtaining or keeping a degree of physical fitness through jogging, swimming, physical exercises, or competing in individual or dual games. A small number may be interested in competing in team events such as basketball, volleyball, softball, and bowling.

The type of program offered for the faculty-staff may be limited due to the unavailability of facilities; however, when the facilities are free for open recreation, the faculty should have the same opportunities as the students to use the facilities on a first-come, first-served basis. Types of programs that can be offered to the faculty-staff include:

Early Bird. The early bird program can provide the faculty-staff with the use of the facilities prior to the regular scheduled classes. The early morning availability of an area in which to work out has proven popular with faculty-staff interest groups. This is a good time for them to run, and play handball, racketball, and indoor tennis. These individuals usually are required to provide their own equipment. Therefore, no equipment clerk need be on duty.

Noon Program. The noon hour provides an excellent opportunity for the faculty-staff group to participate in structured or unstructured activity. This period can be set aside for faculty-staff recreational use of a facility. This is also an excellent time to run an organized program in which members of the physical education or medical staff assist in setting up a program for cardiorespiratory fitness. This type of program would begin with taking measurements of the individuals; then they could choose a program of jogging, swimming, weight training, or stationary bike riding. Periodically throughout the year the initial tests could be repeated so that the faculty-staff members would be aware of the progress made through the program.

Faculty-Staff Leagues. If the faculty-staff members have an interest in team activities, the intramural office should attempt to provide a league for these indiviudals. This should not be combined with the student leagues; it should be separate. If the school does not provide funds to cover the official that will be used in the faculty-staff leagues it may be necessary to charge a user fee to pay for the official. Generally no awards are given in faculty-staff leagues other than golf and bowling. Whenever possible, the intramural director should encourage the faculty-staff members to plan and conduct their own competition with the intramural office providing whatever expertise is necessary to see that the activity runs successfully. One of the most popular events that the intramural office may be asked to help conduct is the golf tournament. Most golf tournaments are used as a good social mixer mong different disciplines in the university; therefore, golfing ability should not be a prerequisite. The intramural department may be asked to conduct this event so that all levels of ability can participate, and this can only be done through a handicap system. The most widely used system for golfers who have not established a handicap is the Calaway system. The

Callaway handicap chart appears in Appendix F.

Wives Program. Although there may not be a great demand for an organized program for faculty-staff wives, the intramural department should encourage this group of individuals to participate in the fitness program and possibly arrange for instruction in recreational activities requiring skill such as golf, tennis, badminton, and racketball. These instructions may be sponsored through the IM office or in conjunction with other campus organizations. Unless qualified instructors are willing to volunteer their services to teach the skills, it will be necessary to charge the wives a fee to pay for the instruction.

Family Recreation. A definite period should be scheduled during the week when the families of faculty-staff and students may use the facilities. The swimming pool is generally the most popular area, and it is advisable to have a portable kiddie pool for the young children. Sundays are traditionally the day of the week that families are together, and this is a good time to schedule their recreation period. Because it is a family recreation period, no children should be permitted to use the facilities unless they are accompanied by a parent or guardian. Intramural directors can create a great deal of good will, as well as provide an educational service, if they sponsor lessons for the faculty-staff children, especially in swimming.

SPORTS CLUBS

Sports clubs have existed for many years in both public schools and on college campuses, but they are currently experiencing a fantastic growth rate because modern educators are not about to discourage students from enjoying a worthwhile activity, no matter what the nature of the activity. School administrators "look good" if they can list a great number of extracurricular activities as part of their program.

Intramural directors should not merely be concerned with listing a number of sports clubs as part of the program. They should take an active part in encouraging the interest groups to organize and become an active part of student life. Intramural directors should realize that sports clubs offer the interested students an excellent opportunity for socializing experiences as well as the chance to develop recreational skills during their leisure.

Sports clubs have expanded well beyond the bounds of the traditional intramural and interscholastic programs. One of the greatest values of this type of program is the fact that segments of the student body may participate in enjoyable activity even though they would never consider the intramural program. These organizations, through their own efforts, may possibly provide the student population with an opportunity to enjoy activities that the educational institution may not feel qualified to offer or may not be willing to support with public funds.

Before discussing the philosophy of various segments of the sports club program, it should be pointed out that there are four basic types of clubs.

Instruction Clubs

This type of club is basically concerned with providing excellent instruction to their members in a particular leisure activity. This is not to say that no competition is held between members of one club even between club members from different institutions. This type of club is generally self-supporting because the members are willing to pay for their instruction, and when a chance arises to display their skills in competition, they are willing to pay for the opportunity to meet the challenge.

Competitive Clubs. These clubs are generally organized around a particular activity. They are composed of highly skilled individuals who want to compete with skilled individuals from other clubs. These clubs desire to become a recognized school athletic team so that they may receive the same benefits offered the athletic squads. Most of their activity is centered around the practice period which will prepare them to compete at a high level with other teams. Although these clubs do not have the philosophy of "win at any cost," they are concerned with belonging to some type of league or conference so they can receive a certain amount of recognition for their efforts.

Recreational Clubs. This type of club is generally made up of members who are more concerned with the social aspect of leisure recreation. These clubs are primarily concerned with providing individuals with the opportunity to enjoy recreation with other individuals in indoor or outdoor activities. They provide an opportunity for individuals to display their learned skills as well as exchange ideas.

Intellectual Clubs. These clubs are formed by individuals who enjoy mental challenge. The clubs are generally self-supporting, and the participants provide most of the equipment necessary to conduct their particular events.

There is no limit to the number of sport clubs which may be sponsored or recognized by an educational institution. In some schools, the sports clubs form the teams which are recognized as varsity teams at other schools. Several factors have contributed to the growth of clubs: (1) students have moved from one region of the country where an activity is played to another and in order to continue in the activity they have had to introduce fellow students to it; (2) television has given vast exposure to different types of leisure activities and created a challenge to students to attempt these activities; (3) less credits may be required to graduate so that students have more time to explore different programs; (4) federal financial assistance enables students to have more free time; (5) some students have a desire to participate with fellow students with the same interests and to practice and play at their convenience at a time not dictated by rigorous scheduling and training procedures. A potential list of sports clubs might include:

Archery	Handball	Rugby
Badminton	Horseback riding	Sailing
Bicycling	Ice hockey	Scuba
Billiards	Jogging	Skeet shooting
Boating	Judo	Squash
Bowling	Karate	Synchronized
Bridge	Lacrosse	swimming
Camping	Models	Table tennis
Canoeing	Orienteering	Team handball
Checkers	Outing	Vans
Chess	Paddleball	Volleyball
Collecting	Parachuting	Water skiing
Dance	Pinball	Weight lifting
Debate	Polo	
Fencing	Riffle shooting	

Administration of Sports Clubs

Just as there is no set number of activities that may be run by sports clubs, there is no definite agreement as to how to adminster a sports club program. Some professional leaders feel very strongly that all sports clubs should be administered under one central office, and others strongly believe that the individuals who elect to seek leisure fulfillment through sports clubs should have the right to self-rule. There is agreement that there should definitely be central administration of the sports clubs if they are receiving funds from a general budget or student activity fees. The individual responsible for this program is usually the sports club coordinator who is a member of the intramural staff.

Before proceeding to organize the various sport clubs at an institution, the sports club coordinators should examine the institution's policies regarding student activities that involve appropriated funds, use of facilities, and legal ramifications. Then a tentative set of guidelines should be drawn up, and the representative of interested sports clubs should be invited to form a sports club council.

The sports club council constitution should contain a section which describes the functions of the council and sets up the rules so that the clubs will be able to operate without violating any institutional regulations. Areas which must be considered are:

Use of the school name. There should be a policy statement covering the clubs use of the name of the institution. It should be established that if these clubs use the institution's name, they are subject when representing the institution to all regulation which the institution feels are necessary.

Advisor. Because the sport clubs represent the university, they should be required to have a faculty or staff advisor who is willing to work with the students in their area of interest.

Membership. There definitely should be a statement defining who is eligible to be a member of a sports club. Any sports club which receives appropriated funds should be limited to students. Faculty, staff, and citizens may be part of the club, but that club should not receive benefits from appropriated student funds.

Eligibility. No student should be declared ineligible to be a member of the sports club because of academic standing or number of years in school; however, each club should be held responsible for the eligibility of its own members if they engage in competition with other schools and they have an agreement on standards for eligibility.

Finances. Most sports clubs derive their revenue from three sources: dues, appropriated funds, and fund raising projects. All funds generated by the clubs should be subject to all of the institution's regulations. The clubs should be encouraged to establish membership dues as a means of supplementing the funds received from appropriated sources. The following is an example of regulations covering the financing of sports clubs, taken from the Western Illinois University Sports Council Constitution:

Article VIII
FINANCES

Section I. The monies for the Council will come from the Council on Student Activity Funds, special fund raising activities, individual club incomes, and other methods authorized by the Sports Council.

Section II. Funds will be distributed according to approved budgets from the individual clubs. If allocations from the Council on Student Activity Funds do not total the requested funds, each club will receive the same percent decrease as was in the Council on Student Activity Funds allotment.

Section III. If one club has excess funds for the year, for whatever reason, they may transfer the excess monies to another club upon approval of the Council.

Section IV. All funds are to be deposited and expended from the Western Illinois University Business Office.

Section V. A yearly audit shall be conducted in compliance with current Western Illinois University policy. A special audit shall be undertaken upon a majority vote of the Council or at the discretion of the advisor.

Section VI. This organization shall submit a detailed financial statement to the appropriate University authorities yearly, in accordance with University policy, by the last Monday of each Spring Quarter.

Section VII. Special funds for National Tournaments or other extraordinary levels of competition may be requested from the Council on Student Activity Funds if approved by the Council.

Facilities. A policy should be established in conjunction with the institution policy regarding the eligibility and priority of the club to use the institution's facilities.

Travel. At state run schools when clubs are eligible to use the school's vehicles, they should be aware of the regulations which govern the use of state owned autos. If commercial or private transportation is used, a policy should be established as to the amount of appropriated funds which may be spent on transportation. There should also be a statement concerning housing and meal allotments. Most clubs require participants to pay their own room and board when away from the campus.

Insurance. There definitely should be a policy statement on insurance coverage for students while they are participating as club members. The clubs should be aware of the amount of coverage provided by students' insurance and decide if they should encourage students to purchase private coverage when they feel that this coverage is inadequate. There are insurance companies who work with members of National Intramural-Sports Association (NIRSA) and American Alliance for Health, Physical Education, and Recreation (AHPER) to offer additional insurance coverage for intramurals and sports clubs.

Medical Care. There should be a definite statement of the steps to follow in caring for students requiring the use of a health center or an emergency room at a hospital. It is advisable to require all members of a sports club who are engaging in strenuous physical activity to have a physical examination before participating; however, it is difficult to enforce this policy because most sports clubs do not have coaches or advisors who take the time to check on physical exams. Injuries can never be completely prevented in an activity which involves physical contact; therefore, sports clubs should be advised to have a student trainer assist them whenever possible.

Equipment. The purchasing of equipment should follow the institution's established policies. All equipment should become the property of the school, and the school should provide adequate storage space and keep an accurate inventory of the equipment that belongs to each club.

Contracts and Scheduling. A stated policy should govern the amount of time that a student is permitted to miss class while representing the university. It is also advisable to state that any contracts that are signed by the sports clubs are the obligations of the sports club, and are not the obligations of the university.

7. Activities

Experience has shown that when children have a chance at physical activities which bring their natural impulses into play, going to school is a joy, management is less of a burden, and learning is easier.

John Dewey

The activities selected for any program will depend largely on the local conditions and facilities that are available; however, the director with imagination, creativity, and organizational skills can plan and offer a maximal program for all students. Almost all activities can be modified to meet the interests and abilities of the participants, no matter the age level or sex.

Geographic location may influence the type of activities which are offered. It is not impossible to offer all types of activities in any geographic area but the facilities and weather conditions make it more meaningful to ski and skate in northern regions whereas beach and water activities are more prominent in southern and coastal areas.

Active engagement by the participants is probably the most important factor in selecting activities to be included in the program. There should be individual, dual, and team activities for both men and women as well as co-recreational events. The activities should range from the highly strenuous, for those who want vigorous exercise, to the purely social, for those individuals that are interested primarily in joining in events with others. The program should include activities which enable highly skilled individuals to compete with other highly skilled individuals and gain a sense of accomplishment. There should also be activities which require no previous training and give all individuals or teams an equal opportunity to be successful.

In recent years, the interest in basic spectator sports has been stabilized and interest has grown in recreational activities. The basic activities of football, baseball, volleyball, and softball still have a place; however, more and more programs are expanding to include different types of team activities, co-recreational activities, and individual activities which the participants can enjoy in later life.

The activities presented in this chapter have been successfully used in intramural programs at all levels. The rules for the acitvities have been written in an attempt to assure safe and enjoyable activities for the participants. It should be kept in mind that "no rules are written in stone"; therefore, the director should modify or change the rules to suit, in the best way possible, the playing conditions for each program.

As previously stated, the participants and officials should be permitted to change the rules if they mutually agree that by changing the rules the game will become more enjoyable for all of the participants. When changes are made in playing rules, the director must be sure to post them so that all participants will be playing by the same rules.

AQUATICS ACTIVITIES

Although the primary use of a swimming pool is for either competitive or recreational swimming, it can serve as an excellent facility for other contests. First and foremost with any activity conducted in the swimming pool, all safety regulations must be observed. They include a lifeguard in the chair and no running on the pool deck, thus limiting certain activities in the area near the water.

Unless individuals are competent swimmers they may have a fear of water; therefore, most of the activities should be conducted in the shallow end of the pool or played with the aid of a flotation device such as an inner tube. By using an inner tube to play a game, individuals will be able to float to the deep end of the pool where they may never have been able to swim. In all games involving teams, at least one team should wear water polo caps so players can be identified.

Swimming Meets

Intramural swimming meets can include free style, backstroke, breaststroke, butterfly, and relay. The distance of the individual events should be 50 yards because these races are for intramural swimmers. The relays could include 150-yard medley (three participants), 200-yard free style (four participants), and 150-yard shuttle (six participants). Diving is not recommended as an intramural event due to the participants' lack of practice time and the lack of trained judges to score the dives. Entrants should be limited to three events, one of which must be a relay. Team scoring can be determined on the basis of 7, 5, 3, 1, for individual events, and 10, 8, 6, 4, 2, 1 for the relays.

Water Polo

Water polo is generally played using the entire length of the pool; however, it can be played in the shallow end although the problem then arises of players walking on the bottom of the pool. Intramural rules for water polo include the following:

1. Seven players make-up a team.
2. Play two 10-minute periods with teams changing goals each period. In case of a tie, flip for goal, and play sudden death.
3. Substitutions—between periods, after scoring, or during official time-out.
4. Goalkeepers may stand on the bottom, jump off, and use two hands on the ball; but goalkeepers may not: push off the side of the pool, go beyond the 4-yard line, or throw the ball beyond the midpool mark.
5. At the start or restart of the game, the players take up positions on their goal lines, outside the goal, and swim or whistle for the ball which is thrown in the middle of the pool.
6. The ball must be played by two or more before a score can be made on a start, restart, or free throw.
7. When the ball is thrown over a team's own goal line, the other team is given a throw at the 2-yard line.
8. When a ball is thrown over the opponents' goal line, the goalie is awarded a free throw.
9. *Free throws and face offs.* Free throws are taken from where the foul occurred or where the ball left the pool. The throw is to be made within 5 seconds. Players are allowed to change positions. The ball cannot be thrown directly at the goal. If one or more players of each team commits a foul, the referee shall call a face off. The ball is thrown into the water between the two players and is played *after* it has touched the water.
10. *Personal Fouls.* Personal Fouls shall be penalized with a free throw and shall be recorded against the offending player. After two fouls, offending players must be removed from the game. They may be replaced with a substitute.
    a. To hold, sink or pull back an opponent.
    b. To kick or strike an opponent, or move with that intent.
    c. To deliberately splash water in the face of an opponent.
    d. To throw the ball away from an opponent who has been awarded a free throw.
    e. To commit any technical foul for the purpose of preventing the scoring of a goal.
11. *Technical fouls.* The penalty for a technical foul is a free throw awarded to the nearest opponent from the spot.
    a. To start before the whistle or to delay the game in any way.
    b. To push off the side of the pool or bottom (except goalie).

c. To hold the ball under the water.

d. To strike at the ball with a clenched fist (except goalie).

e. To be inside the 2-yard line without the ball.

f. To touch the ball before it hits the water on a face off.

g. When taking a free throw, to throw at the goal.

h. To touch the ball with both hands at the same time.

12. *Penalty throws.* When an offensive player is inside the 4-yard line the ball is fouled, the player is awarded a penalty throw from the 4-yard line. The thrower must hold the ball out of water, and it must be thrown on the referee's whistle. The goalie is the only defender and must be on the goal line.

Inner tube Water Polo

Inner tube water polo is played with the same rules as water polo, with a few changes. When using the length of the pool, players should sit in the tubes. Rule differences are:

1. A team consists of nine players.

2. All players must be in inner tubes.

3. Players may not pass the ball more than half the length of the pool.

4. No player may hold the ball longer than 5 seconds.

5. The ball may be held with both hands.

6. Players may walk on the bottom of the pool.

7. Any team that is three goals behind shall put the ball in play at the center line.

8. After score, the ball is put in play at the midline by the team scored on. All players of the team putting the ball in play must be in their end of the pool.

Platform Jousting

Platform jousting is a combative game in which the opponents attempt to knock each other into the water. The platform is a standard ¾-inch piece of 4 × 8 plywood which is attached to two truck tires. A rope is attached to each end to keep the platform from moving off the course. The jousting sticks are made of 1-inch handrails 8 feet long. The ends of the jousting sticks are covered with used 16-inch softballs which have been hollowed out to fit over the end for padding (Fig. 7.1). More than one platform may be used, and a double elimination type of tournament can be scheduled. Rules:

Figure 7.1
The underside of the platform and platform jousting.

1. The contest starts with both contestants touching sticks in the center of the platform.
2. The contestant must push the opponent off the platform by striking against the jousting stick.
3. If the contestant strikes the opponent and not the jousting stick it shall result in a fall being awarded to the opponent.
4. The contestants must hold onto their jousting sticks at all times on the platform or it shall be called a fall.
5. The first contestant to hit the water is declared to have fallen. In case of a tie, replay the fall.
6. Each contest is two out of three falls from the platform.

Water Basketball

Water basketball is generally played in the shallow end of the pool with the baskets placed on the deck of the pool. Participants enjoy this activity because it permits splashing water in the face of an opponent. It is also possible to play water basketball with participants sitting in inner tubes. Special rules:

1. A team shall consist of six players.
2. The game shall be played in two 10-minute periods.
3. Advancing the ball.
   a. Water dribble—pushing the ball ahead of the swimmer.
   b. Passing—the ball must be passed twice before a shot may be taken, except after a foul.
4. Violations. When violations occur, the ball is awarded to the other team at that spot. The exception is that if the ball goes over the end line, it is awarded to teams on the side.
   a. Walking on the bottom of the pool while holding or dribbling the ball.
   b. Being the last to touch the ball before it leaves the playing area.
   c. Having a team control the ball without shooting for 25 seconds.
   d. Holding the ball more than 5 seconds (this does not apply to a player swimming with the ball in front of him).
   e. Shooting the ball inside the goal area (the goal area is the lane nearest the basket).

5. Fouls and penalities. Fouls shall be called for dunking opponents and unnecessary body contact. Four fouls eliminate a player.

   a. If a player is fouled in the act of shooting, the team is awarded one shot from the penalty line, which may be taken by any player on the team. The ball is then awarded to the team on the side at the penalty line. The penalty line is 10 feet from the basket.

   b. If the player is fouled while not in the act of shooting, the player has the option of a free pass or a shot at the goal from the spot of the foul.

   c. After a foul, the team which has been fouled does not have to wait for the defensive team to get in position.

6. Scoring.

   a. Free shot—1 point.

   b. Basket—2 points.

7. No player may block a basket attempt unless they are within 3 feet of the shooter.

8. No offensive player may force the ball in the basket, and defensive players may not interfere with the ball on the rim or on its way down to the basket.

9. IM rules apply for unsportsmanlike conduct.

Water Volleyball

Water volleyball is played in the shallow end of the pool. One standard is placed in the water and the other standard is placed on the deck of the pool. The net is stretched so that it is slightly higher toward the shallow end of the playing area. The boundaries are the edges of the pool and the lane marker which is stretched across the pool at the volleyball standard that is in the pool. Playing rules:

1. Nine players are on a team, and players must rotate each time their team begins a new serve.

2. The team that wins the flip has its choice of service side.

3. Service is made from the last swimming lane line.

4. A point shall be scored for each serve, and games are played to 15 points on the winner's side of the bracket and to 10 on the loser's side of the bracket in double elimination tournaments.

5. The ball may be played four times on each side of the net.

6. Players may not hit or go over the net.

7. Violations shall result in a point being awarded to the opponents. It is a violation to splash water at an opponent.

Inner tube Volleyball

Inner tube water volleyball is played using the same rules as those for water volleyball except players sit in inner tubes. More players should be permitted or the court area should be reduced. It is possible to run both types of volleyball at the same time by playing inner tube volleyball in the deep end of the pool.

Underwater Hockey

Underwater hockey is a very enjoyable game which should be played in the shallow end of the pool for intramurals. Players can wear fins and masks with snorkels; however, it is not necessary to have masks as most players do not know how to breath properly using a snorkel. The goals can be any size (weighted belt or pipe) and just sit on the bottom of the pool. The puck is pushed along the bottom of the pool, using short paddles. This event requires two officials that can swim and use a mask and snorkel because the puck always stays on the bottom of the pool. Rules:

1. The game is played just like regular hockey except that it is underwater.

2. Players may wear masks and fins.

3. Teams consist of five players in the water at one time.

4. The game is played in two 5-minute periods with the clock stopping on score and for official time-outs.

5. To start the game, and after a score, the puck is placed in the middle of the pool and both teams line up on lane marks. All players swim for the puck on the official's command.

6. No artificial weighting of the body.

7. No holding or pushing an opponent (1-minute penalty).

8. No touching of the puck with a free hand; only contact is with the stick (face off).

9. Players in the penalty box may return after a goal is scored.

10. Intentional mistreatment of equipment will result in immediate removal from the game.

11. Intramural rules apply to unsportsmanlike conduct.

Skish

Skish is an individual as well as a team event in which contestants try their skill at casting a plug into inner tubes which are floating on the water. The markers are anchored to the pool at designated lengths in every other lane of the pool.

Course:

1. A small tube is placed 10 yards from the casting end.
2. A 14-inch or 15-inch tube is placed 15 yards from the casting end.
3. A truck tube is placed 22 yards from the casting end.

Individuals score 1 point if the plug strikes the tube in flight; 3 points are scored if the plug lands inside the tube. Each individual is permitted five attempts at each target. An individual's score is the combined total of all attempts, and a team score is the total of the scores of five players.

Water Tug-of-War

This event is held in the deep end of the pool. Five individuals make up a team, and each team is permitted three substitutes. The tug platform is placed in the center of the pool, and each member of the team grasps one of the rope handles. On the whistle, teams swim against each other until they reach the boundary line or edge of the pool. Each contest should be two out of three. The water tug-of-war platform is a standard ¾-inch piece of 4 x 8 plywood. The ropes are attached as in Figure 7.2.

Swimming Carnival

The swimming carnival can be used by men, women, or as a co-rec event. Individual champions as well as team champions can be determined. Teams consist of either four or six individuals. Events might include:

Kickboard Race. Holding kickboard with hands, kick one length of pool.

Sunken Treasure Race. Retrieve objects one at a time from the bottom of the shallow end or deep end of the pool, and place them in a box on the deck. This is a timed event, and the contestant has 2 minutes to gather as many objects as possible.

Pass the Deck Tennis Ring Relay. Teams line up in single file in the shallow end facing the near end of pool. The first player in

Figure 7.2
Water tug-of-war.

line passes the ring between his/her legs to the next player, who passes the ring to the next, and so on down the line. The last person in line carries the ring to the front of the line and starts the process over again until the first player returns to the front of the line.

Water Spaniel Race. Wooden tongue depressors are placed in the center of each lane. Contestants dog paddle to the tongue depressors and grasp them between their teeth; they change directions without touching bottom and dog paddle back to the start.

Balloon Pop Race. Contestants swim with inflated balloons from one end of the pool to the other and pop the balloons.

Match Race. Use the length of the pool with teams in shuttle formation. Swim in any fashion carrying a match stick. Leaders in line swim to the opposite side to teammates and transfer match sticks, and the teammates repeat the same procedure. The first team finished with a match that lights wins. Contestants must try not to let their matches get wet.

Spoon and Ping Pong Ball Race. With the handle of a spoon in their mouths, contestants balance ping pong balls in the spoons and get from one end of the pool to the other. If the ball falls off, the player must stop and replace it using no hands.

T-Shirt Relay. Use the length of the pool with teams in shuttle formation. Leaders in each line put on T-shirts and swim in any fashion to the opposite side to teammates. They remove T-shirts without any help and give it to their teammates who put them on and swim back to the opposite side. The procedure is repeated until the last swimmer takes off the shirt and places it on the deck.

CO-RECREATIONAL ACTIVITIES

A prime consideration when selecting co-recreational activities is that activities can be designed and modified to show an appreciation of the talents of all participants. Care should be taken to assure that embarrassment will not befall any team member. The selection of activities to include in a co-recreational program is limited only by the fact that vigorous physical contact between players of the opposite sex should be avoided.

The most commonly selected co-recreational dual activities include: mixed doubles bowling, dance (social and square), table tennis doubles, badminton doubles, bridge, and two-ball golf.

A number of activities that can be conducted as individual events in either the men's or women's program can also be used as co-rec events. When conducting these activities, a co-rec score may be obtained by adding the scores obtained by each of the partners. Activities which fall into this category are: putt-putt golf, rifle shooting, free throw shooting, football skills, target shooting, archery, field archery, skeet shooting, and hole-in-one.

The key to success in other co-rec activities is the modification of the rules which permits both sexes to work together in enjoyable competition.

Co-Rec Volleyball

Intramural volleyball rules are used with the following modifications:

1. The game is played to 21 points with a point being scored on each serve.
2. The server must serve the ball using the underhand stroke.
3. A team may play the ball four times before returning it.
4. The ball must be played at least twice on each side of the net unless there is a block at the net. Simultaneous blocks are not counted as hits.
5. Each time the ball is played on a side, hitting must alternate between male and female.

Guys and Dolls Basketball

By using the special rules which allow females to score the baskets and avoid unnecessary body contact between the players, the co-rec basketball program has taken on a new emphasis. Rules:

1. Each team consists of three men and three women.
2. The game begins with a jump ball between female players.
3. Individuals will be allowed only 3 personal fouls.
4. The game will be played with no time-outs.
5. On personal fouls which carry a 1-shot penalty, the ball will be awarded out-of-bounds nearest the point of the foul. On personal fouls which carry a 2-shot penalty, the first shot shall be taken and then the ball will be awarded out-of-bounds at the free throw line extended.
6. All fouls in the last 2 minutes result in 2 shots and ball in play on the second shot. Both shots must be taken in 15 seconds.
7. No one-and-one situation.
8. Scoring: Field goals scored by men shall be worth 2 points each; field goals scored by women shall be worth 4 points each. Free throws scored by men shall be worth 1 point each; free throws scored by women shall be worth 2 points each.
9. SPECIAL REGULATIONS: MALE PLAYERS ARE NOT ALLOWED IN THE ENTIRE AREA OF THE FREE THROW LANE FROM THE FREE THROW LINE TO THE BASELINE. A VIOLATION OF THIS PROVISION WILL BE TREATED AS FOLLOWS:

    (*a*). IF THE ENCROACHMENT IS IN THE VIOLATOR'S DEFENSIVE COURT, IT SHALL BE TREATED AS BASKET INTERFERENCE (WHETHER A SHOT HAS BEEN ATTEMPTED OR NOT) AND 2 POINTS SHALL BE AWARDED.

    (*b*) IF THE ENCROACHMENT IS IN THE VIOLATOR'S OFFENSIVE COURT, THE BALL SHALL BE AWARDED OUT-OF-BOUNDS TO THE OTHER TEAM.

Co-Rec Softball

Co-rec softball rules are the same rules as intramural slowpitch, with certain modifications. When playing co-rec softball, the ball in play should have been softened by use. One modification of the rules that has proven successful is having all players bat before the teams change sides, and any runners on base when the last batter has completed his turn at bat are scored as runs. Rules:

1. Teams shall use ten players (five men and five women).
2. The batting order must be drawn up alternating male and female players.
3. Positions in the field must be alternated between male and female players.
4. One pitch rule will be used. (These rules are given in detail later in this chapter.)
5. There is no pitching area, and the pitcher shall not field the batted ball.
6. No sliding—automatic out for sliding.

Co-Rec Bowling Circus

The co-rec bowling circus is an event which can be run either at a bowling facility or by using plastic equipment in a hallway or gymnasium. This event may be a one-day or league event. The co-rec team bowls two games using the following rules:

1. All strikes count 25 pins, and spares count 15. It is possible to score more than 1 strike or spare per frame.
2. In the frame when both players have bowled, the scores are totaled for that frame.
3. Each frame has a different regulation for scoring (Figure 7.3).

Co-Rec Swimming Circus

The co-rec swimming circus is a mixer which can be used by varying the activities commonly associated with swimming meets. The meet may be run as a dual event or team event. Events could include:

Dive for distance. Swimmers dive from the edge of the pool and float as far as possible. The dive ends when the diver moves arms or legs or face comes out of the water. Score is the accumulated distance of both divers.

100-yard free. The women start by swimming 50 yards. Then the men swim 50 yards, and the score is total time.

25-yard boat. The women sit in an inner tube and paddle back-

Game I

1 Woman	2 Man	3 Woman	4 Man	5 Woman	6 Woman	7 Man	8 Woman	9 Team	10	Total
				Man	Man					
Total										

Rules

Frame

1	Woman, 2 balls
2	Man, 2 balls
3	Man, first ball / Woman, second ball
4	Woman, first ball / Man, second ball
5	Blindfold, total of 4 balls; 2 by man, 2 by woman
6	Nondominant hand, total of 4 balls
7	Man, 2 balls
8	Woman, 2 balls
9	Woman—man—woman, total of 3 balls (reset for third roll)
10	Woman, regular tenth frame / Man, regular tenth frame

Strike worth 25
Spare worth 15
(Possible to have more than 1 per frame)

Game II

1 Woman	2 Man	3 Woman	4 Man	5 Woman	6 Woman	7 Man	8 Woman	9 Team	10	Total
				Man	Man					
Total										

Name _____ And _____

Team total _____

Figure 7.3
Co-rec bowling circus score sheet.

ward and the man has both hands on the tube and kicks with his feet.

50-yard free. Same as 100-yard free only each swimmer does 25 yards.

Shuttle boat relay. This race is across the pool with two men and two women per team. Each participant swims the width of the pool while sitting in the tube.

Co-Rec Four Corner Volleyball

A regulation volleyball court is divided by a net that runs lengthwise to provide four separate playing areas. Each section of the court is numbered, and the teams draw for their court each period.

1. Teams consist of two men and two women.
2. The game is played in four 7-minute periods.
3. A point is scored against a team if they fail to return the ball properly from their section or the ball falls in their section after legally being returned from other sections.
4. Co-rec volleyball rules apply to playing the ball (the ball must be played twice and can be played four times).
5. At the conclusion of each period, teams are awarded points based on the number of scores against them. The team with least points receives 4 points, 3 for second, 2 for third, and 1 for fourth. In case of a tie, the teams that tied will divide the points.
6. Each period starts with the teams separated by the four sections, and all scores are zero.
7. The winner of the league will be the team that accumulates the greatest number of points.

Co-Rec Wiffle Ball

A co-rec Wiffle Ball league may be conducted in the gym. More than one field may be set up in the gym at a time as the Wiffle Ball does not carry a long distance.

1. Ten players make up a team. There must be a catcher; except for the pitcher the positions must alternate between men and women.
2. Teams must bat woman, man, woman, etc.
3. Games are 5 innings.

4. All team members bat each inning. No runs score after the last batter has batted out.

5. No walks.

6. Three strikes are out including foul on third strike.

7. No leaving base until the ball is hit.

8. No advance on overthrow.

9. Ball must be pitched underhand with an arc of not more than 3 feet.

10. No automatic homeruns. The ball is played off the ceiling and walls.

11. If fielders from opposing games interfere with each other, the official will use judgment in regard to awarding bases.

Co-Rec Track Relay (Outdoor)

This event can be conducted without men and women ever running against each other. The co-rec score is achieved by adding the times or distances of the two team members. The meet could include the 100-yard dash, 220-yard dash, long jump, high jump, throw put (women throw a softball, and men throw a shot), and distance run (women run a 440 and men run an 880). A medly relay, a team event, could be run by having a woman run 110, a man run 330, a woman run 440, and a man finish with 880.

Co-rec Indoor Track Meet

This is a dual as well as a team event. The times and distances in the 60, 220, high jump, long jump, and shot put (men 12 pounds and women 8 pounds) are added together to determine the score. In the 440 and 880 runs the partners must stay together by holding onto a 2-foot string. An indoor relay would have the women each running 110 yards and the men each running 220 yards.

Co-rec Wrestling

Co-rec wrestling is a form of combative for co-rec activities. The man and woman never actually wrestle each other. They wrestle alternate periods against other members of their own sex. The special rules are:

1. The match consists of three periods. The first and third periods (2 minutes each) will be wrestled by the men. The sec-

ond period will be split into two 45-second periods for the women.

2. Each period will begin in a referee's position. The coin toss will determine which team has top or bottom for the first period as well as the first 45-second section of period two.

3. In case of an escape, the wrestler who escapes will be awarded 1 point and given his choice in the referee's position. No wrestling on feet.

4. Scoring will be cumulative; any points scored in the first period carry over into the succeeding periods. Should a fall occur by one of the men in period one, it shall count 10 points plus any accumulated points tallied before the pin.

5. Period two will begin with that accumulated point total and any points earned in that period will be added on. Should a fall occur in period two, it also will count 10 points on added to the accumulated total earned before the pin. Period three will follow only if a fall did not occur in the first period.

6. Suggested weight classes:

	Men	Women
Bantam	100-136	50-95
Light	137-151	96-110
Welter	152-166	111-125
Middle	167-185	126-140
Bomber	186-	141-

Co-rec Football

Co-rec touch football is played using the regular intramural football rules with the following exceptions:

1. No down field blocking (this includes punts and kick-offs).

2. No rushing on punts.

3. On punts and kick-offs, no players on offense may advance until the ball is kicked.

4. On a scrimmage play, once blockers have taken a position they may not move to ward off defensive players. A defensive player may not run into a blocker.

5. Teams have five downs to make the line to gain.

6. The induvidual who receives the snap from the center must alternate between men and women players.

Co-rec 30-Second Shoot Out

This is a basketball shooting contest in which the women and men each shoot for 30 seconds and their score is the combined total of the baskets made. The partner of the shooter rebounds the shot and returns it to the shooter. Shooting area for women is the free throw line, and for men it is the top of the jump circle. This should be run as a double elimination tournament.

Co-rec 2-on-2 Basketball

Co-rec 2-on-2 basketball is played like one-on-one basketball using the following rule modifications:

1. The ball must be passed twice before a shot may be taken.
2. On any change of team possession, the ball must be cleared out beyond the top of the key area.
3. Play "makers-takers" which means that the team that scores keeps the ball until there is an 8 point difference at which time the other team gets the ball until they tie or are 1 point behind.
4. Male players may not enter the free throw lane area.
5. Fifteen points constitute the game. A goal by a female is worth 4 points and by a male worth 2 points.
6. Players are permitted 4 fouls only. On fouls the shooting team retains the ball whether a basket is made or not.
7. Teams play best two out of three games to determine the winner.

Co-rec Tug-of-War

This co-rec type combative uses an even number of men and women on a pulling team. The same rules apply as for regular tug-of-war.

Co-rec Tandem Bike Race

A bike race using tandem bikes can be run either over a "grand prix" type course or around a track. If tandem bikes are not available, it is possible to conduct the same kind of race using regular bikes that are connected with a 10-foot rope from the seat of the first bike to the neck on the second bike. This is a type of activity that should be run against time, not as head to head competition. When using a track, two teams may start on oppisite sides of the track.

Co-rec Billiards

Partners in co-rec billiards will shoot as a team during each inning by alternating shots, as long as they make a score. If a team scores 10 consecutive points, their inning is over. The female will shoot first and the male will shoot second. If the first shooter fails to make a ball, the partner still has his turn coming in that inning. Games are played until twenty innings have been completed.

Co-rec Cross-Country

A co-rec cross-country race may be run two ways. First, have each member of the team run alone and add the times to get a co-rec score. In this type of race, it is possible to vary the distance that the men and women may run (men 2 miles; women 1 mile). The second method is to have both partners run the same distance while staying together by holding on to a piece of string or cord.

COMBATIVES

The activities listed as combatives are by their nature either strenuous team activities or refer to individuals competing head to head in shows of strength and endurance. Combatives should not be limited to male students, and under proper modifications and supervision they may be conducted at all grade levels.

Pushball

Pushball is played on an open field which has boundaries and a midfield line. If possible, it is best to use a 6-foot pushball; however, the 3-foot cageball is also suitable. Rules:

1. A team may consist of eighteen players or less.
2. The game will be played in two periods (time to be determined by number of entries or age groups).
3. The object of the game is to propel the ball over the opponent's goal line by pushing, rolling, passing, or carrying. Kicking of the ball is not permitted.
4. To start each half and after a score, the ball is placed on the line in midfield. Ball is put in play as for an out of bounds situation.
5. Teams exchange goals after the first period.

6. When the ball goes out-of-bounds, it becomes dead. The teams line up at right angles to the side lines and 1 yard apart. A player from each team holds up the ball, and the referee then pushes the ball between the teams.

7. When for any reason the ball becomes tied up in one spot for five seconds, the referee declares the ball dead. The ball is then put into play as for an out-of-bounds situation.

8. A goal is scored when the ball, or any part of it, is propelled across the opponent's end line.

9. If at the end of the second half the score is tied, the ball is placed in the middle of the field, and the first team to move the ball 15 yards from the center is the winner.

10. Players may not strike an opponent, leave their feet and throw a block, trip, elbow, or clip. If a foul is called, the player is removed and the team is awarded a free push from the spot with the opponents back 5 yards from the ball.

11. Intramural rules regarding unsportsmanlike conduct apply.

12. Anytime a team has a 3-goal advantage, the game shall be terminated.

Cageball Volleyball

Cageball volleyball is played with a 3-foot cageball. The net is stretched across the basketball court; thus the ball may be played off the walls. Rules:

1. Teams shall use fifteen players on a court at a time. Substitutions may be made only when play is stopped.

2. The ball must be clearly hit—no carrying.

3. A team may hit the ball as often as necessary to get it over the net. Players may hit the ball as many times as they desire but not twice in succession.

4. Game shall be to 11 points. A point is scored on every serve.

5. No out-of-bounds—ball is played off the walls.

6. Ball may be hit in the net providing no contact is made with opposing players. Players may play the net, unless action is ruled unsportsmanlike by the official.

7. The server starts the play with the ball in back of the free throw line, and the server may throw the ball or have a teammate hold it while it is pushed.

Tug-of-War

Tug-of-war is an activity which can be conducted indoors and outdoors. It lends itself very well to weight classes which makes for equal competition. When using weight classes, the contestants should weigh in and receive a stamp on the hand to indicate they have made weight. Tug-of-war ropes should be marked with either a knot or tape to indicate positions on the rope for each puller. Rules:

1. Teams are limited to ten pullers with fifteen on a roster.
2. Substitution may be made only when a pull is completed or in intervals between pulls.
3. A match will consist of 1 pull, and the event should be double elimination.
4. There will be a minimum of 3 minutes of rest between team matches, before a team must pull again.
5. A winning pull consists of pulling the losing team's first man across the line, unless a team releases the rope, and surrenders. Anytime a team releases the rope, the match is over.
6. In pulling, rope must be kept at least 6 inches from the ground.
7. Pullers may wear gloves or tape on their hands. They must wear gym shoes or go barefoot.

Pillow Fight

The pillow fight is conducted with two participants sitting on a rail and attempting to knock each other off the rail. A balance beam may be used as the rail; however, a rail may also be constructed as in Figure 7.4. Foam jump pads or gymnastic crash pads should be placed under the bar so that the individual who is knocked off the rail will have a soft landing area. The pillow can be of any soft but sturdy material. The Western Illinois program used burlap sacks which have been washed and then stuffed with towels. This event may also be conducted over water; however, then there is a problem of keeping the pillows dry. Rules:

1. Participants may wear football headgear and swimming goggles if they so choose.
2. Participants sit on the rail and wrap their legs around the rail. They may not grab the rail with either hand.
3. The match is started with both participants holding their

Figure 7.4
Pillow fight stand.

pillows at their sides and they begin on the command to start by the referee.

4. Participants must knock their opponent off the rail by striking him with the pillow. An individual is off the rail when he touches the padding.

5. If neither participant has fallen after 2 minutes, they are notified that the individual to make the most hits to the body in 30 seconds will be the winner of that fall.

6. It is legal to block with the free arm; however, the free arm may not be used to pull the opponent off the rail or pull the pillow.

7. A match shall consist of best two out of three falls, and double elimination tournaments should be used.

King of the Rail

King of the rail is similar to the pillow fight except the participants are standing on the rail (Figure 7.5). In order to be a legal "knock-off", the individual must be struck from the hips up. Striking the legs is illegal. The judge in this event must determine which in-

Figure 7.5
King of the rail contest.

dividual hit the mat first. In case of a tie, the fall is replayed. For this event, contestants are divided into flights of five or six. Then each flight is arranged in order of competition so that they are in line to compete. The first two individuals do battle, and the winner of the match (two out of three falls) stays on the rail to meet the next opponent, while the loser returns to the end of the line. An individual who loses two matches is eliminated. Winners of each flight will then compete using the same procedure.

Wrestling

Wrestling is a very popular combative activity in an intramural program. The tournament is conducted using a weight class method. Standard weight classes for high school are 95, 103, 120, 127, 133, 138, 145, 154, 165, 175 pounds and unlimited. Standard weight classes for college are 118, 126, 134, 142, 150, 158, 167, 177, 190 pounds and unlimited. To arrive at more equal competition for intramurals, there should be more weight classes. A suggested weight division for college age students would be 123, 130, 137, 145, 152, 160, 168, 175, 181, 190, 200 pounds and unlimited.

When a wrestler reports, he is weighed in and assigned a weight class. When all wrestlers have weighed in for that class, the tournament is drawn at the time and everyone wrestles the first night. If a wrestler cannot make weight for 137, then he will not be eliminated because he can be drawn into the 145 bracket.

Example:

```
6:30 — 123 and 130 weigh-in
6:50 — 137 weigh-in, 123 and 130 will begin to wrestle
7:00 — 145 weigh-in, 137 will be drawn
7:20 — 152 weigh-in, 145 will be drawn
7:30 — 160 weigh-in, 152 will be drawn
7:40 —              160 will be drawn
```

Rules:

1. Teams may enter only two men per weight class for team points.
2. Matches will be three periods of 2 minutes each. In case of a tie, two periods of 1 minute each will be used from referee's position.
3. Contestant must weigh in at initial weigh-in only.
4. Forfeit time will be 5 minutes after match time.
5. Team Scoring: each match wrestled and won, 1 point; each match won by a fall, 2 points (1 point plus 1 for a winning); first in weight class, 5 points; second in weight class, 3 points.

Weight Lifting (odd)

As far as weight lifting is concerned, the most important function served by the intramural department is to provide the opportunity for students to participate in weight training. After students have had the opportunity to develop strength and endurance through weight training, they possibly will welcome a weight lifting contest.

The Olympic lifts are the clean and jerk, and the snatch. These two lifts do not make the best lifts for intramurals because of the fine skill required to complete the lift properly, and they are not common in weight training. Three more acceptable lifts for intramural weight lifting are the curl, dead lift, and bench press.

Intramural weight lifting is conducted using weight class. When individuals weigh in, their actual weights should be recorded on the score sheet. In case of a tie in a weight class, the individual with the lower body weight will be classified as winner. Suggested weight

Intramural Activities, Weight Lifting

Name	Organization		Curl			Dead Lift			Bench			Weight Class 160
			1st	2nd	3rd	1st	2nd	3rd	1st	2nd	3rd	
Jim Jones	APO	159	75	(105)	X	210	X	(225)	240	260	(270)	600

Figure 7.6
Weight lifting score sheet.

classes in pounds are 140, 160, 185, 200, and unlimited. Figure 7.6 is an example of a weight lifting score sheet. The rules are as follows:

1. A contestant is given three trials for each of the lifts, and the heaviest lift is recorded as the score for that type of lift.
2. The contestant may choose to start at any time; however, once the contest has started and weight is being added to the

bar, no lesser weight may be attempted.

3. If a lifter fails to complete the lifts at a given weight he may forfeit a turn and attempt the same weight, or 5 pounds must be added for the next lift.

4. Lift regulations:
Curl. Contestants grasp the bar and hold it at a 90° angle at the elbow. Upon the command of the official, the bar is lifted towards the chest, and the lift is completed when the judge claps his hands. No lift is recorded if the contestant moves the feet or bows the back.
Dead lift. Contestants grasp the bar with the palms facing the lifter. When the lifter is ready he picks the bar from the floor and must completely extend the knees and wait for the judge to clap, which signals a good lift. No lift is recorded if the feet move or the bar fails to come parallel to the floor.
Bench press. The lifter may receive assistance in bringing the bar to the chest. Upon the judge's signal the bar must be pushed up in one continuous move keeping it parallel to the floor. Upon full extension of both arms, the judge will clap to signal completed lift. No lift will be recorded if the feet move or the buttocks leave the bench.

Wrist Wrestling

Wrist wrestling is conducted on a stand approximately 42 inches high. On the top of the stand there must be two restrainer areas in which the contestants' elbows fit. These restrainer areas are to keep elbows from sliding along the top of the stand and provide a place to put pieces of foam or carpet under the elbow of the shorter individual's arm in order to make the heights of the hands equal. The competitiors grasp their opponents thumb between their thumb and forefinger and close their other fingers around the hand of their opponents. The noncompetitive hands are also joined by cupping finger to finger underneath the upright arms.

The referee places his hands on top of the upright clasped hands making sure that no one gets a jump. When the referee releases his hands, the contestants begin. The winner is determined when one contestant causes his opponent's arm to touch his nonwrestling arm. Contestants must keep their elbows in contact with the restrainer area. One fall constitutes a contest, and the tournament should be double elimination.

Categories for both left and right handers should be scheduled in the different weight classes. If the number of left handed entrants is not sufficient for a separate category, then the overall structure may be modified to include all individuals, regardless of hand dominance, in one tournament. Each entrant wrestles both left and right handed, and the elapsed time is kept in order to determine the winner.

INDIVIDUAL AND DUAL ACTIVITIES

An intramural program should offer a number of individual and dual events to permit the students with special interests to try their skills. An endless number of activities could be listed as individual events. The most common events are: tennis, golf, paddleball, handball, racketball, billiards, cross-country, badminton, free throw, table tennis, track and field, gymnastics, decathlon, archery and Sigma Delta Psi.

In some of these activities, the intramural departments should modify the standard rules in order to meet the needs of the students. For example: (a) the cross-country run should not be more than 2 miles; (b) in track and field, the participants should receive only two tries in field events, and in the long and triple jumps the measurements should be from the take off spot to the landing spot, thus eliminating scratches; (c) when conducting a decathlon it should be cut to eight events conducted over two days by eliminating the pole vault and triple jump; (d) because judges are hard to find for gymnastics, the gymnast's points should be based on progression in events using a progression chart.

Individual or dual events, which are not as common as those mentioned above, have been sucessfully run in intramural programs. These activities are grouped in related areas. The scores attained by participants in individual events may be combined to get a team score.

Archery

Archery golf is an event in which nine targets are laid on the ground over a large area. The individuals must start at a tee area for each target, and the number of shots needed to stick the arrow in the center of the target face is recorded as the score for that hole.

Field archery is shot by spacing smaller target faces on standards so that the archer must shoot from different distances and at different angles. It may be more enjoyable for the archers, if the targets ressemble animals. There are generally ten stations in a field archery course.

Bowling

King of the hill bowling is an individual event in which the contestants bowl in head to head competition with no handicaps. The bowler who wins remains to bowl against the next challenger. A bowler may be permitted a second challenger after all others have challenged. Where there are a great number of bowlers, a king should be set up for more than one lane; then the kings of each lane will meet to determine the champion (Figure 7.7).

Scratch bowling league is an individual event in which all contestants bowl for the first night by random draw. After each night of bowling, new teams are made up by placing bowlers in rank order based on the previous night's score.

Example:

If there are thirty bowlers, the teams for the second night would have the ranks indicated in this table.

Team	Rank Order				
1	1	12	13	24	25
2	2	11	14	23	26
3	3	10	15	22	27
4	4	9	16	21	28
5	5	8	17	20	29
6	6	7	18	19	30

Each night the bowlers will bowl three games using total pin fall as a team with no handicaps. Members of the winning team will receive 2 points and loser 1 point (1.5 points in case of tie). The top ten individuals will also receive points: 1.0, .9, .8, etc. There will be two individual winners when the competition is over. One winner will be the bowler who accumulated the greatest number of points by the end of the season, and the second winner is the bowler with the greatest pin fall for all games.

Bicycling

The bicycle can be a very useful item in an intramural program. Many different types of races may be run. An intramural director may also conduct "class" events which are determined by the type of

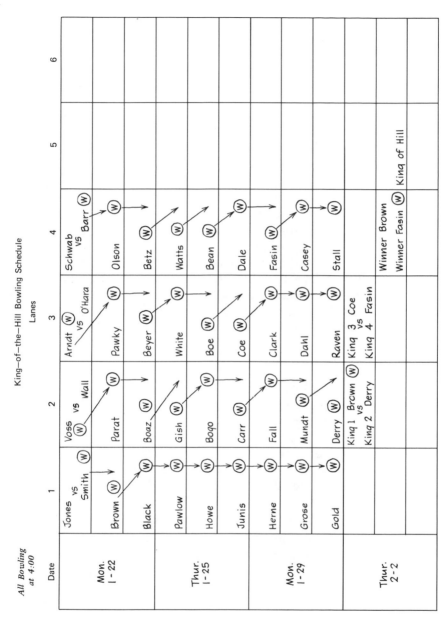

Figure 7.7 King of the hill bowling schedule.

bicycles which are permitted to enter. Three of the more common kinds of bike races are:

Road Race. The bike road race should be run over roads which are not heavily traveled and which offer the riders a chance to cover different terrains. It is a good idea to hold the bike road race over the same course that is used for the marathon run because then you can reproduce only one map for both events.

Grand Prix. The grand prix type of race can be run either on the sidewalks of the campus or on a course which is laid out on the IM playing fields. If good racing bikes are being used by the participants, it is best to keep the races in a smooth area to protect the tires on the bikes.

Lap Race. Lap races are generally held on a track with designated pit areas and are considered team events; however, lap races could be held for individuals by using one or two methods. The first would be head to head competition or time competition with a predetermined number of laps to complete. The second would be to set a time limit, and the winner would be the one who completed the most laps in the given time period. In this type of race, a rider would receive credit for each quarter of a lap completed when the time ends.

Basketball

One-on-one basketball is played between two players using the following rules: (*a*) It is a maker-taker game until a player is 4 points ahead, then the ball goes to the opponent until he/she ties or is 1 point behind. (*b*) Games are two out of three to 11 points. (*c*) On all fouls the shooter gets one free shot and the ball at the top of the key. (*d*) On all exchanges of possession, the ball must be cleared beyond the free throw line. (*e*) Players are permitted only five fouls for all three games.

Shooting skills, or *basketball golf*, is an individual game in which the player shoots from nine spots on the floor, and the player who uses the least amount of total shots to make a basket from each spot is the winner. If players fail to make a basket in the first four tries, they receive a five for that station. The nine stations should be placed around the basket at different angles and distances and be adjusted to the age of the competitors.

Twenty-one elimination can either be an individual or dual contest in which the participants shoot a long shot and a short shot. The long shot has a value of 2 points and the short shot of 1 point. Opponents should shoot at the same time on opposite baskets and the first one to accumulate 21 points win. A player (or pair) cannot shoot a short shot until a long shot has been made to start the game. The game can end only on a long shot. The distance of the long shot will vary with the age level, but the players should be permitted to shoot the short shot from anywhere.

Bloodmobile

If the intramural program uses a participant point system, it would be a good idea to give an organization points for the members who donate blood to a Red Cross bloodmobile. This is an excellent community service project that the intramural department can help promote. There should be no limit to the number of individuals who are encouraged to donate blood, but there should be a limit to the number of points that can be accumulated.

Century Club

The "Century Club" is strictly an individual event in which participants try and see if they can reach the century mark (100 miles). The individuals can run, ride a bike, or swim, at their own pace and on their own time. Each day that the participants complete a distance, they fill out a form and turn it inot the IM office which will record the mileage (Figure 7.8). Each individual who reaches the century mark receives recognition as well as the individual who accumulates the greatest number of miles during the year.

Fishing Derby

A fishing derby can be conducted in two ways. The first, which is generally used for younger students, is to have a lake or stream stocked with special fish for the derby, and different prizes are awarded for first fish, longest fish, heaviest fish, most fish caught during the time period, and fish that have been specially tagged. The second method, which is less expensive, is to have students bring in their big fish or a record of the weight of the fish. The intramural department should then recognize a fishing derby champion for each of the different types of fish that are in the area. This type of fishing derby may last for several months.

Fitness Day

Fitness Day is a day set aside to determine which individual scores best in certain fitness measures. If this is used as a team event the

CENTURY CLUB REPORT

Please record the actual miles in column one and convert your mileage, based on given scale, in column two.

Column I Actual Distance	Scale	*Column II* Converted Distance
Jogging _____	1 for 1	_____
Swimming _____	4 times actual distance swam	_____
Cycling _____	1/5 of actual distance ridden	_____

Name _____

Organization _____

Date _____

Figure 7.8
Century club reports.

score of two or three teammates should be added together to determine places in each event, thus preventing one individual from winning the team title. This also is a day when students may qualify for the President's Physical Fitness Council Award if the intramural departments used their rules at the events. Fitness Day events could include:

Push-ups, as many as possible.

Pull-ups, as many as possible but no hanging between pulls.

Sit-ups, the number in two minutes or unlimited time.

Standing Broad Jump, stand with toes next to mat then jump.

Vertical Jump, using either a jump board or chalk to measure height.

A shuttle run or mile run are sometimes used as a fitness measure.

A very popular Fitness Day running event at Western Illinois University is the bulldog fitness run which requires the student to perform many tasks. This fitness run is as follows. (a) The individual sits on the floor beneath a 20-foot climbing rope and the watch is started when the participant begins to climb the rope; (b) after climbing the rope, the individual runs down a flight of stairs and over a hurdle, through a hurdle, over a hurdle; (c) runs 50 yards going over the foam landing pits; (d) upon touching the line after the last jumping pit, the individual runs backwards the length of the basketball floor; (e) then goes over a low balance beam to pick up a basketball; (f) dribbles the length of the floor and must make a basket; (g) climbs a ladder to the second floor; (h) plunges into the pool (removing shoes first) and swims 25 yards. The watch is stopped when the individual touches the end of the pool.

Football Skills

The *punt, pass, and kick contest* is very popular with both boys and girls of ages eight thru thirteen. Another form of football skill contest can be used for older students and is more meaningful because the two events use the types of skills that they see performed by football players.

Kicking. Each participant is given five tries to kick the football between the goal posts and over the cross from a distance of 20, 25, and 30 yards. The ball should be placed on a kicking tee to eliminate problems of holding the ball.

Passing. A tire or flickerball goal can be hung on a backstop, and the individual is given five throws from a distance of 10, 15 and 20 yards. If the ball passed through the center and hits the fence, a score of 3 is recorded. The ball hitting the tire or goal is scored as 1 point.

Frisbee Golf

Frisbee golf can be played anywhere with a course laid out with varying distances between holes. Participants must throw their frisbee from hole to hole counting each toss until it lands in the hole. A classroom wastepaper basket makes an excellent hole. An interesting golf course can be set up by having holes placed near different buildings on the campus so that students will tour campus throwing their frisbees.

Jai alai

The intramural version Jai alai is a dual event which can be played in the same area used for handball.

The plastic scoops—also used in scoop lacrosse—are used to catch and throw the ball. The modified rules are:

1. The ball must strike the front wall first.
2. The ball must hit the front wall above the 4-foot line on the serve and all plays.
3. The serve must return past the midcourt line and may not strike the side wall before the opponent plays it. Server has two attempts to make a legal serve.
4. A ball which strikes the front wall between the 4-and 6-foot lines and is not returned is scored as 1 point; a ball that is not returned after striking above the 6-foot line is scored as 2 points.
5. The ball may not hit the floor.
6. A player is permitted one step after catching the ball before returning it to the front wall.
7. The game is played to 15 points, and a team scores only when it serves. Match is best two out of three games.

Marathon Run

Many schools hold a cross-country or turkey trot; however, a marathon run can be an enjoyable race for intramural participants. The race should be run on a lightly traveled road and be no longer than 10 miles for intramurals. The local law enforcement office should provide lead cars for the race and a trail car should also be used. Participants should be given a map, and arrows should be placed on the course.

Shooting

There are several types of shooting activities that an intramural department could sponsor. It may be necessary to seek assistance from local gun clubs, law enforcement officials, ROTC, or commercial shooting clubs; however, some activities could be run on campus with BB guns.

Target Shooting with BB guns can be held in the school building or on the grounds. A circular target or regular ten-shoot target should be placed about 20 feet from the shooting line. The target should rest on a cardboard box filled with newspapers so that the BBs may be retrieved and used again. The target may be used more than once by marking the hits on the target with different colored marking pens.

Skeet-Shooting with BB guns is possible when using a device which throws a rubber skeet up into the air. The skeet has an outer ring which holds the target area. When the target is hit the center area falls out indicating a hit. The skeet are all reusable. The BBs are retrieved by using a back drop that keeps the BBs in the area.

Rifle or pistol shooting could be conducted if the proper facilities are available. When using live ammunition it is very important to have proper firing line supervision. Shooters should never be permitted to have more than one shell in the firing chamber.

Two-Man Volleyball

Two-man volleyball is a game that is very popular on the beaches. It can be played in the intramural program by using badminton courts. The net is moved up to the 8-foot mark. The server must serve the ball underhand and teammates must change the server on each change of sides. The ball may be played three times on each side.

TEAM EVENTS

Most of the intramural team activities are modifications of those team events which are conducted in either intercollegiate, or professional athletics. However, a good intramural program should not limit its scope of team activities to those governed by national organization, but should create team activities which may be suitable to the student population.

As enjoyment in participation is a prime factor in selecting an activity, most team games must have the rules modified for intramurals. When modifying the rules, the intent of the game is not changed; however, through modifications some activities become safer and use time periods more suitable for intramurals.

Rules and regulations for each event should be printed and established before the event begins. But in some cases, rules may be changed as the game is being played. Modifications may come from the students playing the game who make suggestions that would make the game more enjoyable, or the director may see that some rules do not permit students with limited physical ability to compete successfully in the activity.

The activities which are listed in this section can be scheduled as a league or one-day event. It is a good idea to conduct a one-day tournament in events which may be established as league events, so that students may become familiar with the modified rules and have an opportunity to practice with teammates.

Touch Football

Injuries are a chief concern when football is discussed; therefore, the rules which are listed for the activity have been modified to protect the students who are participating. It should be understood that there are no rules which will prevent bumps and bruises when you permit students to have body contact while participating in wholesome competition.

The basic rules should be the same as those used in high school because the participants are more familiar with these rules. The biggest difference from the standard rules would be for the penalty modification suggested in rule 12 which prohibits a team from gaining an advantage by committing a foul inside the 30-yard line.

The playing fields may be laid out in an area 70 yards by 40 yards, which would permit a 60-yard playing field that has three zones of 20 yards each and two 5-yard end zones. Special intramural rules:

1. The team shall consist of eight players.
2. No protective equipment may be worn.
3. Tennis shoes, basketball shoes, running shoes, soccer shoes, (molded soles, no detachable spikes) may be worn.
4. The ball shall be kicked off from the goal line.
5. The ball shall be placed on the 19-yard line after a touchback.
6. When the ball touches the ground, the ball is dead at that spot.
7. For the start of each play, the ball should be placed as near the center of the field as possible.
8. First downs shall be awarded on the basis of getting the ball across the 20-yard lines. The field is divided into three sectors, and each time a team crosses a sector it will be awarded a first down.
9. The ball carrier is down when the defensive player touches him with both hands simultaneously below the shoulders (this includes the arm). The decision of the officials on the touch is final. Tackling or restraining the ball carrier in any manner will result in a 15-yard penalty. Abusive violations shall re-

sult in the ejection of the offender from the ball game.

10. A player who has been ejected from the contest shall not be replaced by a substitute. The team must continue minus one man. If two men are ejected from the contest, the game shall be declared a forfeit.

11. No player shall be permitted to use stances except the center.

12. All penalties shall be marked off at full distance. If this would result in the ball being placed in an end zone, the ball will be put on the 1-yard line. Two consecutive penalties, that would put the ball in an end zone, shall results in a score being awarded.

13. The game shall be 50 plays (25 each half). If a penalty is accepted, the down does not count. Extra points and kick-off are not counted as plays.

Offensive team

1. The players may line up anywhere on the field as long as they are behind the ball and at least 5 yards in from the side lines.

2. Once the center has touched the ball, no offensive players may move. No player can be in motion.

3. No QB sneaks or runs right up the middle.

4. No part of the blocker's body except his feet shall be in contact with the ground throughout the block.

5. The offensive blocker can at no time leave his feet to execute a block or excessively swing his elbows to ward off a man (15-yard penalty and ejection).

6. All players are eligible pass receivers with the exceptions of the player who centers the ball.

7. A team will be allowed only 25 seconds in which to put the ball in play for a scrimmage down or a kick-off after a try for a point.

8. The try for the extra point shall be from the 3-yard line. It can be passed or run.

Defensive team

1. Unnecessary roughness on the part of a defensive player while using hands shall result in ejection from the contest.

2. No defensive player is permitted directly over the center.

Tie breaker

During the play-offs, the winner of a tie game will be determined by the results of four plays. A flip of the coin will determine which team will put the ball in play first, and teams will alternate plays until each team has run two plays. The ball is placed on the 20-yard line going towards the goal line. The other goal line is moved up to the other 20-yard line making the field only 40 yards long. If a team scores before the completion of four plays, the game is over.

1. Teams may not kick the ball.
2. All penalties, if accepted, are marked off.
3. When a pass is intercepted, it is the same as incomplete.

After the four plays, the winner is the team which has the ball on the opponent's side of the 20-yard line. If the ball remains on the 20-yard line after four plays, each team will alternate plays until there is a winner.

160 Pound Football

This is a touch football which is played by individuals who weigh in under 160 pounds. The rules are the same as for football except only six individuals make up a team and all players are eligible to receive a pass.

Bowling

Bowling may be conducted at a commercial bowling establishment or in the school using the halls or gymnasium. Bowling teams may be made up of four or five players. It may be necessary to alter the regulations regarding handicaps because in intramurals the same individuals may not bowl each time the team is scheduled, and teams may find it necessary to bowl short a player. In order to allow anyone to bowl at anytime on a team, the following rules may be used:

1. If a team does not have all players present, a dummy score will be used. (Dummy's score is five pins below the score bowled by the bowler who had the lowest score on the other team.
2. To determine the team's handicaps, add the averages of all individuals bowling on the team. (If an individual has not bowled at least three games, compute the handicap as 150.) Determine the difference between the total handicaps of the

two teams, and use 60 percent of this difference as the handicap; however, in no case shall the handicap used be greater than 50 points. For a dummy, use 150 as the average.

Three-man Football

Three-man football is a game which can be played indoors or outdoors. It is a good activity to conduct in the spring. The game is played on an area similar to a basketball floor with only two zones for first downs and end zone areas. Intramural football rules are used with the following exceptions:

1. Three players per team (only six on a roster).
2. Game shall be forty plays (twenty per half).
3. The ball may not be advanced other than by passing. All players are eligible to receive passes, and the ball may be passed anytime. Once a player catches a pass he may take only two steps but he cannot score if near the goal line.
4. Player may run with the ball in back of the line of scrimmage, but may not cross the line of scrimmage.
5. A man is down when touched with two hands anywhere but on the head.
6. There is no first down—a team must score or give up the ball.
7. On interception a player may take only two steps before passing the ball.
8. The game is over if a team has a 4-touchdown lead.

Volleyball

Volleyball is an activity which can be played both indoors and outdoors. Outdoor volleyball may be played wherever courts can be laid out. If the school has a track that is available during intramural time, it makes a fine outdoor facility with the curbs used as the side boundaries of the court. To conserve time and thereby assist in scheduling, a point should be awarded on each serve in intramurals. Rules for intramural volleyball should be modified to encourage more participation. A sample of modified rules would be:

Outdoor—Play two out of three games.

Indoor—Play all three games.

1. A POINT WILL BE SCORED ON EACH SERVICE, and game shall be played to 21 points.

2. Each team may take two time-outs of 1 minute each during the game.
3. The server shall stand with both feet behind the rear boundary line in the right one third of the court.
4. There are no restrictions as to how the ball may be served except that it must be clearly hit, not thrown or pushed. Side-out is declared when a served ball hits the net on the serve.
5. If a player touches a ball or a ball touches a player he is considered as having played it.
6. A ball touching any part of the boundary line is good.
7. It is permissible to run out of bounds to play a ball.
8. Players are not permitted to scoop or hold the ball. THE BALL MUST BE CLEARLY BATTED.
9. A ball touching the body more than once is considered dribbled.
10. A ball, other than a serve, may be recovered from the net, provided the player avoids contact with the net and does not catch the ball.
11. The ball must be returned over the net on the third contact.
12. A player may play the ball twice during a volley but not twice in succession.
13. A player may not go over the net or step on the division line.
14. Teams must rotate each time they win the right to serve, and players in back line may not spike the ball.

Power Volleyball

Power volleyball is a game for the more highly skilled players. USVBA rules should be followed when playing this type of volleyball. Basically the rules differ in how the ball may be played and in allowing players to cross over and under the net.

Soccer

Intramural soccer is generally played on the same fields as IM football, thus preventing the need for additional marking of fields. The goals may be marked using pilons; or if goals are made for IM soccer they should not be more than 5 feet high because the goalies are not permitted to use their hands. Regular soccer rules govern play with the following exceptions:

1. No player may use hands or arms to play the ball.
2. Periods will start with the team that is behind putting the ball in play by a center kick.
3. There are no off sides.
4. Penalty area is 5 yards out from goal.
5. All violations or fouls will result in a *penalty kick* from that spot, and the following rules apply to the kick:
   a. No one can touch the ball except the goalie until the ball is off line.
   b. The first offensive player other than the kicker to touch ball may not score it.
   c. Any violation in 5 yards results in penalty kick from 5-yard line with the ball in the center.
   d. Too many players result in a 20-yard penalty kick.
6. Players must play the ball, no body contact permitted.
7. Ball over end line results in free kick (if touched last by offense), corner kick (if last touched by defense).
8. Team that is scored upon shall put ball in play at midfield.
9. Free substitution at any time.

Softball

There are three different types of softball which may be incorporated into a program for leagues or tournaments. If a program has the opportunity to sponsor all three, it will provide wholesome activity for a great number of students. Limited space or equipment may dictate the type of softball league which is conducted.

Slow-pitch softball may be played using either the 12-inch or 16-inch softball. For intramurals, the 16-inch softball makes for a better game because it is easier to field and is not hit as far. Regular slow-pitch rules are used with the following modifications:

1. A team is composed of ten players. A team may play without forfeiting with seven players.
2. No base stealing is permitted. In 16 inch, a base runner may lead off from any base, and in the event of an attempt to trap him off base he may advance to the next base to avoid being put out. If he is successful in gaining the forward base, he must return to the base he left. While he is returning the game is temporarily stopped and he may not be put out until he has reached the base, and play is resumed. A runner may be tagged out at anytime while off his base. Runner may not

leave base in 12 inch until the ball has crossed over the plate.

3. When the pitcher secures possession of the ball on or around the pitching area, the runner must either continue to next base or return to last base occupied.

4. A base runner may advance only on a fair ball or on a foul fly ball that has been caught. In either case he may not be out if he can advance to a base safely, but they must have tagged up.

5. A pitched ball must arc between the batter and the pitcher. Any pitched ball that does not arc is an automatic BALL count (unless batter strikes the ball). The arc may not be greater than 3 feet in 16 inch; no limit in 12 inch.

6. In 16 inch, the pitcher may stop his pitching motion twice before delivering the ball. The stop is to be only a hesitation. The ball must be pitched with the palm of the pitching hand facing forward. In 12 inch, the pitching motion must be continuous.

7. No bunting. The batter must have a full swing. Batter is out if there is an attempt to bunt.

8. Batter is out on third strike even if foul.

9. The first baseman is the only one permitted to use a glove in 16 inch.

10. No advance on overthrow outside foul lines.

11. Ten run rule after 5 innings.

Fast-pitch softball requires more equipment and is dominated by a good pitcher; however, it makes a good activity for those individuals who have the equipment. In addition to using the basic intramural rules regarding base stealing, advancing a runner, and overthrows, the following modifications of regular softball rules have proven successful.

1. The batter is entitled to 3 balls or 2 strikes.

2. No team may score more than 5 runs per inning.

3. Game time shall be 5 innings or 50 minutes in length, which ever comes first unless (*a*) a team is ahead by 10 runs after the completion of three and a half innings or at anytime thereafter, or (*b*) a team has two players removed from the game or bench for unsportsmanlike action.

4. In case of rain three and a half innings shall constitute a game.

5. The catcher must wear a mask.

6. Pitchers may wear spikes when they pitch but not at bat.

One-pitch softball is a very effective game which can be played both as a coed and a regular intramural event. The basic difference is that the batter receives only one pitch which is pitched by a team-mate. The batters must hit the ball in fair territory or they are out. One-pitch softball enables a director to schedule teams to play two or three games at a time because a game will last approximately 20 to 25 minutes. Rules:

1. A game shall be five innings or ten runs after three complete innings.
2. Each batter will be given only one pitch.
3. The pitcher shall be a member of the batting team and must take his regular turn at bat (at which time another member of the team shall pitch).
4. The pitcher may pitch from anywhere.
5. The one-pitch rule means the batter either hits the ball safely in fair territory or is out.
6. Runners may not leave a base until the ball is *hit*.
7. The fielding team may place their ten players anywhere providing they do not block the batter's view. They must include a catcher.
8. All other rules are the same as IM 16-inch softball.
9. If umpires are not available, the pitcher or an agreed upon official shall make the calls.
10. If the ball hits the pitcher, the batter bats again.
11. In coed softball:
    a. Teams must bat woman, man, woman, etc.
    b. Women and men must alternate in field positions.

Basketball

Each intramural program has its own set of rules pertaining to basketball. The rules discussed here have proven successful because they permit absolute time scheduling and attempt to eliminate a team from gaining an advantage by fouling. By using these rules, it is possible to use one master clock to time all the games for all the courts. The National Federation of State High School Athletics Association rules are used with the following exceptions:

1. Games will consist of two 15-minute halves with 1 minute between halves. The clock will not be stopped. In case of injury, the amount of time elapsed will be played after the

game is over, if it has a bearing on the outcome of the game.

2. If one team is not present and ready to play at game time, the referee will award 2 points to the team present for each minute or fraction thereof that passes before the second team has at least four players on the floor. At the end of the first 10 minutes, the forfeit score is 20 to 0, if one team has been ready to play. If both teams are late in reporting, the game will be started and the first half will be only as long as there is time on the board.

3. If at the end of the official playing period the score is a tie, the ball will again be put in play by center jump and the first team to score wins. This includes shooting the free throws.

4. At any time in second half, if there is a 30-point difference in score the game is terminated.

5. On personal fouls, which carry a one-shot penalty, the ball will be awarded out-of-bounds at the spot nearest the foul. On personal fouls, which carry a two-shot penalty, the first shot will be taken and the ball awarded out-of-bounds at the free throw line extended.

6. In the last 2 minutes of game, all fouls will be two-shot fouls. The teams must line up as quickly as possible. The two inside spots go to defense, but do not have to be filled. The shooter has only 15 seconds to shoot both shots. No shots on double foul. Technical fouls result in two shots and ball is awarded out-of-bounds. (If the basket is made, it is still a two shot foul.)

7. NO ONE AND ONE SITUATION.

8. An individual is entitled to only four personal fouls per contest.

9. Technical fouls. In the following situations, which may result in a technical foul being called, a player will be removed from the contest and a substitute shall not be allowed to enter the contest:
   a. A technical foul, charged against an individual for swearing, unnecessary delay of a game, undue show of temper, or challenging an official decision, shall result in that player being removed from the contest.
   b. Technical charged against a team, bench, or crowd supporting that team shall result in removal of the captain or best player of the team.

10. Any player who is removed from the contest for a flagrant foul or fighting shall:

   a. Jeopardize his chances of playing in any further intra-
      mural basketball.
   b. Not be replaced by a substitute.
   c. Cause a review of the status of his team and of whether or
      not it should be allowed to continue in the basketball
      program.
11. Anytime two players have been removed from the contest
    under either rule 9 or 10, the contest shall be declared a
    forfeit.
12. Each team is responsible for having one person at the scorer's
    table to identify players.

160-Pound Basketball

This game can be used to establish a second basketball league. All
rules are the same as for regular basketball except that players must
weigh 160 pounds at the time they play or during the designated
weigh in period. Any players who fail to weigh in during the weigh in
period must weigh less than 160 pounds every time they play.

5-foot 9 inch Basketball

The 5-foot 9 inch league is an attempt to organize a basketball
league based on height. All players in this league must be 5-foot 9 inches or under. There is no preseason measuring date; however, if
players are challenged, they must stand under a 5-foot 9 inch measuring stick. The measuring stick is a half-T, which is 5-foot 9 inches
long. The players are measured standing against a wall so that heels,
calves, and back touch the wall. The T end of the stick is then pivoted
over their heads and if the stick strikes the head or the player ducks,
they fail to make the height requirement.

Three-Man Basketball

Three-man basketball is played as a half-court game. Some schools
use a three-man basketball league due to lack of facilities. Regular intramural rules are used with the following exceptions:

1. On any change of team control, the ball must be cleared beyond the top of the free throw area, and two passes must be
   made before a basket may be attempted.
2. Events will be two out of three games to 11 points with 1
   minute between games.

3. A shot must be taken within 20 seconds from the time possession of the ball is gained. Failure to do so results in loss of ball.
4. Each player is allowed three fouls per game. When player fouls out, team must play with only two players.
5. Foul shooting is similar to regular IM rules. On all one-shot fouls the foul is recorded and the ball is awarded out-of-bounds. Two-shot fouls result in one free throw and then the ball is awarded out-of-bounds.
6. Any technical foul shall result in removal of the player for that game.
7. After a score is made, the team that scored retains possession if they lead by less than 4 points. When team"A" leads by 4 or more points, they must turn the ball over to team "B" each time they score until such time as team "B" ties the score or is 1 point behind. If either team gains control during play, they may go ahead and score. Then the ball is awarded to the team which is entitled as determined by the point spread.

Hoc Soccer

Hoc soccer is played indoors using soccer and hockey rules. If possible, the games should be played in a gym area that permits the ball to be played off the walls. Modified intramural rules for hoc soccer could be:

1. A team should consist of five players.
2. Goal size: 4 feet by 2 feet.
3. The game is started by a flip of a coin, and the team winning the flip puts the ball in play from the free throw line. All defensive players must be in their half of court.
4. A goal may be scored only when kicked from the offensive half of the court.
5. After a goal, the team scored upon puts the ball in play at the free throw line.
6. On fouls, the offended team is given a penalty kick from spot with only one defender permitted between the kicker and the goal but not in crease and at least three steps from the kicker.
7. Crease rule: no player on the defensive team is permitted in the crease. If any defensive players are in the crease and the ball strikes them, a goal is scored. No offensive players are permitted in the crease, and if they touch the ball while in the crease the defense is awarded the ball.

8. Two-minute penalty in penalty box.
   a. Hands ball (intentional handling only).
   b. Fouls and misconducts: Holding opponents, pushing, striking, kicking, tripping, using knee on opponent, charging, etc.
   c. Slide tackle.

Scoop Lacrosse

Scoop lacrosse is an intramural version of lacrosse played with plastic scoops and a tennis ball. The game can be played either indoors or outdoors. The field should be layed out so that players can go behind the goal area and shoot at the goal. Only one goalie is permitted in the goal area (15-foot radius), and no offensive player is permitted in the goal area. A 50-gallon oil drum, clothes hamper, or something similair should be used as the goal so that it may be hit from any angle. Rules:

1. A team consists of nine players.
2. The game is played in two halves (the time is determined by the number of entries).
3. The teams shall be designated by the color of the scoops.
4. The ball may be moved by batting with the scoop or catching the ball in the scoop and throwing it.
5. No individual may carry the ball in the scoop for more than two steps; however, if players wish to air dribble the ball in the scoop they are permitted to run as long as they continue to air dribble.
6. NO BODY CONTACT. The ball can be taken away from the opponent by hitting the scoop or catching the ball when thrown in the air.
7. To strike an opponent from the back will result in a free shot from the spot.
8. Free shots which hit the goal are scored as 1 point the same as any ball which strikes the goal. On a free shot only the goalie may make an attempt to stop the ball and this must be done with his scoop.
9. Goalies may not use their body in any way to deflect the ball. If there is an attempt at the goal and the ball strikes the goalie's body, a point is scored.
10. At anytime the ball is deflected by anyone using his body other than the arm attached to the scoop, it shall be a free

shot for the opponents from the spot.

11. If the ball goes out of the playing area, the opponents of the team to last touch the ball shall have a free toss from that spot. A goal may not be scored on a free toss.

12. It is legal to score from in front, on the side, or behind the goal.

13. The ball may not be kicked or hit with the hand other than with the one holding the scoop.

Team Handball

Team handball can be played both indoors and outdoors. For intramurals it makes a fine indoor game to be played either early in the fall or in spring when the gymnasium is not being used. A regular team handball may be purchased, but a playground ball or even volleyball can be used as the ball. In order to produce scoring the net should be the width of the free throw lane area. Outdoor rules would be similiar to the indoor rules stated below, but a goal area would have to be marked to take the place of the free throw lane area. Rules:

1. The game is played with nine players on a team. Free substitution.

2. Teams will flip a coin to determine team with first throw-in. Throw-in is from free throw line.

3. Game is played in two timed halves.

4. The goalkeeper is the only individual permitted in the free throw lane area.

5. Ball is out-of-bounds when it leaves the basketball playing area. Throw-in rule is the same as for basketball.

6. A goal may not be scored on the throw-in. NO player of the offensive team is permitted in the offensive end of the court during throw-in from back court.

7. The ball may be advanced by:
   a. Passing it; it may not be "held" for longer than 3 seconds.
   b. Running three steps with the ball, bouncing it once, and running for not more than three additional steps.

8. There must be no purposeful contact with the ball below the knee.

9. Blocking is permitted. It must be a passive obstruction with the body only (principle same as basketball screen).

10. The defender may attempt to:
    a. Intercept passes.
    b. Block; same rules as offensive blocking on a player with or without the ball.
    c. "Play" the ball from an offensive player with one flat *hand*. Ball may not be pulled from player in control.
11. All fouls shall result in a shot at the goal or pass to teammate from spot of foul (unless foul occurs between free throw line and end line, then shot is from top of key). On foul shot only the goalie may be between the thrower and the goal, and he must be in goal area.
12. Technical foul shots are from free throw line, and goalie must be no more than 4 feet in front of goal. Technical fouls are:
    a. Unnecessary delay in returning to defensive side of court for throw-in.
    b. Intentionally throwing the ball out-of-bounds or over the end line.
    c. Unsportsmanlike conduct (IM rule for unsportsmanlike conduct applies).

Goofy Olympics

The goofy Olympics is an event in which five students compete as a team in contests that are similar to individual track events.

Pollock high jump is an event in which four members of the team throw the fifth member over a bar. In college, the pole vault standards should be used as the players are thrown over a height of 10 feet or more.

Shanty Irish potato relay is a relay race in which two team members carry a third member as the baton for 110 yards; then the person carried is passed to the other two teammates who finish the race. The baton teammate must be carried by both runners; he/she may not ride on just one runner.

Dago dash is a 60-yard dash in which all five team members must cover the 60-yard distance together. The race is run with the racers on hands and knees, and they stay together in file order by holding onto the ankles in front of them.

Kraut long-shot jump. The four tossers throw the human shot as far as possible. The team is given two tosses, and the best distance is recorded. The distance is measured from where the front man is standing to where the human shot lands on the mat.

Limey wall vault is a timed event in which all five teammates must scale a bank of bleachers. The race starts will all participants sitting on the floor, and the time ends when the last man is on top of the bleachers. Climbers may be assisted by teammates; however, a climber may not start up the bleachers until teammates before him have reached the top.

Hungarian hurdle hop is a timed event in which the team forms a human chain by holding hands, and the end member of the chain must jump over four obstacles as he/she is turning in a complete circle. The outside teammate must complete five laps. If the chain is broken, the race must be started over with a different team member on the end of the chain.

Team relays

Team relays use track events but combine times, heights, or distances of team members to get a single score. Any number of individuals can make up a team. In a college program, three individuals are used; however, at the junior high or elementary level it is a good idea to use all the members of the unit to arrive at a score. When running a team relay event it is not necessary that all team members run, jump, or throw at the same time because their scores will be added together.

Tandem bike race

This is a bike road race using tandem bikes. There are ten riders on a team and two teammates each ride one lap of the race. This event should be run against time in the interest of safety. If tandem bikes are not available, two regular bikes may be connected with a 10-foot rope.

8. Facilities and Equipment

Man should not consider his material possessions his own, but as common to all, so as to share them without hesitation when others are in need.

St. Thomas Aquinas

Although facilities and equipment are essential to any intramural program, they should not limit the scope of the program. This chapter will attempt to point out ways an individual may make better use of existing facilities and equipment.

FACILITIES

It has been an axiom for many years that there will never be enough indoor or outdoor facilities for intramurals and recreation because intramurals and recreation have an unlimited scope of activites. However, most educational institutions are not about to build any new facilities; therefore, the intramural personnel must plan to make the best use of all existing facilities.

Probably the most important function to be performed by the intramural director in planning for the use of facilities is the co-ordinating of scheduling. It is a known fact that intramurals and recreation must schedule their activities after physical education and athletics have completed their day's activities. The intramural director should receive a definite commitment from the administration concerning the use of the facilities. It is a good policy to establish a set of priorities.

In the public school system scheduling is generally determined by the time periods given to classes and athletic contests; however, the intramural director should establish policies in regard to using facilities before school, during the noon hour, after school, evenings, and on the weekends. One of the most important considerations is that not all facilities should be constantly used for scheduled activities; the students need some area for recreational activities.

At the college or university level it is common practice to have a committee establish a set of priorities for a multiuse facility. The committee generally acts as the policy making body and settles

191

disputes in regard to scheduling. Priorities for the use of facilities might be ordered as follows:

1. Classes take precedence over all other programs from 8:00 A.M. to 3:00 P.M., Monday through Friday.
2. Intercollegiate athletics take precedence over all other programs from 3:00 P.M. to 5:00 P.M., Monday through Friday.
3. Scheduled intercollegiate contests have priority over all other events for time specified after 3:00 P.M., on weekdays and on Saturdays.
4. University sponsored programs, such as lectures and entertainment, or other large university sponsored programs.
5. Intramurals and recreation.
6. Recognized student and faculty organizations such as sports club and faculty leagues.
7. Off-campus groups such as community, county, or statewide organizations, that have been declared eligible to use the facilities by established university policies.

Although classes have top priority during the weekdays, it has been a common practice to schedule no classes during the lunch hour to permit faculty and staff to use the areas for recreation. Some colleges and universities also permit students to check out recreational equipment during the day as long as they do not interfere with classes.

Indoor Playing Areas

Once the facility has been scheduled for intramurals and recreation, the director must then make the best possible use of the facility for the program. Many floors are already marked with multicolored lines for use in different types of activities. If the floor is not already marked for multiuse, it might be suggested that additional lines be added to provide for different courts. In order to avoid a mass of lines which could cause confusion, common boundaries should be used for the different courts.

An example of common boundaries on a regulation basketball court would be to have the basketball lines in black, the volleyball in light blue, and the badminton in light green, except where these lines would fall side by side: the players should realize that the black lines on the outside serve as the outside boundary for all three courts. An example of a basketball court with common boundaries is presented in Figure 8.1. It should be noted that in order to use common

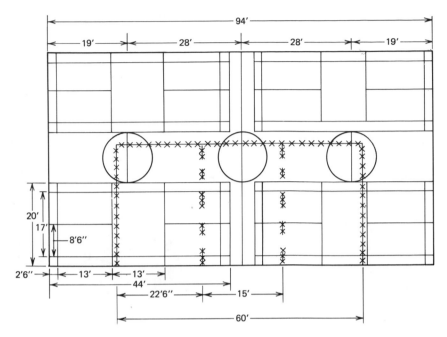

× × × × Represent volleyball

Figure 8.1
Multimarked basketball court.

lines, the basketball court must be 52 feet wide.

When it is impossible to add additional permanent lines to the area, elastic binding may be used to superimpose lines over the existing court. Although the elastic may not be 2 inches wide, it makes excellent lines because it will spring back into place after it has been kicked. The courts can be laid out rather quickly if small markers are placed on the area to indicate the corners of the court and if the connecting corners are sewed together to limit the number of places that the elastic must be taped to the floor. In small enclosed playing areas, it is also possible to stretch the elastic to hooks which have been placed for permanent markers of such courts.

Other areas of the buildings, such as lobbies, hallways, and areas in back of bleachers, may be used by the director for activities which do not require large floor space. The lobby area in many schools is used for the playing of inactive games, shuffleboard, bowling, table tennis, or weight training when weight machines that have different stations are placed in this area.

Figure 8.2
Portable handball courts.

The area between bleachers and a wall may serve as handball or paddleball courts. The courts may not be of regulation size, and it may only be possible to play either one-wall or two-wall (front and back) handball. If funds are available, portable handball walls can be purchased from commercial companies which can be attached to other walls and moved out of place when it is necessary to use the area for the bleachers. Because the courts may not be regulation, it is best to use the soft paddleball instead of the regulation handball. Figure 8.2 shows portable handball courts which has been placed between the bleachers and the wall. The handball walls fold back against the wall when it is necessary to use the bleachers.

Outdoor Areas

Ideally, the outdoor facilities are easily accessible to the participants and located adjacent to the indoor dressing areas. This is not always possible because outdoor areas that belong to the school are limited, and the intramural program may be required to use outdoor areas that belong to the community. One of the major concerns in the use of outdoor playing areas is safety. All playing areas should be smooth, free of holes, and located at an adequate distance from hazardous structures.

Outdoor areas should be planned so that they are multipurpose. It is possible to play soccer, football, and softball in the same area if proper planning is used in laying out the field. It is a good idea not to use permanent backstops for softball because they may obstruct play in other activities as well as create worn spots in the surface by necessitating bases to always be placed in the same locations. Figure 8.3 shows a 550 x 550 foot square area used for four softball fields and six football fields. The six football fields would be 70 X 40 yards, and the softball diamonds would have 250 feet of playing area down the foul lines.

With the emergence of sports clubs, it may become necessary

Figure 8.3
Football and softball fields.

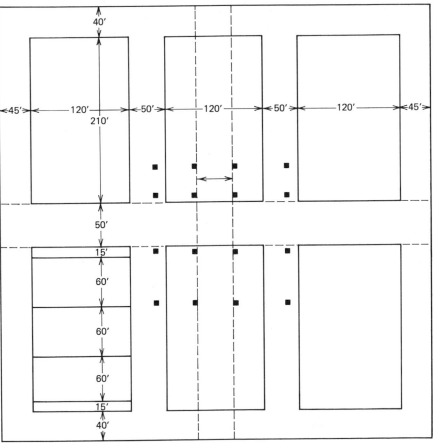

to establish a playing area which can be used when these clubs compete with other clubs. Because of the premium placed on outdoor space it may not be practical to provide a field for each interest group; therefore, one common field should be used by different clubs. Figure 8.4 is an example of how one field may be used by rugby, soccer, and lacrosse; all three games can be played on a field which is 330 feet long by 210 feet wide (additional space—not to exceed 25 yards—on each end is needed for the rugby in-goal area). Rugby and soccer could use the same set of goal posts by placing an extension over the soccer goal to provide the posts necessary for rugby. Different colored paint could be used to indicate the different areas for each game which are not bounded by common lines.

Tennis courts may be used for many activities; however, due to the popularity of tennis it is difficult to use this area for anything but tennis. The tennis practice board may also be used for one-wall handball or paddleball. If there is hard surface outside the tennis fences, the practice boards should be on the outside of the fences to permit more use of the area. Baskets could be placed on the fences

Figure 8.4
Lacrosse, rugby and soccer fields.

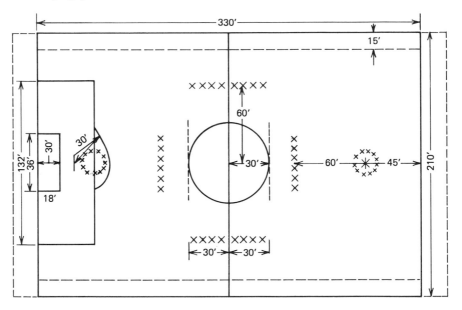

——————— Represents soccer and common lines
— — — Represents rugby
×××× Represents Lacrosse

to permit basketball to be played. If the area is to be used for many activities, such as handball, basketball, volleyball, badminton, and tennis, movable posts are placed in preset holes to accommodate particular sports. The courts could be multimarked; and tennis courts should have the dominant white lines.

The intramural department should also try and provide a jogging area for those individuals who are interested in jogging. The jogger should be able to determine the distance that has been run. Determining distances is made possible by either (a) painting a small mark on fence parts or trees which indicates each quarter of a mile so that individuals may keep track of the distance or (b) duplicating a map of different courses which may be run on the campus that indicates the amount of miles that the different courses cover (Figure 8.5).

Parks and golf courses may be used for conducting such activities as cross-country, turkey trots, or orienterring. It is not absolutely necessary to line the course; however, if the varsity teams use a lined course, the intramural department should plan to conduct the intramural meet when the course has been marked for their use.

The outdoor track should be used not only for conducting track meets and fitness runs but for bike races and outdoor volleyball. The curb on the track can serve as the sidelines for volleyball, and if it is not possible to mark the track for the center and back lines then elastic binding could be attached to the curb to serve as the lines.

Commercial Facilities

The use of commercial facilities can increase the scope of any intramural program. Proprietors of commercial facilities generally welcome the opportunity to work with the intramural program because it offers the student a chance to become familiar with their facilities. Scheduling is once again an important concern when using a commercial facility. The intramural director should try and schedule the use of the commercial facility when it is not in use. By scheduling during "nonpeak times," when the proprietor would not be receiving any income, the intramural department may receive a rate good for the use of the facility.

Whenever the intramural department uses a commercial facility, a written agreement should be drawn up covering costs and supervision during the use of the area. There is also an opportunity—if this is part of the agreement—to have the professional at the facility offer some instruction either during or before the activities begin.

Geographical location often determines what commercial facil-

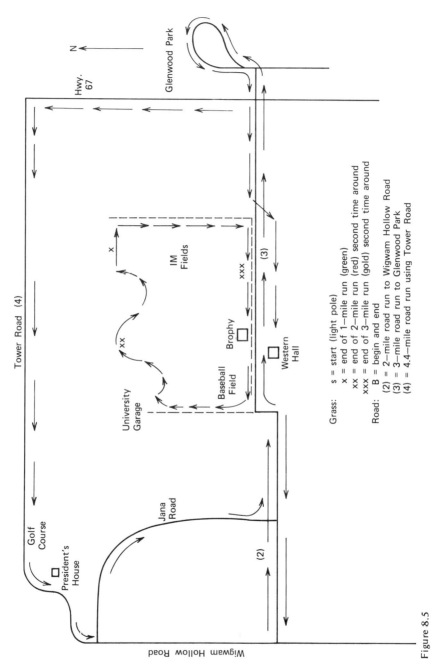

Figure 8.5

Jogging map (Western Illinois University F.I.T. jogging program grass and road trails).

198

ities are available to the intramural program. Commercial facilities which might be used by the intramural department include: bowling lanes, family billiard centers, shooting (skeet, trap, rifle) ranges, raquet clubs, golf courses, karate or judo centers, skiing facilities, roller skating arenas, ice skating arenas, archery ranges, go-cart tracks, miniature golf, and family recreation centers.

Facility Shorts

1. Softball fields should be laid out from the center of playing area for safety as well as more central supervision.
2. The master score clock in the gymnasium should be used for all contests to keep the program on schedule.
3. Karate kick boards and a mirror should be located in a small area for use by both clubs and individuals who have an interest in improving their skills.
4. When the track is used for jogging, hurdles should be placed in different lanes so that the joggers will not always use the same lane. Signs should indicate which lanes are to be used for jogging.
5. To prevent repeated wear on the grass, football and softball fields should not be located in exactly the same area each year.
6. Construct a record board out of plywood with slots for cards so that records may be changed as soon as they have been established.

EQUIPMENT

The equipment that is used in the program and that students check out for recreation should be the best equipment possible. The intramural directors should never object to sharing equipment with athletics and physical education departments as long as they are sharing good equipment and the intramural department does not receive the "hand-me-downs."

The highest standards should be followed when purchasing equipment. Many institutions require that all equipment be purchased through the bid process. Although bidding will enable a department to receive a lower price on the items, the director should make sure that inferior items are not substituted when the merchandise is received. It is possible to stretch the budget by purchasing equipment during a close-out sale or year-end sale if the items are of the quality that are used in the department.

As a general rule, the intramural departments provide the necessary equipment to conduct the activities, but this does not include any personal items for the participants; however, it is a good idea for the department to have different colored pinnies for the teams who arrive with jerseys that are alike. The department should also purchase the jersey's that are to be worn by the intramural officials. These should be checked out to the officials by the season.

For several activities the participants may sometimes be asked to provide the balls that are necessary to compete. Tennis is one activity for which opponents are asked to bring a new can of balls, one can is used and the winner receives the unused can for the next match. Participants are often asked, because of the expense, to provide golf balls, paddleballs, handballs, and table tennis balls.

Some activities require the intramural department to construct the equipment necessary to play a contest. The constructed equipment should be of top-grade materials and finished in such a way as to insure that it is safe for use by the students. This equipment should be marked and numbered, because if the activities are enjoyable the students may wish to check this equipment out for recreational use.

Much of the equipment can be used by the intramural department for more than one activity. Examples of multiuse of equipment would be:

1. *Balance beam* used for pillow fights and obstacle races.
2. *Hockey goal* used also as goal for team handball.
3. *Pylons and corner flags* used in football, cross-country, archery, bike races, etc.
4. *Inner tubes* used for water events, wiffle golf, three-legged races, raft races.
5. *Plastic scoops* used for jai-alai and hybrid lacrosse.
6. *Small archery targets* used also for BB-gun shooting.

Care of Equipment

The first step in caring for the equipment is to mark it so that it can be identified as belonging to the program. If items are part of permanent equipment then most institutions require that an inventory number be attached to the items. For nonpermanent items, such as balls, bats, etc., a definite type of a marking should be used. One of the most successful ways of marking this type of equipment is to use colored paint and a number so that the equipment may be identified by number when checked out.

Manufacturers' suggestions should be followed when cleaning and storing equipment. If the school has its own washing machine most of the rubber balls used in the program may be washed in that machine. Proper storage of equipment in a dry area will increase its longevity.

The keeping of accurate inventory records is a must in order to assure that the proper equipment is either on hand or will be purchased before it is next needed in the program. Institutions may have a standard inventory form which they require the intramural director or equipment personnel to use. If there is no standard inventory form for intramural and recreational equipment, the intramural department should devise a form which will enable them to keep an accurate record of the available equipment. An example of an inventory form appears in Figure 8.6.

This type of inventory form not only provides the information on what equipment is available but also assists the director in planning for future purchasing and serves as a guide for budgeting equipment. After the inventory has been taken, the director must indicate, in the fourth column, the anticipated needs for equipment of each activity. If the inventory falls below anticipated needs, then the director can plan for each activity by listing the amount of equipment required and the total cost for all equipment.

Checking Out Equipment

There are two different kinds of occasions when intramurals and recreational equipment must be checked out, and each should have its own procedure to assure that all the equipment is returned: First, when a supervised intramural activity is being conducted, the equipment should be checked out to the supervisor, and this individual should then be responsible for the equipment. The supervisor can then in turn assign the equipment to either an official of the contest or a team captain. If the equipment is being assigned to a team captain, he/she should leave either an ID card or some item of identification for security until the equipment is returned. Second, when students check out equipment for unsupervised intramural activities or recreational play, the equipment personnel should require the student to leave an ID card until the equipment is returned.

It is not a good practice to require a deposit on equipment, because this may discourage students from using the equipment during

Intramural Equipment Needs and Inventory

Date _____

Sport	Inventory			Anticipated Need	Need to Purchase	Price		Sport Total Cost
	New	Used	Total			Per Item	Total	
Softballs	25	10	35	150	10 Doz.	$3.80 each	$456.00	
Throw Down Bases	1 Set	6 Sets	7 Sets	12	5 Sets	$11.60 set	$58.00	
Bats	7	7	14	24	10	$9.00 each	$90.00	$604.00
Football								
Footballs	4	10	14	24	10	$18.00	$180.00	
Corner Flags	—	12	12	32	2 Doz.	$14.00 doz.	$28.00	$208.00

Figure 8.6
Inventory form.

their recreation. Students should not be charged for natural wear and breakage of equipment; however, they should be held responsible for items that are lost. It is a good practice to charge the students a retail price for the equipment that is lost, otherwise, if they know they can purchase the equipment at the school price which is generally below the common retail price, they might say they lost the equipment.

Ideas for Use of Equipment

1. To facilitate putting up and taking down of badminton nets, instead of using strings, attach bands cut from old inner tubes to top and bottom of nets.

2. Attach turn buckles to the ends of volleyball nets to insure that the cable may be stretched to the proper height.

3. Fill cardboard boxes with newspapers to use as backing for BB-gun events and permit the reuse of the BBs.

4. In the weight room, weld the weights to the bars and mark the total weight on the bars to prevent loss as well as make them convenient for the lifters.

5. Encourage the industrial education department to assist in the construction of equipment.

6. Purchase large sheets of table tennis rubber to resurface paddles when they are worn out.

7. Purchase a racket stringer and string so that both badminton and tennis rackets can be restrung.

8. Use four-wheel clothes hampers to move equipment from the equipment room to the playing area.

9. Use rubber throw-down bases for softball, because they may be moved to dry areas and strapped-down bases increase the chances of injury.

9. Structuring Competition

*Don't waste time in doubts and fears; spend
yourself in the work before you, well assured
that the right performance of this hour's
duties will be the best preparation for the
hours or ages that follow it.*

Ralph Waldo Emerson

Every director should have a working knowledge of the mechanics necessary to draw up the various kinds of tournaments which are available for organizing competition. In selecting the best tournament for the activity, one must consider such factors as age group, playing time, facilities, equipment, and number of entries. This chapter will discuss the mechanics and procedures required to set up the various tournaments.

It should be understood that unless it is absolutely necessary to complete a tournament in a short time with the least number of games, the single elimination tournament should not be used. The director should clearly understand that minimum participation will be achieved when using this type of tournament.

The random selection of places in the tournament bracket is the best method to use for intramurals, because all teams have an equal right to compete; however, a director should have an understanding of proper seeding techniques and the use of byes in case these methods are needed when drawing up tournaments.

SEEDING

Seeding is a method used in elimination tournaments that attempts to have the best players or teams on the opposite sides of the bracket so that they have an opportunity to meet in the finals. The general rules for seeding are:

1. Place in rank order those teams or players which have the best performance records.
2. No more than half the teams or players should be seeded.
3. Place the number one seeded individual or team in the first bracket place at the top of the tournament and the number two seed in the last bracket of the tournament. The number four seed is then placed in the bottom of the top bracket with

the number three seed on the top line of the bottom bracket. Not all directors agree on how to place the seeded players on the brackets. Some directors feel that to insure the number two seed a better chance to reach the finals, the number four seeded team or player should be placed on the lower bracket.

4. Other seeded teams or players are then placed in opposite quarters of the tournament so that the higher seeded teams have the best opportunity to advance to the quarterfinals of the tournament. Also the top seeded team or player should be scheduled to play the lowest rated team or player in the first round, with other seeded teams and players arranged accordingly. Figure 9.1 is an example of seeding for 8-, 16-, 32-team brackets.

It should also be kept in mind that if organizations enter more than one team they should be placed on opposite sides of the brackets, so that they have an opportunity to advance as far as possible before they play each other. This principle also determines that if an elimination tournament is to follow a round robin tournament and two teams from the same section go to the elimination tournament, they should be placed on opposite sides of the bracket.

Seeding is also used in track and swimming, when heats are held, to have the best competitors meet in the finals. All competitors must run or swim an equal number of heats to reach the finals. The number of participants will determine the number of heats necessary to reach the finals. A table for the forming of trial heats, which depend upon the number of lanes and number of participants, appears in Appendix A.

The contestants in the preliminary heats should be placed in rank order. The best performer should be placed in the first heat, and then other contestants are alternated from left to right, and the right to left. For 24 competitors who are attempting to become the 12 semifinalists, the seeding would be as indicated in the table.

	Heat 1	Heat 2	Heat 3	Heat 4
	1 (best time)	2	3	4
	8	7	6	5
Preliminary	9	10	11	12
(3 to semifinals)	16	15	14	13
	17	18	19	20
	24 (poorest time)	23	22	21

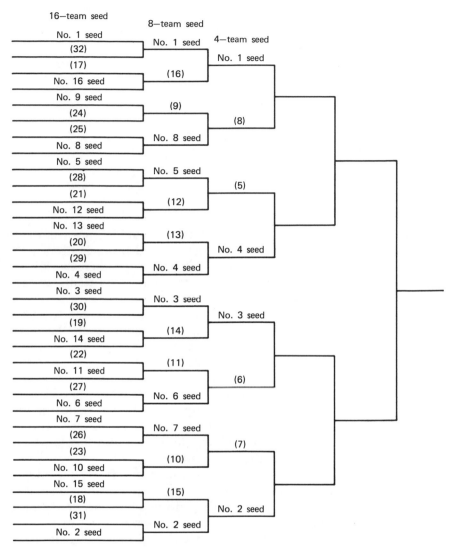

Figure 9.1
Seeding.

The exception to this procedure would occur when two members of the same organization are drawn into the same heat; in this situation the slower individual should be moved to the next heat.

The procedure used to form the heats for the semifinals is as follows: seed each group of place finishers as a unit by their times; seed winners, then seconds, etc., using the principle of left to right then right to left.

	Heat 1	Heat 2
	1a*	1b†
Semifinal	1d	1c
(3 to finals)	2a‡	2b
	2d	2c
	3a	3b
	3d	3c

*1a = fastest first.
†1b = second fastest first.
‡2a = fastest second.

Just as in the preliminary race, if two individuals are from the same organization, the slower individual should be exchanged with the nearest place winner with comparable time. If there is not an even number of contestants for all heats, extra contestants are assigned heats by the draw.

In swimming and races that are to be run in lanes, the top two seeded individuals draw for the middle two lanes. Then the next two individuals draw for the adjacent lanes. For races that are not run in lanes, the participants should draw for lanes.

There is also a method of seeding for field events and distance races where the winner will be determined based on time or distance. The seeding is to place the best competitors in the same flights. The flights are arranged so that the best competitors, based on previous time and distance records, compete after those flights which have individuals with poorer times or distances.

In intramural track and swimming, the selection of individuals who are to compete in the finals should be based on time. It is difficult to seed heat leaders, because they do not have previous times and intramural participants may not be in shape to run or swim a number of heats. In the prelims, runners should draw for lanes, but in the finals the lane assignments should be made in the same manner as described above so that the best runners or swimmers are in the center of the tracks or pool. In case of a tie for the qualifiers they should be given their choice of a run-off or flipping a coin for position in the finals.

BYES

Byes may be necessary when there are not enough players or teams to fill all the brackets for first games. The use of byes is similar to the procedure for seeding. The byes are placed on the opposite ends of the bracket so that an equal number are in each quadrant of the tournament. The order in which byes are placed on a bracket is illustrated in Figure 9.1 with the higher seeded (lower numbered) teams receiving the byes.

The principle of placing byes in the opposite quadrants of the bracket is only practical if there are a few byes. Whenever the number of byes exceeds one half the number of entrants it is advisable to use the "play-in method." The "play-in method" allows teams or individuals, when they draw a bye, to begin play immediately without waiting for the results of the other games.

Figure 9.2 is a example of 21 teams being placed on a 32-team bracket using the "play-in method." By using this method 20 of the 21 teams can begin play immediately as opposed to the bye method, as illustrated in Figure 9.3, where five teams must wait because of byes for the results of first-round games.

The number of first-round games for the "play-in method" is determined by subtracting the number of games possible on the standard bracket (8, 16, or 32) from the number of entries. In Figure 9.2, the five first-round games were determined by subtracting 16 from 21. The table lists the number of first-round games necessary for the different standard brackets.

Number of Teams	8-Team Bracket	Number of Teams	16-Team Bracket
9	1	17	1
10	2	18	2
11	3	19	3
12	4	20	4
13	5	21	5
		22	6
		23	7
		24	8
		25	9
		26	10

The "play-in" games should always be placed at the top of the bracket. During a one-day tournament, the "play-in method" would permit a late entry to play team K (Figure 9.2). If all games did not begin at the same time, it would also permit more late entries because they could be placed against teams L, M, etc., or even teams in the bottom of the bracket.

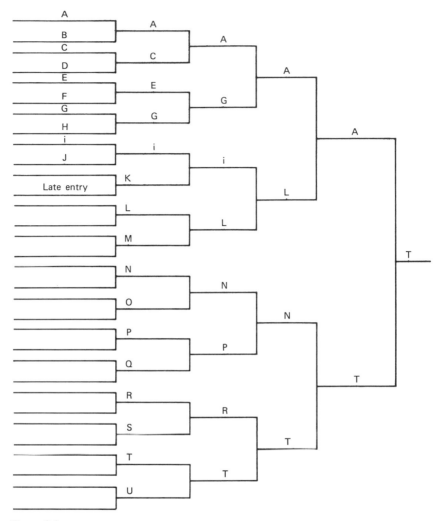

Figure 9.2
Play-in method.

The "play-in method" is also very practical in a double elimination tournament when the standard double elimination bracket, as illustrated in Figure 9.8 is used.

SINGLE ELIMINATION TOURNAMENTS

The single elimination tournament involves the elimination of all participants except the one who wins. This type of tournament is

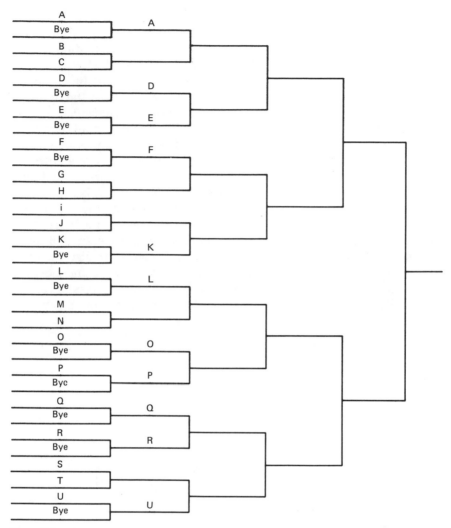

Figure 9.3
Twenty one teams on bye method.

especially advantageous when a winner must be determined in a short period of time. The formula to determine the number of games in a single elimination tournament is n-1 where n represents the number of entries. For 22 teams, there would be 21 games (22-1).

A basic fundamental in drawing up elimination tournaments is the use of "powers of 2" (2, 4, 8, 16, 32, 64). If the number of entries is even and equals a power of 2, then every line of a tournament bracket will be filled. When the number of entries are uneven or not an exact power of 2, byes or the "play-in method" must be used and a "power of 2" must be obtained in the second round. The intramural department should duplicate single elimination blanks which are designed to handle 8-, 16-, or 32-team entries.

For all elimination tournaments, the games should be numbered and the date, time, and playing area should be placed in the brackets. If the game number is placed at the point on the bracket where the winner's name will be written, the other information may be written under the line, thus making it clear to the participants when that game will be played (Figure 9.4). Not all directors agree with this method; some put all the information in the area between the brackets as in Figure 9.4, game number 3. Either method is acceptable; however, when using a duplicated 32-team bracket there is hardly enough room in the first round to put the names of the contestants along with the other information about playing time and places. It is also a good practice to use an additional sheet to list the game numbers, times, and participants for first-round games and post this alongside the tournament. As discussed earlier in Chapter 4 this additional list will enable the partcipants to check off their names to indicate they know when they are playing.

Figure 9.4
Game number, time, court.

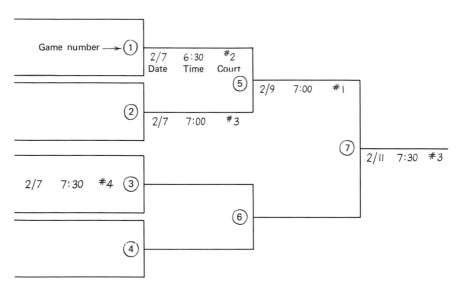

CONSOLATION TOURNAMENTS

This tournament is a better tournament than the single elimination tournament because it assures all players or teams of at least two games. There are two different types of consolation tournaments:

The first type of consolation tournament permits only the first-round loser or second-round loser, who drew a bye, to play another single elimination type tournament to determine the consolation winner. Figure 9.5 illustrates both methods.

The second type of consolation tournament is very similar to a double elimination tournament because all losers, regardless of what round they lost (except final round), have a chance to play for the consolation championship. This type of tournament can be modified to allow the losers in the semifinal round to either play each other for third place or loop back to the consolation side and play for that championship (Figure 9.6).

Figure 9.5
Consolation tournament, first round and byes.

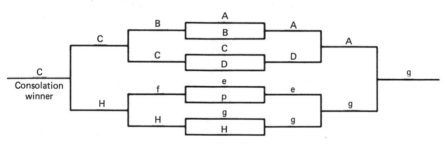

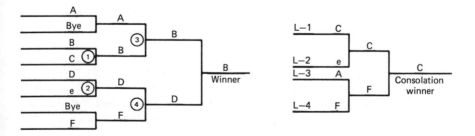

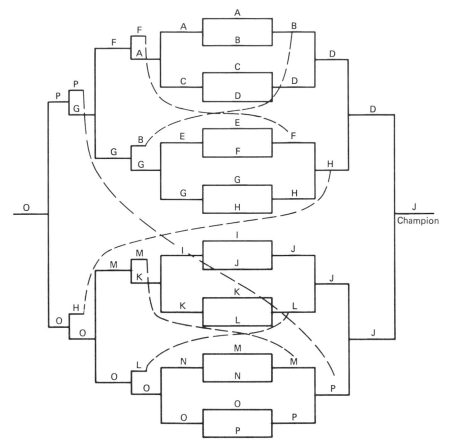

Figure 9.6
Consolation tournament, all losers play. This tournament may also be run without letting losers cross-over but letting them play for third place.

DOUBLE ELIMINATION TOURNAMENTS

The double elimination tournament provides at least twice as much play as a single elimination tournament, and it provides for a fairer championship as by random draw the best teams may have met in the first round. In a double elimination tournament, a team must be defeated twice before they are eliminated. The first defeat will drop the team into the loser bracket, yet they still have a chance to come back and win the championship.

The number of games may be determined by using the formula

$2n - (1$ or $2)$ when n is the number of entries. The number of contests will vary by one game if the winner of the losers' bracket defeats the winner of the winners' bracket when they meet. The same basic principles regarding drawing up the tournament (the use of powers of 2 and the "play-in method" or the bye method) should be followed in setting up the first round of a double elimination tournament.

The basic principle in back of a double elimination tournament, other than allowing a team two defeats before being eliminated, is to prevent teams from playing each other for the second time until the latest possible time. This is accomplished, after the first round, by having the losing teams cross over into different quadrants of the bracket. The cross-over to different quadrants may be accomplished by drawing arrows to the losers' side of the bracket (Figure 9.7).

A much clearer and easier method is to use a 32-team bracket, as illustrated in Figure 9.8, which can handle all double elimination tournaments with any number of entries up to 32 teams. If there are between 17 and 32 entries, the first-round game and byes are put in the spaces for a 32-team draw. With 9 to 16 entries, the first-round games and byes are placed on spaces for games 17 through 24. For 5 to 8 entries, first-round games will be placed on spaces 45

Figure 9.7
Sixteen team double elimination cross-over method.

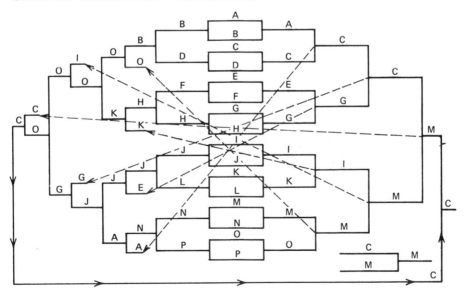

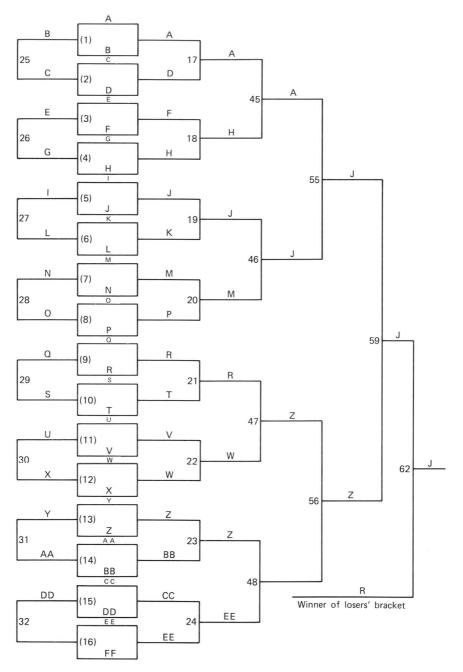

Figure 9.8
Double elimination tournament, winners bracket and first-round losers.

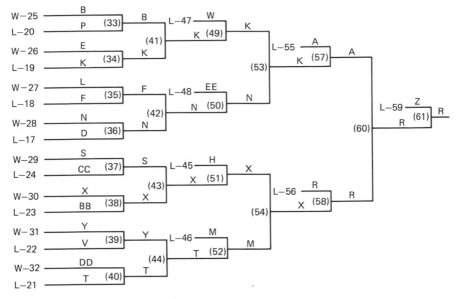

Figure 9.9
Double elimination tournament loser bracket (second-round on).

through 48. After the first round, the winner advances to the right of the bracket and the losers take their predetermined position on the losers' bracket (Figure 9.9).

BAGNAL-WILD ELIMINATION TOURNAMENTS

This is a modification of a single elimination tournament which selects a winner and a true second and third place finisher. The one disadvantage of this tournament is that the competitors cannot begin to compete until the finalists have been decided. When the finalists have been determined, the competitors who were defeated by the finalists compete against each other in separate elimination tournaments. Those individuals who were defeated by the winner will compete for the right to meet the defeated finalist for a second place. To determine third place, an elimination tournament is conducted among those defeated by the loser in the finals. The winner meets the loser of the second-place match for third place. If the defeated finalist loses in the match for second place, then the winner takes second place and the loser automatically becomes the third place winner. However, if the defeated finalist wins the second-place,

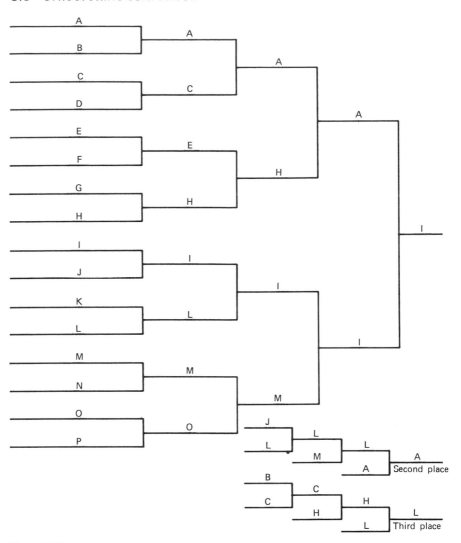

Figure 9.10
Bagnal-wild tournament.

then another elimination tournament involving those individuals he defeated is conducted to determine who contests the loser for third place. Figure 9.10 is an example of a 16-team Bagnal-wild elimination tournament.

This is a type of tournament common in wrestling meets where points are awarded for second and third places. It should be noted that some wrestling tournaments are set up so that second place is determined by who loses in the finals, and individuals compete for positions from third to sixth place.

ROUND ROBIN TOURNAMENTS

The round robin tournament is considered to have a great advantage over other tournaments because individuals or teams are not eliminated until they have completed the schedule. This method of competition is adaptable to both teams and individuals and is appropriate for small numbers in league play. For a large number of teams involved in league play, the round robin tournament may be divided into six- or eight-team sections and the top teams then advance to a single elimination tournament to determine the winner. When there is a tie for the top two places, all teams should be placed in the play-off tournament.

To determine the number of games to be played in a round robin tournament, the following formula should be used:

$$\frac{n(n\text{-}1)}{2} \quad n \text{ represents the number of entries}$$

Substituting 6 or n in a 6-team section, the result would be:

$$\frac{6(6\text{-}1)}{2} \quad \text{or 15 games for each section}$$

To determine the number of rounds in each section, the number of matched pairs is divided into the total number of games. Using 6 teams, there would be 3 sets of matched pairs; the 15 games would then be divided by 3 and 5 rounds in order to complete the section.

To determine the number of days necessary to complete the league, the total number of games should be divided by the number of playing areas.

Example:
Given
        4 sections with 6 teams each and 6 fields each day,
Then
      15 games per section × 4 = 60 games; 60/games/6 fields = 10
                      days to complete section play

A prepared blank schedule sheet should be used when setting up the schedule (Figure 9.11, section I). The teams should be written or typed on the schedule sheet along with the playing date, time, and court. A time saving method is to either write the schedule on a ditto and duplicate the work sheet by using a Spirit Master Machine, which produces a ditto master.

To draw up a round robin tournament schedule, the entries should be placed in two vertical columns which indicate the first-round games. To schedule subsequent games, the top left team is held constant and other teams are rotated counterclockwise. When an uneven number of teams is entered, the same procedure is used but a bye is placed in the top left spot and teams are rotated around the bye counterclockwise. Section II of Figure 9.11 is an example of a completed 6-team section.

	Even		*Odd*	
	Cats	Bills	BYE	Cats
Round one	Stars	Dons	Stars	Bills
	Owls	Shots	Owls	Shots
	Cats	Dons	BYE	Bills
Round two	Bills	Shots	Cats	Shots
	Stars	Owls	Stars	Owls
	Cats	Shots	BYE	Shots
Round three	Dons	Owls	Bills	Owls
	Bills	Stars	Cats	Stars

The playing times and courts should be rotated so that each section has a chance to play on a different court and at different times. If all teams in a section play at the same time on the same day, it is easier to read if the date and time appear only once for each section. Both methods of indicating playing dates and time appear in Figure 9.11, section II.

Some intramural programs use a standard number chart for round robin tournaments and assign teams numbers; however, it is clearer to the students to see their team name on the schedule. A complete listing of games for round robin tournaments from 6 teams to 16 teams appears in Appendix B.

Once the sections have been established, the next step is to assign the sections playing dates. In a round robin tournament it is important that all teams play their first game before any team plays its second contest. An efficient and easy way to do that scheduling in a logical order is to stack all work sheets in a pile and begin

Section I			Date	Teams	Court	Time

	W	L				

Section II

	W	L	Date	Teams		Court	Time
			Mon. Jan. 3	Vets	High	1	6:30
				Sams	Red	2	
				8-Balls	Joes	3	
			Wed. Jan. 12	Vets	Red	2	7:00
				High	Joes	3	
				Sams	8-Balls	1	
			Tues. 1-17	Vets	Joes	3	7:30
			Tues. 1-17	Red	8-Balls	1	7:30
Vets			Tues. 1-17	High	Sams	2	7:30
Sams			Thur. 1-19	Vets	8-Balls	1	8:00
8-Balls			Thur. 1-19	Joes	Sams	2	8:00
High			Thur. 1-19	Red	High	3	8:00
Red			Mon. 1-24	Vets	Sams	2	8:30
Joes				8-Balls	High	1	
				Joes	Red	3	

Figure 9.11
Round robin work sheet.

Time	Court 1							Court 2							Court 3							Court 4						
	I-4	I-5	I-6	I-12	I-13	I-14	I-18	I-4	I-5	I-6	I-12	I-13	I-14	I-18	I-4	I-5	I-6	I-12	I-13	I-14	I-18	I-4	I-5	I-6	I-12	I-13	I-14	I-18
6:05	✓	✓	Fa	✓	Fa	Pl	✓	✓		Fa		Fa	Pl	✓	✓		Fa		Fa	Pl	✓	✓	c		c			Fa
6:40	✓	✓	culty	✓	culty	ayOffs	✓	✓		culty		culty	ayOffs	✓	✓		culty		culty	ayOffs	✓	✓	lu		lu			culty
7:15	✓	✓	League	✓	↓	↓	✓	✓		↓		↓	↓	✓	✓		↓		↓	↓	✓	✓	b		b			↓
7:50	✓	✓	✓	✓	Pla	↓	✓	✓				Piay											Pra		Pra			
8:20	✓	✓	✓	✓	yOf		✓	✓				Offs											cti		cti			
9:00	✓	✓	✓	✓	fs		✓	✓				↓											ce		ce			
9:35	✓	✓	✓	✓			✓	✓																				
10:10	✓	✓	✓	✓	↓		✓	✓				↓																
10:45																												
11:20																												

Figure 9.12
Volleyball scheduling work sheet.

with section I, put in the date for the first contest, then proceed to the first contest in section II. Follow this procedure and turn over each page until all sections have their first game scheduled. Next, merely turn the work sheets over and repeat the procedure for the second playing date in each section.

To assure that there is no duplication of times and dates, the director should use a field and floor form on which he has listed available dates and times and check off those that are scheduled. Figure 9.12 is an example of how field and floor sheets can be used to check dates, floors, and times for the volleyball season where teams play games. This also serves as a check for the director as to what dates are available for scheduling the league.

There are three methods that can be used to determine the winner of a round robin tournament: Percentage, British, and Canadian. If all contests are played until there is a winner and no ties are possible, then the Percentage Method is most widely used.

Percentage Method. If the final standings are determined by the percentage of wins, the percentage is obtained by dividing the number of games won by the total number of games played and is usually expressed as a decimal carried to three places. Tie games are customarily counted as games not played when the percentage is computed. For example, if 8 games are played and a tie is not counted, a team with a 5-2-1 record would have a percentage of 0.625 (5 ÷ 8) A fairer method is to consider each tie as half a win and half a loss; thus the team that is 5-2-1 would have a percentage of .687 (5.5 ÷ 8).

Canadian Method. In the Canadian method, points are given for each victory and each tie. The most commonly used method is to award 2 points for a victory, 1 point for a tie, and no points for a loss. The team which accumulates the greatest number of points is the winner. Using the example above, the team would accumulate a total of 11 points.

British Method. The British method goes one step farther, than the Canadian method, the total number of points obtained are divided by the total possible points had the team won all the games. For the above example the team would accumulate a percentage of 0.687 (11 ÷ 16).

PLACE TOURNAMENTS

A place tournament is one in which teams play until they have reached a place in the tournament. This type of tournament requires more games than other elimination tournaments. It can be used in intramurals for interest groups which continually play or as an evaluative technique for classes.

The tournament's basic design is similar to that of a consolation tournament with the addition of tournament brackets for the losers. After the first round games, when winners advance right and losers advance left; the winners will remain playing on the tournament

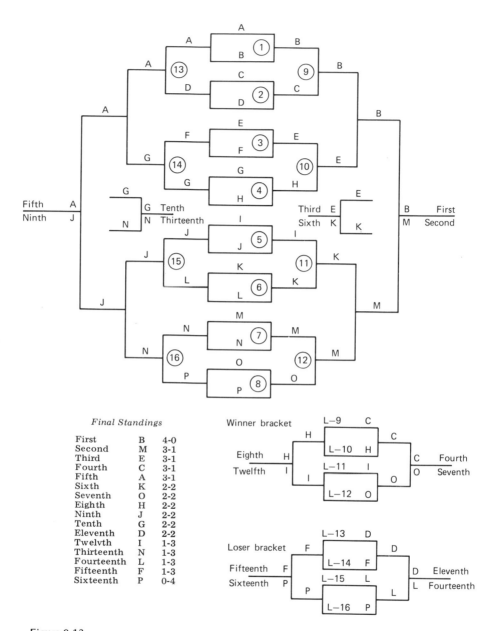

Final Standings

First	B	4-0
Second	M	3-1
Third	E	3-1
Fourth	C	3-1
Fifth	A	3-1
Sixth	K	2-2
Seventh	O	2-2
Eighth	H	2-2
Ninth	J	2-2
Tenth	G	2-2
Eleventh	D	2-2
Twelvth	I	1-3
Thirteenth	N	1-3
Fourteenth	L	1-3
Fifteenth	F	1-3
Sixteenth	P	0-4

Figure 9.13
Sixteen team place tournament.

bracket and the losers will be placed on a predetermined tournament bracket.

The final standings in a place tournament are based on (1) the won-loss record and (2) how far the entries advance in the winners' bracket before losing. If there are identical won-loss records at the conclusion of the tournament, the team which advances the fastest on the winner's side of the bracket receives the highest place in the tournament. Figure 9.13 is an example of a completed 16-team place tournament.

In Figure 9.13, teams M, E, C, and A have identical records of 3 and 1. It is obvious that M receives second, and team E is awarded a higher place (third) than C, because of advancing farther in the winner bracket. Team C has a higher place (fourth) than Team A, which the same record, because it advanced farther on the winner side before being defeated. The same principle holds true for those teams who fall into the loser side of the bracket. Note that the only team that the fifteenth place team defeats is the sixteenth place team. A 24-team and 32-team tournament appears in Appendix C.

Figure 9.14 is an example of how to combine a consolation and a place tournament. Those individuals or teams who lose in the first

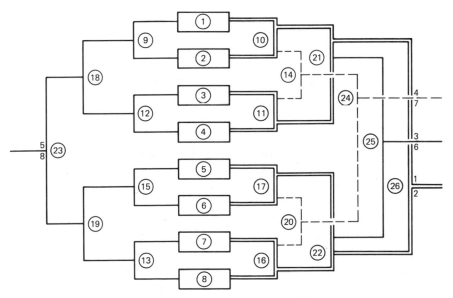

Figure 9.14
Consolation tournament with eight places.

round continue to play for the consolation championship. The teams who advance in the winners' bracket continue to play until they reach the end of the bracket or lose two games.

LOOP TOURNAMENTS

The loop tournament will determine a winner from the positions of all participants in the tournaments. There is no limitation to the number of contestants who can participate. The basic design of the tournament is to divide the participants into equal halves by any means and place one half in the upper division, one half in the lower division, so that each contestant in the upper division is paired with a contestant in the lower division. (If there is an odd number, place the unpaired contestant at the right end of the upper division, and he/she will have no match in the first round.)

Example A:

Basic design	A	B	C	D
	E	F	G	H

Once the tournament has been set up two basic steps are required to conduct the tournament:

1. After each round, place the winner of the match in the upper division, the loser in the lower division.
2. Rotate all the winners one position to the left, the contestant in the upper left position will move to the lower left. Rotate all the losers one position to the right; the contestant in the lower right position will move to the upper right.

Example B:

Rotation of winners and losers (winner in each round is circled).

Round 1 (A)   B   (C)   (D)
           E   (F)   G   H

Intermediate step, move winners up, losers down.

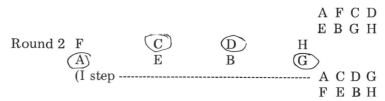

```
                                    A F C D
                                    E B G H
Round 2  F        (C)      (D)      H
        (A)        E        B      (G)
        (I step ------------------------------------------- A C D G
                                    F E B H
```

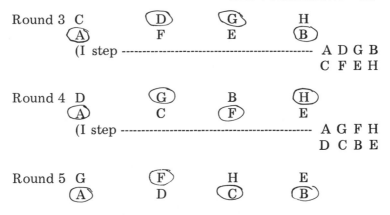

Round 3 C   D   G   H
         A   F   E   B
         (I step -- A D G B
                                                            C F E H

Round 4 D   G   B   H
         A   C   F   E
         (I step -- A G F H
                                                            D C B E

Round 5 G   F   H   E
         A   D   C   B

Because the loop tournament is a continuous tournament, it is not necessary to stop play after a certain number of games. To insure the individual or team that draws the lower right-hand position at the start of the tournament a chance to advance to first, there should be at least one round more than matched pairs. In the example above, there should be at least five rounds played.

The places in the tournament are determined after the last round by placing the winners in the upper division and awarding places as follows:

| First | Third | Fifth | Seventh |
| Second | Fourth | Sixth | Eight |

In the previous example, the won-loss records and places after five rounds would be as shown in the table.

Team		Score	Position
A	=	5-0	First
G	=	3-2	Second
F	=	3-2	Third
D	=	3-2	Fourth
C	=	3-2	Fifth
B	=	2-3	Sixth
H	=	1-4	Seventh
E	=	0-5	Eighth

Although four teams have identical records, their places are determined when the tournament is halted.

The loop tournament has two definite advantages. First, its effectiveness as an evaluative technique is not limited by the number of contestants. Second, the tournament, as designed, prevents the control of the upper end of the tournament, which may occur in other types of challenge tournaments, because after each round all contestants must rotate allowing winners to meet at the left side of the rotation design.

CHALLENGE TOURNAMENTS

Challenge tournaments are excellent for informal competition or competition between special interest groups. One of the biggest advantages of a challenge tournament is that contestants are never eliminated.

The rules for challenge tournaments will vary with each tournament and modification; however, general rules are:

1. Players advance by challenging and defeating the player challenged (default also results in advance).
2. A challenge starts at the bottom and a player may challenge any of the three above. In tournaments where a number of players are on an equal line, they must win a challenge on that line before challenging up.
3. If the challenger wins, the names switch places in the tournament. When a challenger is defeated, names stay in the same places and the challenger may not rechallenge that player for a set period of time.
4. Challenges may not be refused and must be accepted in the order they were offered.
5. Definite time periods are established for the games of challengers, and those who fail to appear or accept challenges shall be placed at the bottom of the challenge board.

Before discussing the various types of challenge tournaments, it should be noted that most of the tournaments can be easily administered by setting up predesigned challenge boards. These boards can either be made of wood with hooks, positioned on the board in the shape of the tournament, so that the contestant can change the name easily, or they can be made out of cardboard or other soft material so that the contestants can change positions by using thumbtacks.

Ladder Tournament

The ladder tournament is a challenge tournament in which names are listed vertically. Players may challenge those in positions above in accordance with predetermined rules. If the challenger wins he exchanges positions on the ladder with the loser. The winner of this tournament is the person who is at the top of the ladder at a predetermined termination date (Figure 9.15).

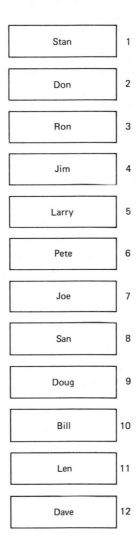

Figure 9.15
Ladder tournament.

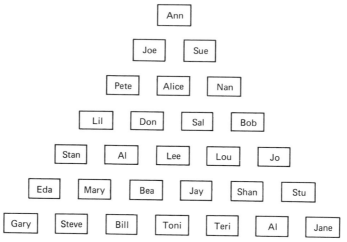

Figure 9.16
Pyramid tournament.

Pyramid Tournament

The pyramid tournament provides more entries and a broader challenge base than the ladder tournament. In this tournament, the challengers are arranged in a pyramid with one on the first line, two on the second line, three on the third line, etc. Challengers must defeat someone on their line before challenging up in this tournament (Figure 9.16).

Inverted Funnel Tournament

The inverted funnel tournament is a combination of the ladder and pyramid tournaments. The object of this tournament is to determine the top six places. This type of tournament allows for a great number of entries. The players who are in the bottom of the inverted funnel follow the rules of the pyramid tournament while those who have reached the top of the inverted funnel follow the rules of the ladder tournament (Figure 9.17).

Spider Web Tournament

This tournament allows for more individuals to challenge the individual or team who is in the number one spot. However, it is also a disadvantage that the leader has so many (six) potential challengers. It is a good idea to modify the challenge rules to re-

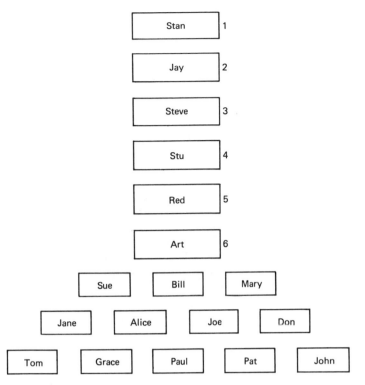

Figure 9.17
Inverted funnel tournament.

quire challengers to defeat an individual on their level before being permitted to challenge an inner level. Once the leader moves out of the center, he/she should be required to defeat a player or accept a challenge from another level before being permitted to challenge for the leadership position again (Figure 9.18).

Record Challenge

This is an individual or team effort where the competitors attempt to better an existing record. The number of times they may try to break the record is not limited.

Ringer Challenge

The ringer tournament permits the contestant a given number of times to better his or her score, or contestants may submit a given

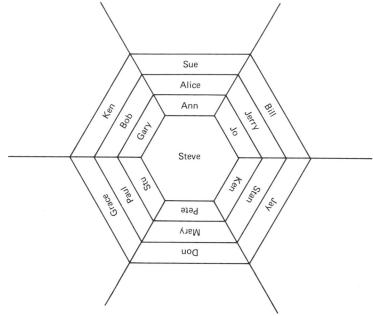

Figure 9.18
Spider web tournament.

number of best scores for a total entry in the tournament. As an example, after six rounds of golf, the player may submit the best scores for each hole and this total is the tournament score.

LOMBARD TOURNAMENT

The Lombard tournament is a round robin tournament that is completed in a relatively short length of time. The teams play "limited" games which are fractions of a regular game.

Each team's score is determined by adding all game scores and subtracting the total of its opponents' scores. The teams with the largest positive scores are selected to play a "full game" in either a round robin or an elimination tournament to determine the winner.

This tournament method can be adapted to team games, as well as individual sports, and can be played on a limited time, reduced number of games, or reduced number of points basis.

TIME-LIMIT TOURNAMENT

Many students can compete simultaneously in a variety of activities in this tournament play. Activity stations are set up, such as badminton horseshoes, tennis, and throw for distance. Groups of contestants compete at the various stations. At the end of "time" all teams or individuals rotate to a new station. Competition is continued until all contestants have visited all stations. Scores are totaled to determine the winner.

TOMBSTONE TOURNAMENT

This kind of competition involves the accumulation of a best score over a specified period of time or reaching an established goal in the shortest period of time. For example, in golf, contestants might submit their total score of ten rounds; or, in swimming, contestants might indicate on a chart the distance covered each day. At the end of a certain period of time, that swimmer who has the greatest charted distance is the winner. If a distance is specified, such as ten miles, the first individual to swim that far is the winner. This tournament may be used for group or individual competitions in activities such as hiking, track and field events, and basketball shooting.

ONE-DAY TOURNAMENTS

One of the major objectives of a good intramural program is to get as many participants in an activity as possible, and a good method of encouraging participation is by conducting one-day tournaments in which the winner will be determined at the conclusion of the day's activity. One-day tournaments have been very popular in activities such as table tennis, badminton, golf, bowling, tennis, or other individual events; however, it is possible to conduct one-day tournaments in football, soccer, basketball, volleyball, or any other team sport. These tournaments can be very popular if properly organized and conducted.

The intramural department may run either of two different types of one-day tournaments. The first is used when a great number of entries are expected; the entries are required in advance of the playing date so that the tournament may be drawn. The second type of one-day tournament is conducted by having the teams enter at the starting time on the date of the event. Different practices are used for administering the two types of one-day tournaments.

When a great number of entries are received in advance, it is a good practice to schedule teams in the first quadrant of the tournament to play two games before other teams are scheduled. The reason for this is that teams will be in the area and then there will not be a long wait for their second game. When the teams reach the quarterfinals and semifinals, they should all play at about the same time if possible. If it is not possible to have them play at the same time, a rest period for the last team to play should be scheduled before the finals begin.

A key to a good one-day tournament that allows entries at the starting time is to get the tournament punctually started. Two easy methods for placing the teams on the tournament bracket are available. The first method is to have each team sign a small slip of paper which is dropped in a box and then drawn out to be placed on the bracket. The second method is to have the bracket already numbered and then the teams merely draw a number to determine their place in the tournament. If an organization has more than one entry, they should go on opposite sides of the bracket. The tournament can be drawn at anytime there are at least eight teams; and if more show up, then the "play-in method" can be used by drawing for positions against those teams who have not already started to play.

As previously stated, it is best to run a double elimination tournament if it is at all possible. To save time, the teams should sign in all players when they start their first contest, and these should be the only players who are eligible for the day's event. When a game is over, the teams are responsible for reporting the results to the supervisor and picking up their cards for the next contest.

In order to conduct such tournaments, the director must first set up revised rules to accommodate the number of teams and the number of games necessary to determine a champion in one day. Rules must be revised for playing time, playing area, and playing rules.

Playing time. The amount of actual playing time should be determined by the number of entries and the number of games necessary to eliminate all teams but the two finalists. In order to obtain the approximate playing time available for each contest, divide the number of games, into the total time allotted for the tournament. It must be remembered that time is needed for warm-up, unforeseen delays, and tie contests. In a timed contest run on a tight schedule, it is advisable that the contest be timed on a running-time basis. If more than one playing area is being used, a master clock will help in keeping the tournament on schedule because it will start and stop all contests at the scheduled times.

If it is necessary to play two games an hour per area, then the contests should be played in two 11-minute halves, with a 3 minute break. If it is necessary to play three games an hour per area, then the contests have to be cut to 15-minute games. If four contests per area an hour are needed, then the playing time of the contests would only be 10 minutes. These contests would all be played on running time and the scheduling would allow for a 5-minute warm-up period. The Figure 9.19 shows the possibilities for conducting one-day tournaments within an eight-hour period which depend upon the type of tournament number of entries, and the number of playing areas. The times listed are actual game times taking into consideration the 5-minute warm-up periods for each game.

Figure 9.19
Playing Time for One-day Tournament

No. of Entries	Type of Tournament	No. of Floors	No. of Games	Actual Playing Time
16	Single	1	15	22*
		2	15	48†
	Double	1	31	10
		2	31	22*
24	Single	1	23	15
		2	23	40
		3	23	48†
24	Double	2	47	15
		3	47	22*
32	Single	2	31	22*
		3	31	40‡
	Double	2	63	10
		3	63	15
64	Single	3	63	15

*Two 11-minute halves with 3-minutes between halves.
†Four 12-minute quarters with 1 minute between quarters and 5 minutes at half time.
‡Four 10-minute quarters with 1 minute between quarters and 6 minutes at the half.

Playing Area. The standard size basketball and volleyball courts are suitable for one-day tournaments, but it would be advisable to cut down the size of the playing areas in softball, soccer, and football to increase the chances of scoring and thus produce a winner in a shorter period of time. The size of the football field would be determined by the number of players that constitute a team. In softball the size of the infield should remain standard, but a designated fence should be nearer home plate than regulations perscribe to increase the possibility of homeruns and thus of getting a winner of the contest sooner.

Playing Rules. The special rules for a one-day tournament should be set up with the specific purpose of allowing individuals to participate in contests under game conditions that will produce a winner to advance in the tournament. It must be remembered that there should be no drastic deviation from standard playing rules, merely an abbreviation of some parts of the games. In a double elimination tournament the length of the games on the loser side of the bracket should be just one half of that on the winner side because teams on the loser side must play more games to remain in the tournament.

SPECIAL EVENT DAYS

Special event days have become more popular at all levels because these competitions are set up on a recreational basis. It is true that the individuals are competing to determine who is the winner but usually the activities are enjoyed for their own value. The special events day permits the director to conduct activities which will allow for competition between men, women, and co-rec.

The director's objectives when planning and conducting special event days should be:

1. To interest as many individuals as possible by providing wholesome recreational experiences.
2. To provide for both individual and group competition. The socializing influence of a group contest ought to be available to all students.
3. To equalize competition. Close competition makes the day more interesting to all participants.
4. To provide students with a chance to practice acquired skill and to attempt to develop new skills.
5. To assist in selling the program to students and the administration.

Special event days should be an integral part of the school life.

The basic design requirement of a special event day is to have various stations set up where individuals, partners, or teams may use their skills in a variety of different activities. Most of the activities should be of the kind that are not generally practiced by the students. Then they will feel that they have an equal chance in competition. The number of activities which may be offered is unlimited. Games and activities may be modified for any age level and either sex. Many of the activities that were discussed in Chapter 7 might be included as well as the following abbreviated list of "unpracticed" activities.

Wiffle Ball hit for distance
Bowling with plastic equipment
Basketball obstacle dribble, left and right hand
Scooter races
Ring toss
Hula hoop races
Drop the pin in the bottle
Frisbee
Jump rope
Jarts
Darts

The following is an example of a list of a special events day contests with special rules set up for unpracticed activities. These games could be conducted for individuals or as co-rec events. A champion could be selected in each event as well as an over-all champion found by awarding points for placing in each event as in a track meet.

Scooter race. Contestants sit on scooters and push backward with their feet the length of the gym; then the contestants lay on their stomachs and pull forward with their hands back to the other end of the gym.

Bowling. The object is to gain the highest pin fall out of five frames using a playground ball instead of a bowling ball.

Bean Bag Shuffleboard. Shuffleboard is played using bean bags instead of shuffleboard discs.

Ring Toss. Rings are tossed to land around numbered pegs. Each person will have five tosses of four rings each.

Hula Hoop Race. Contestants race with hoops going around their waists the length of the gym, and return to the other end of the gym with hoops going around their necks. If a hoop falls off, the contestant must stop and start from that spot.

Drop the Pin in the Bottle. Each person gets ten pins. Pins must be kept waist high.

TOURNAMENT TIPS

1. For individual or dual events, place the phone numbers of the contestants on the tournament bracket.

2. When players put their names up as winners in a tournament, they should also fill out a slip indicating the date, time, and score so that disputes may be settled if both players claim a win.

3. It is a good practice to have a location for notes near tournaments so that players may leave each other messages if they are unable to get together.

4. Leave a few blanks on the tournament sheets in which late entries may be written.

5. When drawing up tournaments in which organizations have multientries, start by placing the organization with the most players in different quadrants of the tournament brackets.

6. Keep a duplicated copy of the tournament in the office in case the original is torn off the bulletin board.

10. Point Systems and Standards for Individual Performance

Keep on going and the chances are you will stumble on something, perhaps when you are least expecting it. I have never heard of anyone stumbling on something sitting down.

Charles F. Kettering

This chapter will discuss different methods used to award points to individuals and organizations who attempt to achieve an all-school championship. A section also deals with different types of events in which individuals may participate to test their skills against established standards.

Using a point system has long been accepted as a motivational device by intramural directors. There is no uniform agreement as to which type of point program is the best. In fact, some programs do not use any point system, because the director feels that point systems take away from the true meaning of voluntary participation or that it is too time consuming to keep the necessary records. This author feels that point systems enhance the program because they encourage more individuals to participate in new activities.

Before discussing the different types of point systems, it should be pointed out that the numerical values placed on the various activities may vary with age levels. When working with elementary or junior high school programs, the points may have a value of 1000 instead of 10, because students at a young age are impressed with large numbers. The keeping of records when using point systems is not difficult or time consuming if the method of record keeping discussed in Chapter 4 is followed. There are two basic types of point systems.

A participation point system awards points for individuals participating in activities. The individuals receive a point each time they participate, and the organization also receives credit for the individual's participation.

A winner point system awards points for entry into an event and has scaled values for high-place finishers in the activity. The individual may receive a share of the points that are credited to the organization.

PARTICIPATION POINT SYSTEM

The participation point system is the more educationally justifiable of the two systems, because it stimulates interest in the program and builds a certain esprit de corps within the organization. Because points are awarded for participating, and not for performance on highly skilled tasks, many students will attempt new and different activities. The winner point system, places far too much emphasis on winning by rewarding points on the basis of how high an organization finishes in the competition.

By using the participation point system, a director can determine organizational participation point champions as well as individual participation point champions. Champions may be determined for each league classification as well as an all-school champion using the figures which were accumulated by the participants.

A good program has many different activities, and therefore the director must devise regulations which establish the number of participation points that may be received in each event. This also prevents an organization from winning the participation championship just because they have more members than other organizations. It should be pointed out that although an organization may receive a limited number of points in team events, each individual will receive credit for participating. An example of rules for standardizing participation points would be:

1. In round robin league events, a team shall receive the number of points equivalent to the number of players necessary to play the event for each contest played in the league. (Example: 5 points for basketball, 10 for softball, 6 for volleyball, for each game played.) If a team plays with less than the minimum, it will receive participation points for the number that played.

2. For one-day team tournaments each team will receive points equivalent to the number of players necessary to participate in the event. Team points will not be given for each contest played.

3. For one-day individual or dual events, organizations should be

encouraged to enter as many individuals they desire; however, there should be a maximum as to the number of points that can be received. For example: 2-man volleyball would get a maximum of 6 points, canoe jousting a maximum of 4 points.

4. For individual or dual events (not one day) organizations should enter as many participants as they desire. After completion of the tournament, the organization will receive 1 point for each participation by the 2 players who advance the farthest in the tournament.

Although the participation point system is basically established to give credit for participation, some incentive could also be attached to winning an event. The point values for winning should not be out of balance with the participation points gained for competing in the events. The following is an example of how incentive points may be assigned:

10 Points	Winner of league event
	Winner of major one-day team event
5 Points	Runner-up in league and major one-day team event
	Winner of minor one-day team event
3 Points	Runner-up in minor one-day team event
	Team winner of skill oriented event
2 Points	Team runner-up in skill oriented event
	Individual winner of any event
1 Point	Second-place finisher in any individual event

The incentive point values and the participation point limitations should always be listed on the entry blanks.

As discussed in Chapter 4, the team participation points can be recorded for each event on the entry check-off form. The accumulation of participation points could be placed on a form which lists the organizations and the events. Figure 10.1 is an example of a record of participation points and incentive points for six organizations that competed in six events.

Football. All teams played in the football league with 8 players on a team and played 5 games. Teams A, B, C, and D were in the play-offs, with team A winning the play-off and team B finishing second.

Volleyball. All teams played in a one-day volleyball tournament (major), with team C winning and team D finishing as the runner-up.

Soccer. All teams played in a one-day soccer tournament (minor), with team D the winner and team E the runner-up.

Skills. In the football skills event, only teams C and D entered full 5-men teams; team D won and team C finished second. An individual from team A was the individual winner, and team B has the individual runner-up.

(one-day event) each team entered 3 teams; team F won and team A finished second.

Tennis. In the tennis tournament, which was not a one-day event, team A had no players advance beyond the first round; team B's best 2 players played in 2 and 3 matches; team C did not enter; team D had the winner who played 5 matches and 1 player who was eliminated in the first round; team E had the runner-up who played 5 matches and no other entry; team F had 2 players who reached the semifinals by playing 4 matches.

A good method of assuring a close race for the all-school participation championship is to convert the standings at the end of each quarter or semester to a point value scale. By converting to a point value scale, each organization has the opportunity periodically to start new. The reasoning in back of this conversion is to allow an organization that falls way behind in point total in a quarter or semester to retain a chance for the championship if they have good participation.

The tables illustrate why converting to a value scale is superior to totaling the points: without converting to a point scale team C had little or no chance to win as they were behind over 200 points.

	Fall	Winter	Spring
Team A	350	185	280
Team B	325	230	275
Team C	150	190	250

A point value score could be set up in which first place receives 15 1/3, second 14, third 13, etc. Giving the 1/3 point for first rewards a team just a little extra and it assures that the only way a tie could result at the end of the quarter or semester is if three organizations had identical placements. An example would be team A winning 2 quarters and finishing third the other quarter, while team B was first one quarter and second the other two quarters:

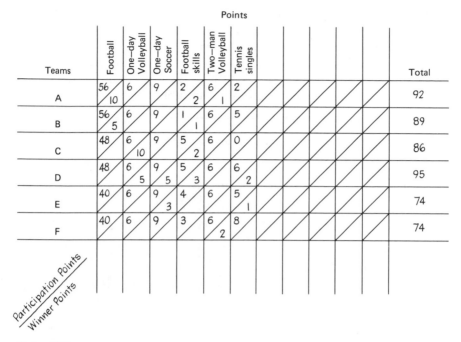

Figure 10.1
Team participation and incentive points. The participation points are written above the line, winner points below.

	Fall	Winter	Spring	Total
Team A	15 1/3	13	15 1/3	43 2/3
Team B	14	15 1/3	14	43 1/3
Team C	13	14	13	40

Using the point value table, it would have been possible for the teams to tie for the championship had team C won the spring quarter, team A come in second, and team B finished third in back of team A.

WINNER POINT SYSTEM

The winner point system does not use the participation of the players for awarding points. In most winner point systems, the teams receive points for entering an event, and there is generally a penalty for forfeiting a contest. The practice of deducting points for forfeiting is not a good practice because it makes participation mandatory for the students. When an organization fails to participate, they lose credit for those points they would have received for entering the event; therefore, they should not be penalized doubly by having forfeit penalty points deducted from the total. An example of the use of the winner point system is given in the table.

Event	Entry Points	Finish								Forfeit Penalty Points per Contest
		1	2	3	4	5	6	7	8	
Football	50	100	75	50	40	30	20	10	5	10
Basketball	25	75	60	45	30	25	20	10	5	5
Track	1 for each man	50	40	30	25	20	15	10	5*	5
		6	5	4	3	2	1†			None
Tennis‡	1 for each man	4	3	2	1					2
Wrestling	1 for each man	40	35	30	25	20	15	10	5*	
		4	3	2	1†					2
Free throw	5 for team	15	12	10	8	6	4	2	1	None

*Team winner.
†Individual winner.
‡Team limited to 1 player per event.

If more value is to be placed on winning, then a greater point spread would be used. The differences in the values are generally based on whether the activity is considered a major or a minor event. The record keeping for this method is similar to that illustrated in Figure 10.1. It is possible to convert the winner points each quarter to scale values to create more interest.

Individual Champion

The individual champion or outstanding intramural athlete may be determined by using either method. When using the participation point system, this individual should be determined by totaling all of the points that the individual accumulated through participation—1 point for entering each event. The recording of these points was discussed in Chapter 4. In the winner point system, the individual could receive a percentage of the points given for being on a winning team or the individual could be credited with the points awarded the team.

ESPRIT DE CORPS WINNER

Another type of recognition which may be given organizations is the esprite de corps award for the year. This award requires no additional events but is compiled from the entries in selected events. The intramural department should list the events which are esprit de corps events on the entry sheets and give the teams credit for the number of individuals who enter the event. The organization that has the greatest number of individuals listed in each event receives points on a conversion scale of 10 to 1, with each place having one less value. These points are easily recorded on the entry check-off form (Figure 4.1) as discussed in Chapter 4, and the year's totals may be kept on a form similar to Figure 10.1. The purpose of this type of team award is to give recognition to the organizations that encourage their members to participate in a spirit of competition and for the good will it creates between the members who join in some activity.

SPORTS SKILL CHAMPION

In addition to selecting a participation champion or an outstanding athlete, an intramural director can determine a sports skill champion by converting the results in selected sports events. The recognition of this type of champion would give credit to the individual who has the greatest individual sports skill.

It is not necessary to run an additional event to get this champion; a director merely needs to record the places of the individuals in the selected events, and the winner is the individual who accumulates the greatest number of points. A director may select any events as part of this program. The following list gives examples of selected sports skill events and values.

Football Skills	Half of the score of the 20-yard kick and the 15-yard pass.
Golf	Five points for finishing in the top 5, 3 for finishing in the next 10, and 2 for finishing in the next 10.
Tennis Singles	One point for each match won; 5 for first place, 3 for second, and 2 for reaching the semifinals.
Free Throw	Half of the number of free throws made.
Badminton Singles	Same as for tennis.
Billiards	Same as for tennis.
Table Tennis singles	Same as for tennis.

Track In the 100-yard dash, use the same points as for golf.

Archery One tenth the score from 20 yards.

A simple method of keeping the records for the sports skill champion is to have an alphabetical file of 5 × 8 cards. When the results of the selected events are turned in, the office personnel needs only to list the names on the alphabetical cards of the individuals who receives points in that event.

SIGMA DELTA PSI TEST

Sigma Delta Psi is a national honorary athletic fraternity which has chapters in colleges and universities throughout the United States. The Sigma Delta Psi test uses standards that have been set up to give recognition to college students for their athletic ability. If the college or university is a member of the national organization, upon completing the test, an individual is eligible to become a member of this organization.

Requirements for Sigma Delta Psi[1]

1.	100-yard dash	11.6 seconds
2.	120-yard low hurdles	16 seconds
3.	Running high jump	Height and weight classification
4.	Running long jump	17 feet
5.	16-pound shot put	30 feet
6.	20-foot rope climb or	12 seconds
	golf	4 out of 5 shots
7.	Baseball throw or	250 feet
	javelin throw	130 feet
8.	Football punt	120 feet
9.	100-yard swim	1 minute, 45 seconds
10.	1-mile run	6 minutes
11.	Front handspring, landing on feet	
12.	Handstand or	10 seconds
	bowling test	160 average (3 games)
13.	Fence vault	Chin high
14.	Good posture	Standard B (H.B.M.)
15.	Scholarship	Eligible for varsity competition

See the following sections for additional requirements.

[1] reproduced with permission of Sigma Delta Psi.

A. *Test No. 2.* Five standard low hurdles, placed twenty yards apart, hurdles must remain upright from their bases.

B. *Test No. 3.* The high jump requirement is based on a graduated scale that considers the height and weight of each individual.

C. *Test No. 5.* Thirty feet is the requirement for a man of 160 pounds or over, the requirement to be scaled down in accordance with the following proportion for candidates of less weight:

160 pounds is the candidates weight as 30 feet is to the requirement.

D. *Test No. 6. Rope Climb.* The candidate shall start from a sitting position on the floor and climb rope without use of legs. Legs may be used in the descent.

Golf. Four out of 5 shots must land on the fly in a circle (10-foot radius) from a distance of 75 feet.

E. *Test No. 12. Handstand.* The candidate shall not be compelled to remain stationary during the test, neither shall he be allowed to advance or retreat more than 3 feet in any direction.

Bowling. The candidate must average 160 for 3 games. Only 3 games may be bowled in any one day.

F. *Test No. 14.* The candidate shall be required to pass the B Standard of the Harvard Body Mechanics Posture Chart, page 12. These charts will be furnished all local chapters. The Director or Committee on Certification should observe the candidate's posture when he is not aware of the fact.

G. *Test Numbers 1, 2, 5, 7,* and *8* shall be attempted crosswise into the wind to be accepted by the Director or Committee on Certification.

H. The national collegiate rules for the various activities of the tests are the accepted standards.

Intramural departments, although not members of the national organization, could use these standards to recognize outstanding athletic ability. If an intramural department were interested in having their institution become a member of the national organization, it should contact the Sigma Delta Psi Fraternity.

DECATHLON AND PENTATHLON

The decathlon and pentathlon events may be used either in competition or with standards against which men and women test their skills. The decathlon, when conducted as a college or Olympic meet, consists of ten events; however, it is most common in intramural college and high school decathlon meets to run only eight events. The pole vault and the javelin throw are usually eliminated because of the safety hazards involved in both events. The pentathlon is a five event meet for women. When conducting either meet the events should be scheduled over at least two days.

A copy of the decathlon tables for intramural use appears in Appendix D. These tables contain more than ten events so that the director may choose which events are most suited for the student population. It is possible to use the softball or football throw in place of the javelin or discus, and convert the scores to the appropriate standards. Although most states do not permit junior high students to compete in more than four events, a decathlon type event can be run over a several week period with the students entering the events they feel capable of competing in. The table in Appendix D could be used for junior high students; however, they will not attain as high a total score as older students.

A copy of the pentathlon table appears in Appendix E. This table also contains more than five events so that directors may select what events they wish to use. The recommended events for the pentathlon are the 100-yard hurdles, shot put, high jump, long jump, and the 200-meter race.

PHYSICAL FITNESS STANDARDS

Although the intramural department or recreation department may not be directly responsible for conducting physical fitness tests, they are often called upon to assist in testing the fitness of the local population. Many different types of physical fitness tests may be administered. The most popular of these tests is the AAHPER Youth Fitness Test which may qualify students for the Presidential Physical Fitness Award.

The President's Physical Fitness Award program was begun in 1966 through the efforts of the President's Council on Physical Fitness and Sports. This program established standards for boys and girls between the ages of ten and seventeen. When an individual scores higher than the eighty-fifth percentile on all six test items, they are eligible to receive an award certificate that indicates the accomplishment. Scores for the eighty-fifth percentile appear in the Figure 10.2 that follows. The AAHPER publishes a youth fitness manual which has standards for all percentiles.

Eight-Fifth Percentile National Fitness Test, 1976

						600-Yard, Run—Walk				
						Ages 10-12 1 mile or 9-Minute Run		Ages 13 and Over 1½ mile or 12-Minute Run		Shuttle Run
Age	Situps (Flexed Leg) 1 Minute	Pullups 1 Minute	Standing Long Jump	50-Yard Dash	Options—	(Time)	(Yards)	(Time)	(Yards)	
BOYS										
10	42	5	5'8"	:7.7	2:11	7:06	2081			:10.4
11	43	5	5'10"	:7.4	2:09	6:43	2143			:10.1
12	45	6	6'1"	:7.1	2:0	6:20	2205			:10.0
13	48	7	6'8"	:6.9	1:54			9:40	3037	:09.7
14	50	9	6'11"	:6.5	1:47			9:40	3037	:09.3
15	50	11	7'5"	:6.3	1:42			9:40	3037	:09.2
16	50	11	7'9"	:6.3	1:40			9:40	3037	:09.1
17	49	12	8'0"	:6.1	1:38			9:40	3037	:09.0
GIRLS		(Flexed Arm Hang)								
10	38	:24	5'5"	:7.8	2:30	8:33	1801			:10.9
11	38	:24	5'7"	:7.5	2:25	8:02	1824			:10.5
12	38	:23	5'9"	:7.4	2:21	7:28	1847			:10.5
13	40	:21	6'0"	:7.2	2:16			14:00	2232	:10.2
14	41	:26	6'3"	:7.1	2:11			14:00	2232	:10.1
15	40	:25	6'1"	:7.1	2:14			14:00	2232	:10.2
16	38	:20	6'0"	:7.3	2:19			14:00	2232	:10.4
17	40	:22	6'3"	:7.1	2:14			14:00	2232	:10.1

Source. AAHPER Youth Fitness Manual, American Alliance for Health, Physical Education and Recreation, 1976

Figure 10.2

The President's Council on Physical Fitness and Sports has also established standards in forty-one recreational activities by which adults may qualify for awards from this council. Further information regarding the standards for each event may be obtained from the President's Council on Physical Fitness and Sports, Washington, D. C. 20201.

In addition to assisting with the administration of actual fitness tests, the intramural department should post physical fitness standards in a prominent place so that students may test themselves to see how they "stack-up" with the established norms. Physical fitness tests make good challenge activities; students who make the top ten in a particular test can have their names posted on the challenge board.

A HEAT CHART

Number of Entries	Number of Trial Heats	Number Qualifying	Number of Semifinal Heats	Number Qualifying	Number in Finals
For six lanes					
1 to 6	0	—	0	—	6
7 to 12	2	3	0	—	6
13 to 18	3	4	2	3	6
19 to 24	4	3	2	3	6
25 or more requires quarterfinals following above pattern.					
For seven lanes					
1 to 7	0	—	0	—	7
8 to 14	2	3	0	—	6
15 to 21	3	4	2	3	6
22 to 28	4	3	2	3	6
29 or more requires quarterfinals following above pattern.					
For eight lanes					
1 to 8	0	—	0	—	8
9 to 16	2	4	0	—	8
17 to 24	3	4	2	4	8
25 to 32	4	4	2	4	8
33 to 40	5	3	2	4	8
41 or more requires quarterfinals following above pattern.					
For nine lanes					
1 to 9	0	—	0	—	9
10 to 18	2	4	0	—	8
19 to 27	3	3	0	—	9
28 to 36	4	4	2	4	8
37 to 45	5	3	2	4	8
46 to 54	6	3	2	4	8
55 or more requires quarterfinals following above pattern.					

ROUND ROBIN TOURNAMENT

No. of Teams	Rounds									10	11	12	13	14	15
	1	2	3	4	5	6	7	8	9	10	11	12	13	14	15
6	1-2	1-4	1-6	1-5	1-3										
	3-4	2-6	4-5	6-3	5-2										
	5-6	3-5	2-3	4-2	6-4										
7	1-2	2-4	4-6	6-7	7-5	5-3	3-1								
	3-4	1-6	2-7	4-5	6-3	7-1	5-2								
	5-6	3-7	1-5	2-3	4-1	6-2	7-4								
8	1-2	1-4	1-6	1-8	1-7	1-5	1-3								
	3-4	2-6	4-8	6-7	8-5	7-3	5-2								
	5-6	3-8	2-7	4-5	6-3	8-2	7-4								
	7-8	5-7	3-5	2-3	4-2	6-4	8-6								
9	1-2	2-4	4-6	6-8	8-9	9-7	7-5	5-3	3-1						
	3-4	1-6	2-8	4-9	6-7	8-5	9-3	7-1	5-2						
	5-6	3-8	1-9	2-7	4-5	6-3	8-1	9-2	7-4						
	7-8	5-9	3-7	1-5	2-3	4-1	6-2	8-4	9-6						

10

1-2	1-4	1-6	1-8	1-10	1-9	1-7	1-5	1-3
3-4	2-6	4-8	6-10	8-9	10-7	9-5	7-3	5-2
5-6	3-8	2-10	4-9	6-7	8-5	10-3	9-2	7-4
7-8	5-10	3-9	2-7	4-5	6-3	8-2	10-4	9-6
9-10	7-9	5-7	3-5	2-3	4-2	6-4	8-6	10-8

11

1-2	2-4	4-6	6-8	8-10	10-11	11-9	9-7	7-5	5-3	3-1
3-4	1-6	2-8	4-10	6-11	8-9	10-7	11-5	9-3	7-1	5-2
5-6	3-8	1-10	2-11	4-9	6-7	8-5	10-3	11-1	9-2	7-4
7-8	5-10	3-11	1-9	2-7	4-5	6-3	8-1	10-2	11-4	9-6
9-10	7-11	5-9	3-7	1-5	2-3	4-1	6-2	8-4	10-6	11-8

12

1-2	1-4	1-6	1-8	1-10	1-12	1-11	1-9	1-7	1-5	1-3
3-4	2-6	4-8	6-10	8-12	10-11	12-9	11-7	9-5	7-3	5-2
5-6	3-8	2-10	4-12	6-11	8-9	10-7	12-5	11-3	9-2	7-4
7-8	5-10	3-12	2-11	4-9	6-7	8-5	10-3	12-2	11-4	9-6
9-10	7-12	5-11	3-9	2-7	4-5	6-3	8-2	10-4	12-6	11-8
11-12	9-11	7-9	5-7	3-5	2-3	4-2	6-4	8-6	10-8	12-10

13

1-2	2-4	4-6	6-8	8-10	10-12	12-13	13-11	11-9	9-7	7-5	5-3	3-1
3-4	1-6	2-8	4-10	6-12	8-13	10-11	12-9	13-7	11-5	9-3	7-1	5-2
5-6	3-8	1-10	2-12	4-13	6-11	8-9	10-7	12-5	13-3	11-1	9-2	7-4
7-8	5-10	3-12	1-13	2-11	4-9	6-7	8-5	10-3	12-1	13-2	11-4	9-6
9-10	7-12	5-13	3-11	1-9	2-7	4-5	6-3	8-1	10-2	12-4	13-6	11-8
11-12	9-13	7-11	5-9	3-7	1-5	2-3	4-1	6-2	8-4	10-6	12-8	13-10

ROUND ROBIN
TOURNAMENT (cont.)

No. of Teams							Rounds								
	1	2	3	4	5	6	7	8	9	10	11	12	13	14	15
14	1-2	1-4	1-6	1-8	1-10	1-12	1-14	1-13	1-11	1-9	1-7	1-5	1-3		
	3-4	2-6	4-8	6-10	8-12	10-14	12-13	14-11	13-9	11-7	9-5	7-3	5-2		
	5-6	3-8	2-10	4-12	6-14	8-13	10-11	12-9	14-7	13-5	11-3	9-2	7-4		
	7-8	5-10	3-12	2-14	4-13	6-11	8-9	10-7	12-5	14-3	13-2	11-4	9-6		
	9-10	7-12	5-14	3-13	2-11	4-9	6-7	8-5	10-3	12-2	14-4	13-6	11-8		
	11-12	9-14	7-13	5-11	3-9	2-7	4-5	6-3	8-2	10-4	12-6	14-8	13-10		
	13-14	11-13	9-11	7-9	5-7	3-5	2-3	4-2	6-4	8-6	10-8	12-10	14-12		
15	1-2	2-4	4-6	6-8	8-10	10-12	12-14	14-15	15-13	13-11	11-9	9-7	7-5	5-3	3-1
	3-4	1-6	2-8	4-10	6-12	8-14	10-15	12-13	14-11	15-9	13-7	11-5	9-3	7-1	5-2
	5-6	3-8	1-10	2-12	4-14	6-15	8-13	10-11	12-9	14-7	15-5	13-3	11-1	9-2	7-4
	7-8	5-10	3-12	1-14	2-15	4-13	6-11	8-9	10-7	12-5	14-3	15-1	13-2	11-4	9-6
	9-10	7-12	5-14	3-15	1-13	2-11	4-9	6-7	8-5	10-3	12-1	14-2	15-4	13-6	11-8
	11-12	9-14	7-15	5-13	3-11	1-9	2-7	4-5	6-3	8-1	10-2	12-4	14-6	15-8	13-10
	13-14	11-15	9-13	7-11	5-9	3-7	1-5	2-3	4-1	6-2	8-4	10-6	12-8	14-10	15-12
16	1-2	1-4	1-6	1-8	1-10	1-12	1-14	1-16	1-15	1-13	1-11	1-9	1-7	1-5	1-3
	3-4	2-6	4-8	6-10	8-12	10-14	12-16	14-15	16-13	15-11	13-9	11-7	9-5	7-3	5-2

5-6	3-8	2-10	4-12	6-14	8-16	10-15	12-13	14-11	16-9	15-7	13-5	11-3	9-2	7-4
7-8	5-10	3-12	2-14	4-16	6-15	8-13	10-11	12-9	14-7	16-5	15-3	13-2	11-4	9-6
9-10	7-12	5-14	3-16	2-15	4-13	6-11	8-9	10-7	12-5	14-3	16-2	15-4	13-6	11-8
11-12	9-14	7-16	5-15	3-13	2-11	4-9	6-7	8-5	10-3	12-2	14-4	16-6	15-8	13-10
13-14	11-16	9-15	7-13	5-11	3-9	2-7	4-5	6-3	8-2	10-4	12-6	14-8	16-10	15-12
15-16	13-15	11-13	9-11	7-9	5-7	3-5	2-3	4-2	6-4	8-6	10-8	12-10	14-12	16-14

THIRTY–TWO PLACE
TOURNAMENT WINNERS

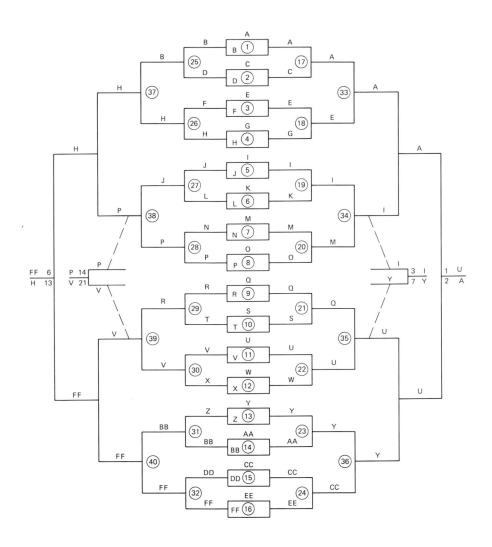

THIRTY-TWO PLACE
TOURNAMENT (cont.)

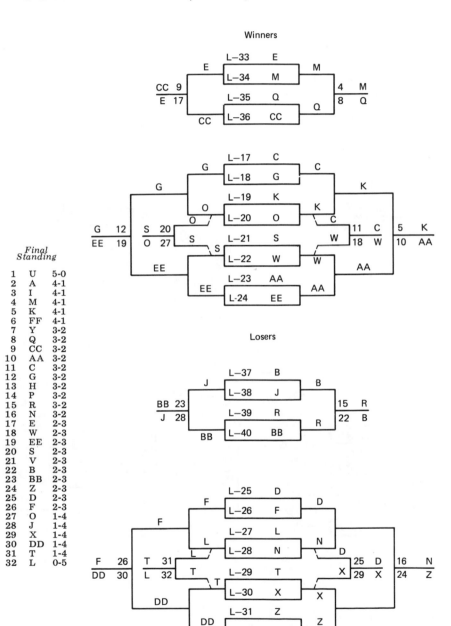

Winners

Losers

Final Standing

1	U	5-0
2	A	4-1
3	I	4-1
4	M	4-1
5	K	4-1
6	FF	4-1
7	Y	3-2
8	Q	3-2
9	CC	3-2
10	AA	3-2
11	C	3-2
12	G	3-2
13	H	3-2
14	P	3-2
15	R	3-2
16	N	3-2
17	E	2-3
18	W	2-3
19	EE	2-3
20	S	2-3
21	V	2-3
22	B	2-3
23	BB	2-3
24	Z	2-3
25	D	2-3
26	F	2-3
27	O	1-4
28	J	1-4
29	X	1-4
30	DD	1-4
31	T	1-4
32	L	0-5

259

TWENTY – FOUR PLACE TOURNAMENT

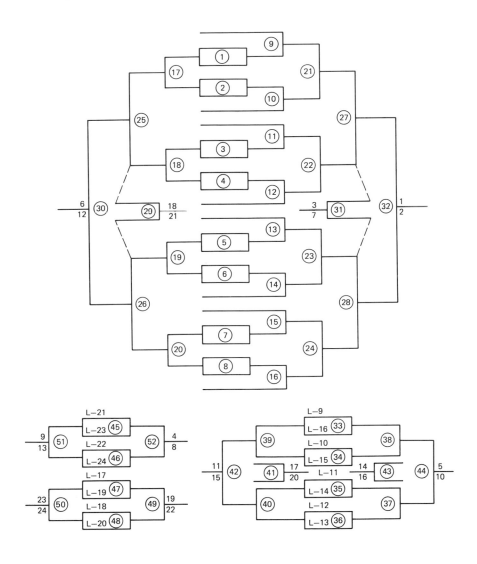

DECATHLON TABLE, I

Points	100 Yards	220 Yards	660 Yards	120 Low Hurdles Yards	70 High Hurdles Yards	High Jump
1000	:09.3	:20.2	1:17.0	:12.3	:08.1	6'11"
990	—	—	1:17.3	—	—	—
980	—	—	1:17.6	—	—	—
970	—	:20.3	1:17.9	—	—	—
960	—	—	1:18.2	:12.4	:08.2	—
950	—	—	1:18.5	—	—	6'10"
940	:09.4	:20.4	1:18.8	—	—	—
930	—	—	1:19.1	—	—	—
920	—	:20.5	1:19.4	:12.5	:08.3	—
910	—	—	1:19.7	—	—	—
900	—	:20.6	1:20.0	:12.6	—	6'9"
890	—	—	1:20.3	—	—	—
880	:09.5	:20.7	1:20.6	—	:08.4	—
870	—	—	1:20.9	—	—	—
860	—	:20.8	1:21.2	:12.7	—	—
850	—	—	1:21.5	—	:08.5	6'8"
840	—	:20.9	1:21.8	:12.8	—	—
830	:09.6	—	1:22.1	—	—	—
820	—	:21.0	1:22.4	—	—	—
810	—	—	1:22.7	—	:08.6	6'7"
800	—	:21.1	1:23.0	:12.9	—	—

DECATHLON TABLE, I (cont.)

Points	100 Yards	220 Yards	660 Yards	120 Low Hurdles Yards	70 High Hurdles Yards	High Jump
790	—	—	1:23.3	—	—	—
780	:09.7	:21.2	1:23.6	—	:06.7	6'6"
770	—	—	1:23.9	:13.0	—	—
760	—	:21.3	1:24.2	—	—	6'5"
750	—	—	1:24.5	:13.1	:08.8	—
740	:09.8	:21.4	1:24.8	—	—	—
730	—	—	1:25.1	—	—	6'4"
720	—	:21.5	1:25.4	:13.2	:08.9	—
710	—	—	1:25.7	—	—	—
700	—	:21.6	1:26.0	—	—	6'3"
690	—	—	1:26.4	:13.3	:09.0	—
680	:09.9	:21.7	1:26.8	—	—	—
670	—	—	1:27.2	—	—	6'2"
660	—	:21.8	1:27.6	:13.4	:09.1	—
650	—	—	1:28.0	—	—	—
640	—	:21.9	1:28.4	—	—	6'1"
630	:10.0	—	1:28.8	:13.5	:09.2	—
620	—	:22.0	1:29.2	—	—	—
610	—	:22.1	1:29.6	—	—	6'0"
600	—	:22.2	1:30.0	:13.6	:09.3	—
590	:10.1	:22.3	1:30.4	—	—	—

No.						Height
580	—	:22.4	1:30.8	—	—	—
570	—	:22.5	1:31.2	—	:09.4	5'11"
560	—	:22.6	1:31.6	:13.7	—	—
550	:10.2	:22.7	1:32.0	—	—	—
540	—	:22.8	1:32.4	:13.8	:09.5	5'10"
530	—	:22.9	1:32.8	—	—	—
520	—	:23.0	1:33.2	—	:09.6	—
510	:10.3	:23.1	1:33.6	:13.9	—	5'9"
500	—	:23.2	1:34.0	—	:09.7	—
490	—	:23.3	1:34.4	—	—	—
480	:10.4	:23.4	1:34.8	:14.0	:09.8	5'8"
470	—	:23.5	1:35.2	:14.1	—	—
460	—	:23.6	1:35.6	:14.2	:09.0	—
450	:10.5	:23.7	1:36.0	:14.3	—	5'7"
440	—	:23.8	1:36.4	:14.4	:10.0	—
430	:10.6	:23.9	1:36.8	:14.5	:10.1	—
420	—	:24.0	1:37.2	:14.6	:10.2	5'6"
410	:10.7	:24.1	1:37.6	:14.7	:10.3	—
400	—	:24.2	1:38.0	:14.8	:10.4	—
390	:10.8	:24.3	1:38.4	:14.9	:10.5	5'5"
380	—	:24.4	1:38.8	:15.0	:10.6	—
370	:10.9	:24.5	1:39.2	:15.1	:10.7	5'4"
360	—	:24.6	1:39.6	:15.2	:10.8	—
350	:11.0	:24.7	1:40.0	:15.3	:10.9	5'3"
340	:11.1	:24.8	1:40.4	:15.4	:11.0	—
330	:11.2	:24.9	1:40.8	:15.5	:11.1	5'2"
320	:11.3	:25.0	1:41.2	:15.6	:11.2	—

DECATHLON TABLE, I (cont.)

Points	100 Yards	220 Yards	660 Yards	120 Low Hurdles Yards	70 High Hurdles Yards	High Jump
310	:11.4	:25.1	1:41.6	:15.7	:11.3	5'1"
300	:11.5	:25.2	1:42.0	:15.8	:11.4	—
290	:11.6	:25.3	1:42.4	:15.9	:11.5	5'0"
280	:11.7	:25.4	1:42.8	:16.0	:11.6	4'11"
270	:11.8	:25.5	1:43.2	:16.1	:11.7	4'10"
260	:11.9	:25.6	1:43.6	:16.2	:11.8	4'9"
250	:12.0	:25.7	1:44.4	:16.3	:11.9	4'8"
240	:12.1	:25.8	1:44.8	:16.4	:12.0	4'7"
230	:12.2	:25.9	1:45.2	:16.5	:12.1	4'6"
220	:12.3	:25.0	1:45.6	:16.6	:12.2	4'5"
210	:12.4	:26.2	1:46.0	:16.7	:12.3	4'4"
200	:12.5	:26.4	1:46.5	:16.8	:12.4	4'3"
190	:12.6	:26.6	1:47.0	:16.9	:12.5	4'2"
180	:12.7	:26.8	1:47.5	:17.0	:12.6	4'1"
170	:12.8	:27.0	1:48.0	:17.2	:12.7	4'0"
160	:12.9	:27.2	1:48.5	:17.4	:12.8	3'11"
150	:13.0	:27.4	1:49.0	:17.6	:12.9	3'10"
140	:13.1	:27.6	1:49.5	:17.8	:13.0	3'9"
130	:13.2	:27.8	1:50.0	:18.0	:13.2	3'8"
120	:13.3	:28.0	1:50.5	:18.2	:13.4	3'7"
110	:13.4	:28.2	1:51.0	:18.4	:13.6	3'6"

100	:13.5	:28.4	1:51.5	:18.6	:13.8	3'5"
90	:13.6	:28.6	1:52.0	:18.8	:14.0	3'4"
80	:13.7	:28.8	1:53.0	:19.0	:14.2	3'3"
70	:13.8	:29.0	1:54.0	:19.2	:14.4	3'2"
60	:13.9	:29.5	1:55.0	:19.4	:14.6	3'1"
50	:14.0	:30.0	1:56.0	:19.6	:14.8	3'0"
40	:14.2	:30.5	1:57.0	:19.8	:15.0	2'11"
30	:14.4	:31.0	1:58.0	:20.0	:15.5	2'10"
20	:14.6	:31.5	1:59.0	:21.0	:16.0	2'9"
10	:14.8	:32.0	2:00.0	:22.0	:17.0	2'8"

APPENDIX D

DECATHLON TABLE, II

Points	Long Jump	Hop, Step, Jump	Pole Vault	Javelin	Discus	Shot Put	Mile
1000	26'8"	52'6"	15'8"	250'	180'0"	62'0"	4:40
990	26'7"	52'4"	15'7"	249'	179'3"	61'10"	4:41
980	26'6"	52'2"	15'6"	248'	178'6"	61'8"	4:42
970	26'5"	52'0"	15'5"	247'	177'9"	61'6"	4:43
960	26'4"	51'9"	15'4"	246'	177'0"	61'4"	4:44
950	26'3"	51'6"	15'3"	245'	176'3"	61'2"	4:45
940	26'2"	51'3"	15'2"	244'	175'6"	61'0"	4:46
930	26'1"	51'0"	15'1"	243'	174'9"	61'10"	4:47
920	26'0"	50'9"	15'0"	242'	174'0"	60'8"	4:48
910	25'11"	50'6"	14'11"	241'	173'3"	60'6"	4:49
900	25'10"	50'3"	14'10"	240'	172'6"	60'4"	4:50
890	25'9"	50'0"	14'9"	239'	171'9"	60'2"	4:51
880	25'8"	49'9"	14'8"	238'	171'0"	60'0"	4:52
870	25'7"	49'6"	14'7"	237'	170'3"	59'8"	4:53
860	25'6"	49'3"	14'6"	236'	169'6"	59'4"	4:54
850	25'5"	49'0"	14'5"	235'	168'9"	59'0"	4:55
840	25'4"	48'9"	14'4"	234'	168'0"	58'8"	4:56
830	25'3"	48'6"	14'3"	233'	167'0"	58'4"	4:57
820	25'2"	48'3"	14'2"	232'	166'0"	58'0"	4:58
810	25'1"	48'0"	14'1"	230'	165'0"	57'8"	4:59
800	25'0"	47'9"	14'0"	228'	164'0"	57'4"	5:00
790	24'11	47'6"	13'11"	226'	163'0"	57'0"	5:01
780	24'10"	47'3"	13'10"	224'	162'0"	56'7"	5:02

770	24'9"	47'0"	13'9"	222'	161'0"	56'2"	5:03
760	24'8"	46'9"	13'8"	220'	160'0"	55'9"	5:04
750	24'7"	46'6"	13'7"	218'	159'0"	55'4"	5:05
740	24'6"	46'3"	13'6"	216'	158'0"	54'11"	5:06
730	24'4"	46'0"	13'5"	214'	157'0"	54'6"	5:07
720	24'2"	45'9"	13'4"	212'	156'0"	54'1"	5:08
710	24'0"	45'6"	13'3"	210'	155'0"	53'8"	5:09
700	23'10"	45'3"	13'2"	208'	154'0"	53'3"	5:10
690	23'8"	45'0"	13'1"	206'	153'0"	52'10"	5:11
680	23'6"	44'9"	13'0"	204'	152'0"	52'5"	5:12
670	23'4"	44'6"	12'11"	202'	151'0"	52'0"	5:13
660	23'2"	44'3"	12'10"	200'	150'0"	51'7"	5:14
650	23'0"	44'0"	12'9"	198'	148'6"	51'2"	5:15
640	22'10"	43'9"	12'8"	196'	147'0"	50'9"	5:16
630	22'8"	43'6"	12'7"	194'	145'6"	50'4"	5:17
620	22'6"	43'3"	12'6"	192'	144'0"	49'11"	5:18
610	22'4"	43'0"	12'5"	190'	142'6"	49'6"	5:19
500	22'2"	42'9"	12'4"	188'	141'0"	49'1"	5:20
590	22'0"	42'6"	12'3"	186'	139'6"	48'8"	5:21
580	21'10"	42'3"	12'2"	184'	138'0"	48'3"	5:22
570	21'8"	42'0"	12'1"	182'	136'6"	47'10"	5:23
560	21'6"	41'9"	12'0"	180'	135'0"	47'5"	5:24
550	21'4"	41'6"	11'11"	178'	133'6"	47'0"	5:25
540	21'2"	41'3"	11'10"	176'	132'0"	46'7"	5:26
530	21'0"	41'0"	11'9"	174'	130'6"	46'2"	5:27
520	20'10"	40'9"	11'8"	172'	129'0"	45'9"	5:28
510	20'8"	40'6"	11'7"	170'	127'6"	45'4"	5:29

DECATHLON TABLE, II (cont.)

Points	Long Jump	Hop, Step, Jump	Pole Vault	Javelin	Discus	Shot Put	Mile
400	20'6"	40'3"	11'6"	168'	126'0"	44'11"	5:30
490	20'4"	40'0"	11'5"	166'	124'6"	44'6"	5:31
480	20'2"	39'9"	11'4"	164'	123'0"	44'1"	5:32
470	20'0"	39'6"	11'3"	162'	121'6"	43'8"	5:33
460	19'10"	39'3"	11'2"	160'	120'0"	43'3"	5:34
450	19'8"	39'0"	11'1"	158'	118'6"	42'10"	5:35
440	19'6"	38'9"	11'0"	156'	117'0"	42'5"	5:36
430	19'4"	38'6"	10'10"	154'	115'6"	42'0"	5:37
420	19'2"	38'3"	10'8"	152'	114'0"	41'7"	5:38
410	19'0"	38'0"	10'6"	150'	112'6"	41'2"	5:39
400	18'10"	37'9"	10'4"	148'	111'0"	40'9"	5:40
390	18'8"	37'6"	10'2"	146'	109'6"	40'4"	5:41
380	18'6"	37'3"	10'0"	144'	108'0"	39'11"	5:42
378	18'4"	37'0"	9'10"	142'	106'6"	39'6"	5:43
360	18'2"	36'9"	9'8"	140'	105'0"	39'1"	5:44
350	18'0"	36'6"	9'6"	138'	103'6"	38'8"	5:45
340	17'10"	36'3"	9'4"	136'	102'0"	38'3"	5:46
330	17'8"	36'0"	9'2"	134'	100'6"	37'10"	5:47
320	17'6"	35'9"	9'0"	132'	99'0"	37'5"	5:48
310	17'4"	35'6"	8'10"	130'	97'0"	37'0"	5:49
300	17'2"	35'3"	8'8"	128'	95'0"	36'7"	5:50
290	17'0"	35'0"	8'6"	126'	93'0"	36'2"	5:51
280	16'10"	34'6"	8'4"	124'	91'0"	35'9"	5:52

270	16'8"	34'0"	8'2"	122'	89'0"	35'4"	5:53
260	16'6"	33'6"	8'0"	120'	87'0"	34'11"	5:54
250	16'4"	33'0"	7'10"	117'	85'0"	34'6"	5:55
240	16'2"	32'6"	7'8"	114'	83'0"	34'1"	5:56
230	16'0"	32'0"	7'6"	111'	81'0"	33'8"	5:57
220	15'9"	31'6"	7'4"	108'	79'0"	33'3"	5:58
210	15'6"	31'0"	7'2"	105'	77'0"	32'10"	5:59
200	15'3"	30'6"	7'0"	102'	75'0"	32'5"	6:00
190	15'0"	30'0"	6'10"	99'	73'0"	32'0"	6:01
180	14'9"	29'6"	6'8"	96'	71'0"	31'6"	6:02
170	14'6"	29'0"	6'6"	93'	69'0"	31'0"	6:03
160	14'3"	28'6"	6'4"	90'	67'0"	30'6"	6:04
150	14'0"	28'0"	6'2"	87'	65'0"	30'0"	6:05
140	13'9"	27'6"	6'0"	84'	63'0"	29'6"	6:06
130	13'6"	27'0"	5'10"	81'	61'0"	29'0"	6:07
120	13'3"	26'6"	5'8"	78'	59'0"	28'6"	6:08
110	13'0"	26'0"	5'6"	75'	57'0"	28'0"	6:09
100	12'9"	25'6"	5'4"	72'	55'0"	27'6"	6:10
90	12'6"	25'0"	5'2"	68'	53'0"	27'0"	6:11
80	12'3"	24'6"	5'0"	64'	51'0"	26'6"	6:12
70	12'0"	24'0"	4'10"	60'	48'0"	26'0"	6:13
60	11'9"	23'6"	4'8"	56'	45'0"	25'6"	6:14
50	11'6"	23'0"	4'6"	52'	42'0"	25'0"	6:15
40	11'3"	22'6"	4'4"	48'	38'0"	24'6"	6:16
30	11'0"	22'0"	4'2"	44'	34'0"	24'0"	6:17
20	10'6"	21'0"	4'0"	40'	30'0"	23'0"	6:18
10	10'0"	20'0"	3'10"	36'	26'0"	22'0"	6:19

APPENDIX E

PENTATHLON TABLE

Points	50-Yard Hurdles	60-Yard Hurdles	100-Yard Hurdles	Shot Put	High Jump	Long Jump	200 Meters	800 Meters
1100	:5.9	:7.1	:12.4	62'1"	6'1½"	22'8"	:22.4	1:59.1
1075	:6.0	:7.2	:12.6	60'5¼"	6'½"	22'3¼"	:22.7	2:00.6
1050	:6.1	:7.3	:12.7	58'9½"	5'11½"	21'10½"	:22.9	2:02.1
1025	:6.2	:7.4	:12.9	57'2¼"	5'10½"	21'6"	:23.2	2:03.6
1000	:6.2	:7.5	:13.1	55'7¼"	5'9¼"	21'1¼"	:23.4	2:05.1
975	:6.3	:7.6	:13.2	54'½"	5'8¼"	20'8½"	:23.7	2:06.7
950	:6.4	:7.7	:13.4	52'6¼"	5'7¼"	20'4"	:23.9	2:08.4
925	:6.5	:7.8	:13.6	51'	5'6½"	19'11½"	:24.2	2:10.1
900	:6.6	:7.9	:13.8	49'6"	5'5½"	19'7"	:24.4	2:11.8
875	:6.7	:8.0	:14.0	48'½"	5'4½"	19'2½"	:24.7	2:13.6
850	:6.8	:8.1	:14.2	46'7"	5'3½"	18'10"	:25.0	2:15.4
825	:6.9	:8.2	:14.4	45'2"	5'2½"	18'5½"	:25.3	2:17.3
800	:7.0	:8.3	:14.6	43'9¼"	5'1½"	18'1¼"	:25.6	2:19.2
775	:7.1	:8.5	:14.8	42'5"	5'½"	17'9"	:25.9	2:21.2
750	:7.2	:8.6	:15.0	41'¼"	4'11½"	17'5"	:26.2	2:23.2
725	:7.3	:8.7	:15.3	39'8"	4'10½"	17'½"	:26.5	2:25.3
700	:7.4	:8.8	:15.5	38'4½"	4'10"	16'8½"	:26.8	2:27.5
675	:7.5	:9.0	:15.7	37'1"	4'9"	16'4½"	:27.2	2:29.7
650	:7.6	:9.1	:16.0	35'9½"	4'8¼"	16'½"	:27.5	2:32.0
625	:7.7	:9.3	:16.3	34'6½"	4'7½"	15'8¼"	:27.9	2:34.4

600	:7.8	:9.4	:16.5	33'4"	4'6½"	15'4½"	:28.2	2:36.9
575	:8.0	:9.6	:16.8	32'1½"	4'5½"	15'¼"	:28.6	2:39.4
550	:8.1	:9.7	:17.1	30'11¼"	4'4½"	14'8½"	:29.0	2:42.0
525	:8.3	:9.9	:17.4	29'9½"	4'4"	14'4½"	:29.3	2:44.7
500	:8.4	:10.1	:17.7	28'8"	4'3½"	14'1"	:29.7	2:47.5
475	:8.6	:10.3	:18.1	27'6¼"	4'2¼"	13'9"	:30.2	2:50.4
450	:8.7	:10.5	:18.4	26'5"	4.2"	13'5½"	:30.6	2:53.4
425	:8.9	:10.7	:18.7	25'4½"	4'1¼	13'2"	:31.0	2:56.5
400	:9.1	:10.9	:19.1	24'4"	4'½"	12'10"	:31.5	2:59.7
375	:9.2	:11.1	:19.5	23'3½"	3'11½"	12'6½"	:31.9	3:03.0
350	:9.4	:11.3	:19.9	22'3¼"	3'11"	12'3"	:32.4	3:06.4
325	:9.6	:11.5	:20.3	21'3½"	3'10½"	11'11¼"	:32.9	3:10.0
300	:9.8	:11.7	:20.7	20'4"	3'9½"	11'7½"	:33.4	3:13.7
275	:10.0	:12.0	:21.1	19'5"	3'9"	11'4½"	:33.9	3:17.6
250	:10.2	:12.2	:21.6	18'6"	3'8½"	11'1"	:34.5	3:21.6
225	:10.4	:12.5	:22.1	17'7"	3'7½"	10'9½"	:35.0	3:25.8
200	:10.6	:12.8	:22.6	16'8½"	3'7"	10'6½"	:35.6	3:30.2
175	:10.9	:13.1	:23.1	15'10¼"	3'6½"	10'3¼"	:36.1	3:34.8
150	:11.1	:13.4	:23.6	15'¼"	3'5½"	10'	:36.7	3:39.6
125	:11.4	:13.7	:24.2	14'3"	3'5¼"	9'9"	:37.4	3:44.5
100	:11.7	:14.0	:24.8	13'5½"	3'5"	9'5½"	:38.0	3:49.8
75	:12.0	:14.4	:25.4	12'8"	3'4¼"	9'2½"	:38.7	3:55.2
50	:12.3	:14.8	:26.1	11'11¼"	3'3½"	8'11½"	:39.4	4:01.0
25	:12.7	:15.2	:26.8	11'3"		8'8¼"	:40.1	4:07.0
0	:13.1	:15.7	:27.6	10'6"		8'6"	:40.8	4:13.1

CALLAWAY ONE-ROUND GOLF HANDICAP SYSTEM

		Guide Scores			*Handicap deduction*
—	—	70	71	72	Scratch and no adjustment
73	74	75	—	—	½ highest hole and adjustment
76	77	78	79	80	1 highest hole and adjustment
81	82	83	84	85	1½ highest holes and adjustment
86	87	88	89	90	2 highest holes and adjustment
91	92	93	94	95	2½ highest holes and adjustment
96	97	98	99	100	3 highest holes and adjustment
101	102	103	104	105	3½ highest holes and adjustment
106	107	108	109	110	4 highest holes and adjustment
111	112	113	114	115	4½ highest holes and adjustment
116	117	118	119	120	5 highest holes and adjustment
121	122	123	124	125	5½ highest holes and adjustment
126	127	128	129	130	6 highest holes and adjustment

Adjustment: add to or deduct from handicap   −2   −1   0   +1   +2

Notes: 1. No hole can be scored at more than twice its par.
        2. Half strokes count as whole strokes.
        3. The *seventeenth* and *eighteenth* holes are never deducted.
        4. In case of ties lower handicap or adjustment should be given preference.

ADJUSTED CALLAWAY
FOR 9-HOLE TOURNAMENT

The same procedure is used as for the 18-hole handicap system placing score values as indicated in the table.

Gross Scores					Handicap Deduction
—	—	34	35	36	Scratch and no adjustment
37	38	39	40	41	½ highest hole and adjustment
42	43	44	45	46	1 highest hole and adjustment
47	48	49	50	51	1½ highest holes and adjustment
52	53	54	55	56	2 highest holes and adjustment
57	58	59	60	61	2½ highest holes and adjustment
62	63	64	65	66	3 highest holes and adjustment

Adjustment: add to or deduct from handicap   —2   —1   0   +1   +2

Notes: 1. No hole can be scored at more than twice its par.
2. Half strokes count as whole strokes.
3. The *eighth* and *ninth* holes are never deducted.
4. In case of ties lower handicap or adjustment should be given preference.

Index